NAVIGATION

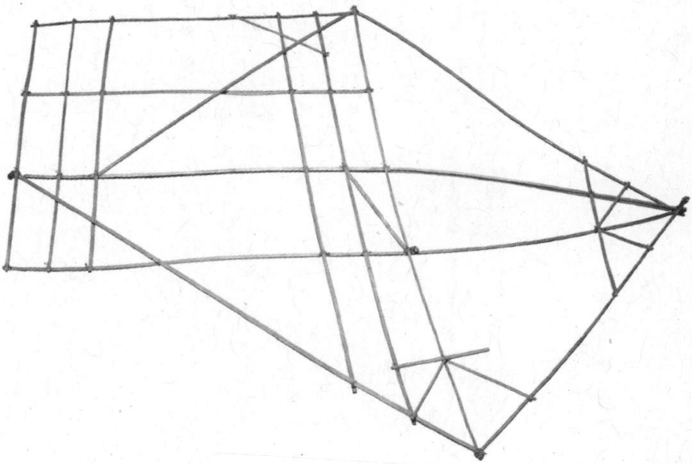

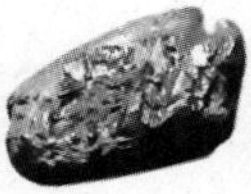

NAVIGATION. A PUBLICATION FOR A PLACE WITHOUT A HISTORICAL CENTER, CREATED CONTINUOUSLY ANEW IN MEETINGS AND EVENTS THAT OCCUR IN EMPOWERED SPACES, SIMULTANEOUSLY

Edited by
Hinrich Sachs, Kirke Hundevad Meng,
Samuel Richter, Rikard Heberling

Onomatopee 162
cabinet project

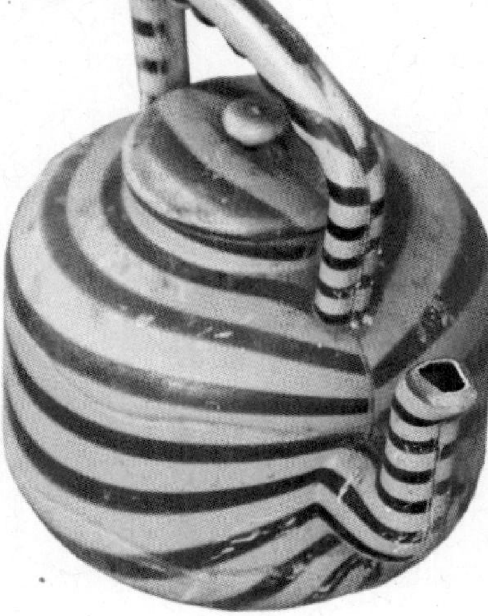

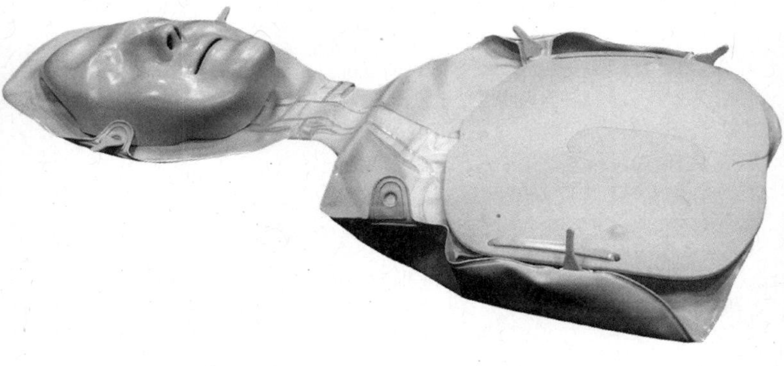

CONTENTS

NAVIGATION. BEFORE AND AFTER
Introduction
9

BIRD FLIGHT, STONE FLIGHT, A THOUSAND DESCRIBED ROUTES
Ellie Ga
25

WAITING, WANDERING, AND WONDERING. "POST-CINEMATIC" SPACES IN THE MULTIPLE PRESENT
Robin Curtis
49

THE NAME OF THE ROSE
Lili von Wallenstein
73

SOMEWHERE ELSE AND OTHER PLACES
Hana Jaber
97

THE LONG MARCH THROUGH THE INSTITUTIONS. A STRATEGY FOR TODAY?
Mikkel Bolt Rasmussen
121

LEARNING FOLLOWING MAKING
Tim Ingold
145

SOFT MACHINE ORALITY
Rikard Heberling, Kirke Hundevad Meng, Lisi Raskin, Samuel Richter, Hinrich Sachs, Barbara Wien
169

FLOTSAM AND JETSAM
Catalina Aguilera, Ehab Aljaby, Søren Andreasen, Isak Anshelm, Malou da Cunha Bang, Donatella Bernardi, Ludvig Briland, Anton Brolin, Dector & Dupuy, Marjolijn Dijkman, Tomas Kominis Endresen, Helena Fernández-Cavada, Yara Flores, Gideonsson/Londré, Goldin+Senneby, Cecilia Grönberg, Karin Hald, Marcus Harrling, Mohomodou Houssouba, Jacob Grønbech Jensen, Sophie Jung, Oscar Lara, Lars Bang Larsen, Doris Lasch, Leonela Lilja, Cecilia Luzon, Toby Lynas, Jonas (J) Magnusson, Kirke Hundevad Meng, Nanna Nordström, Mateusz Nowak, Kristoffer Ørum, Asier Perez, Daniel Pianetti, Falke Pisano, Samuel Richter, Hinrich Sachs, Gabriel Säll, Eran Schaerf, Jacques Henri Sennwald, Adam Shiu-Yang Shaw, Aron Skoog, Simon Starling, Jonathan Terry, Yusuke Toda, Hedda Viå, Gitte Villesen, Apichaya Wanthiang, Johan Widén, Filippa Wikner, Yun Yu, Klara Zetterholm
193

Contributors
221

Colophon
224

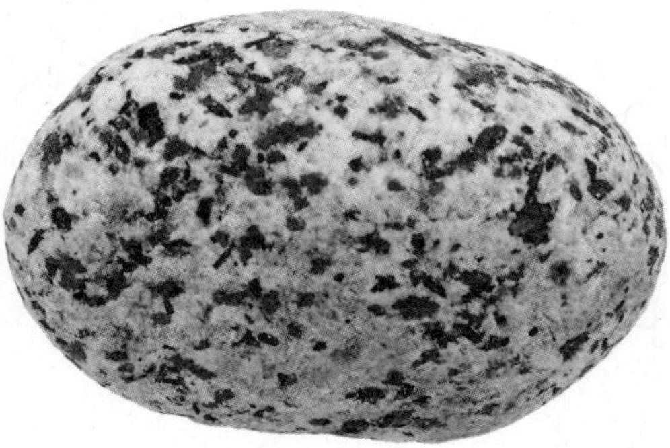

NAVIGATION. BEFORE AND AFTER

Introduction

> On the planking, on the ship's bulwarks, on the sea, with the course of the sun through the sky and the ship, an unreadable and wrenching script takes shape, takes shape and destroys itself at the same slow pace—shadows, spines, shafts of broken light refocused in the angles, the triangles of a fleeting geometry that yields to the shadow of the ocean waves. And then, unceasingly, lives again.
> — Marguerite Duras[1]

How we perceive the land at our front door on any particular day is determined not only by the daily journey of Helios, but also, and perhaps even more importantly, by what is touched by the light of our telematic devices. The land is not a given land; our perception of it depends on so many things: what we consider urgent or of importance on that day, where we want to be or ought to be, how we feel, who we are to meet, where we get the best baked goods. So let us dwell on this notion of having a relative position in the world, a position from which one's quest of undertaking meaningful and purposeful work breaks against the contemporary condition of a normalized state of crisis.

From navigation's original, grand meaning of planning and directing often extensive travels on water, the word has become a discharged metaphor for basically living or "dealing" with anything. *Anything*, because an individual life's relationship to global forces—financial economics, high-tech warfare, fake news, surveillance, and so on—that shape the social, political, and economic reality on a local and a personal level are veritably real, but at the same time impossible to perceive. Thus, from software to the heart, anything may be subject to the desire to navigate. And what can't be detached from desire is the market; the offerings of bestselling self-help books, political seminars asking perplexing questions such as "what to do?," advice on where to place your money in the global gamble of the contemporary economy, and other forms of guidance is overwhelming.

Friction, however, is what will inevitably emerge when established explanatory models, tools, and abstract schemes are applied to an individual's perception, agency, and horizon *in situ*. These points of friction affect how we localize ourselves and navigate what David Harvey, among others, has designated as a "relational space": a space that cannot be separated from the processes that define it, be it a spontaneous mass demonstration or the devaluation of a currency.[2] Navigation relates to what is *assembled* together in such a space as various motions stream through the past, becoming concentrated and fixed at a certain point in the present to momentarily define the nature of that specific point—

•

—but this act of assembling involves an interpretive aspect: setting the point in motion once again, always relative, pragmatic, and informed by an ulterior motive for further navigation.

The present book contains an array of positions. Images of personal and staged narratives emerge across the pages: narratives that are made of movement, teaching, learning, and unlearning processes that unfold in the trails of human beings, and various apparatuses that determine the agency of individuals and collectives. The cargo is an assemblage of materials, heterogeneous and asynchronous in terms of language, form, and content, produced by a set of practitioners from a variety of professions and personal backgrounds. The aim was not to create a coherent whole in order to canalize a "problem" or an "answer," but rather to compose a context of momentary use. Instead of resembling a map, in which the vertical relation to what is represented generates a vision of definitive space, the publication can be compared to the record in a logbook: the kind of book in which a ship's crew registers surroundings and important events during a voyage. In contrast to the idea of definitive space, the metaphor of the logbook opens up what Ezra Pound might have had in mind when he employed the term "periplum" in his poetry, referring to how land is perceived by the sailors at sea, rather than the cartographical image of it.[3]

This focus also sheds light on navigation's often idiosyncratic biographical aspects, as well as its material markings. After all, how we orientate, identify, and relate ourselves with regard to the imperceptible global forces that, to a large extent, constitute the space we inhabit is often done via mediating items.

These are not so much conventional tools with an explanatory use value: instead, they appear to give access to those external movements that define the space. Somewhere in Japan, the influence of a tsunami swirling over a space in the past congeals in a granite pebble, whose material presence on a studio worktable becomes the point of departure for drifting reflections on nature beyond control, drifting velocities that, in turn, will equally partake in the complex relations that momentarily define that pebble on the worktable, in a studio, somewhere in Japan.

At regular intervals, the reader of this book will encounter images of items such as that pebble—or toothpicks, lotion, a CPR doll, a protractor, a wooden sword, and a cassette voice recorder, among many others. Like flotsam and jetsam, the kind of debris found floating on or washed up by the sea, the constellation of images may be seen as an inventory of movement. The need to find one's way, using the guidance of knowledge accumulated by others, is represented here not only by such obvious tools as a signpost and various maps, but also by accessories relating to linguistic navigation in the form of a dictionary, or modes of communication such as the analogue emergency phone or the digital chatbot. Instruments that might serve a more material purpose in the process of movement are also depicted—a walking stick, a backpack, a horse halter, a pocketknife—as well as facilities for resting and standing still, such as a tent, a folding chair, a plastic kettle, a fan, an ashtray, and books. In many cases, however, the items have nothing to do with efficacy, but have instead been selected for the personal memories they evoke.

Stripped back to its most basic meaning, navigation implies the orientation and identification of the relationship between self, Other, and the relative location of each in time and space. It may be argued, however, that digital image environments render this operation difficult, as our contemporary sense of space is increasingly represented through aesthetic strategies defined by "post-continuity," in which the cohesion of time and space is disrupted. New technologies enable material places with local memory and tradition to constantly become more and more intertwined with nonlocal "spaces of flow" (that of the high-tech transformation of information, communication, and capital). Studies of these profound changes in social space tend to focus on everyday informational phenomena and omit the specific effects of the aesthetic experience of inhabiting and orienting one's way through such transformed spaces.

In contrast to such an omission, Robin Curtis' essay, *Waiting, Wandering, and Wondering: "Post-cinematic" Spaces in the Multiple Present*, suggests that a certain aesthetic sensibility—immersion—can make palpable a number of features that we have become accustomed to in everyday routines. By discussing three different contemporary phenomena that let one inhabit such immersive spaces—an augmented reality game, an immersive theater, and a 4-D cinema—Curtis offers a critical reflection on the physical orientation and movement that is brought about by the multiple layers of space and time in audiovisual epistemes of contemporary media. Such movement would include, to a certain extent, idiosyncratic trajectories caused by hesitations and detours with aimless waiting, wandering, and wondering in these environments. This may, in turn, disrupt any narrative framework of the game, film, or theater, since the participant or the audience is no longer guided by a goal or an interpretation. What opens up instead is another understanding of objects that offers an insight into the "space of flows" from a "non-interpretative micro perspective," in contrast to both a hermeneutic interpretation of these aesthetic phenomena, as well as the macro perspective of a media ecology, whose objects are large-scale structures and networks beyond the individual's interpretative intentions.

Ellie Ga's contribution, *Bird Flight, Stone Flight, a Thousand Described Routes*, brings together drifting individuals and histories by following, interpreting, and retelling the routes of explorers, refugees, beachcombers, and messages in bottles. The story departs from the Greek island of Lesbos, where Ga worked as a volunteer during a period of what has been termed the 2015 European refugee crisis. Encounters here are interwoven with histories of the Norwegian explorer Fridtjof Nansen's expedition through the Arctic pack ice, as well as Ga's firsthand experience onboard the *Tara*, a scientific research vessel built to replicate Nansen's drift in the Arctic. Further connections are made to Nansen's later work as the first High Commissioner for Refugees for the League of Nations, and his involvement in the 1923 population exchange between Greece and Turkey, in which approximately two million people were forcibly denaturalized from their homelands. Such stories of displacement and exile are echoed in the writings of Osip Mandelstam and Paul Celan, forming the underlying current by which the reflections of the essay move forward open-endedly.

Somewhere Else and Other Places by Hana Jaber is inspired by her path through life as a migrant, a citizen, and a social scientist specializing in migration. The essay is a flow of reflections ruptured by scraps of theses and conclusions, fragments of testimonies and private memories, facial features and emotions that explore the meaning of the verb "to navigate." Jaber addresses the "metamorphoses" and the "invisibilization" of migrants in the process of transcending the borders between the Other and the citizen. Such an act of reciprocal overcoming, Jaber argues, can only transpire through a form of reification—one that lies at the very core of politics—of a value that seems to have become obsolete: hospitality.

Even though, as Jaber writes, "we cannot ignore that globalization is transforming the concept of civilization and culture" as it "interferes with the landmarks traced by national territories, hardening some and smashing others," liberal prophets still seem to express a faiblesse for declaring the death of the nation-state as well as anything that had if not a real, then at least a symbolic, prominent status before neoliberal globalization: socialism, the welfare state, the proletariat, the avant-garde, etc. These declarations of death could be seen in relation to a history that appears, to quote Slavoj Žižek, "as a closed continuity of 'progression' leading to the reign of those who rule today. It leaves out of consideration what failed in history, what has to be denied so that the continuity of 'what really happened' could establish itself."[4] But what has been denied will resurface. The break is never definitive. Instead, it can open up a space to look back at past shortcomings in order to evaluate the projects of today.

Mikkel Bolt Rasmussen's contribution, *The Long March Through the Institutions: A Strategy for Today?*, addresses a historical notion of the institution and the limits of a progressive use for it. It begins with the well-known quote by the German student movement leader, Rudi Dutschke, who in 1967—paraphrasing the Long March of Mao Zedong and the Communist Red Army in 1935—advocated a "long march through the institutions" in order to radically transform society from within. Bolt Rasmussen asks whether this strategy might be relevant for the contemporary situation. He traces parallels between the ideas espoused by Dutschke and recent discussions of a return to or critical use of the institution for artistic and political purposes, recalling, for our orientation, the possibility of a theoretical as well as a lived exterior to the institutional.

In Bolt Rasmussen's essay, we are once again exposed to two of the main pitfalls of the avant-garde tradition. On the one hand, the Situationist International aspired to radicalize the projects initiated by Surrealism and Dada in order to give art a revolutionary dimension, which ironically resulted in a dispute regarding the redundancy of art and was eventually abandoned in favor of revolutionary activities outside the institutions. On the other hand, the so-called neo-avant-garde's practice of "institutional critique": instead of seeking profound transformation, the critical art in question took place within the same institution that the classical avant-garde had challenged. Since then, institutional critique has become, in the words of Bolt Rasmussen, a kind of "Biedermeier version of criticality" with no lines of flight in sight.

Light should be shed upon contemporary theories concerning the status of the institution by means of such a historical orientation. Today, theorists are once again quoting Dutschke as they criticize the hegemony of neoliberal ideology. In contrast to the common understanding of a mere "political" redefinition of institutions, be it the institutional art system or the institutional building blocks of parliamentary democracy as key agents of capital, Bolt Rasmussen argues that a moving through institutions should be remembered and projected as a "dismantling" process toward a larger issue: leaving behind capitalist society.

The Name of the Rose, by Lili von Wallenstein, is a short story set in the semi-fictional first-person experiences of Colleen LaRose. After converting to Islam in 2009, LaRose took part in a plot to assassinate the artist Lars Vilks, who had previously published anti-Islamic caricatures. It is a pulp story of sliding identities—of crossing out the past, of transforming into something new—in which isolation alongside the limitless comfort and community of the Internet plays a crucial role. The story equally slips between narrative levels, imposing grand diagnostic explanations onto Colleen's microhistory. Behind the act of appropriating and recombining narrative fragments that generate identity in digital social networks and elsewhere, one can hear the echoes of Hannah Arendt's famous statement that "nobody is the author or producer of his own life story [...] the stories, the results of action and speech, reveal an agent, but this agent is not an author or producer."[5] Further layers to this story are added by the fact that its writer is using a pseudonym, as well as an appropriated title. As for today, *The Name of The Rose* is no longer a classical murder-mystery novel, written by a seminal linguist and turned into a blockbuster movie, but a semiotic landscape washing biographical fragments ashore.

In contrast to the other forms of writing included in this book, *Soft Machine Orality* tests language itself—in this case the language of the editors—and transcription as a text genre. Differentiated from transcriptions of so-called unstructured interviews (common in social sciences as well as in market research), with an awareness typical for the twentieth-century activity called "contemporary art," the text unfolds the intent of highlighting the leaps and digressions one makes when thematizing the particular role of oral communication in various contexts. The flow of the discussion focuses on the instantaneous character of orality, saturated with social relations and inequalities, and some of the deeper implications of the contrast between the act of speaking and its representation within an array of parameters—the written word being one of them. Hence, what is readable are the voices of six people—four editors and two guests—as they were in the late summer of 2016. As Mladen Dolar has stated, the voice is projected from the body to circulate "out there."[6] However, the voice does not move away from the body, but carries it forward instead. Focusing on orality is thus a focus on the body *in situ*, bound to its politics and poetics, its accents and dialectics, its grammars as well as its handicaps. With the launch of Apple's Siri in 2011, followed by other competing services like Microsoft's Cortana, S Voice, Google Now, and Amazon's Alexa, the experience of speaking to digital devices directly, in natural language, has slowly reshaped the realm of orality.

Movement comes into focus once more in Tim Ingold's *Learning Following Making*, which argues for a forward-moving anthropology whose temporal orientation is the same as the orientation of the lives it studies. This means moving and thinking with people and things rather than about them, following their trails, and allowing our knowledge to grow and flourish amid the movements of the world. Ingold argues that knowledge is carried on through wayfaring, not through transmission. He explores how learning in practice has to be conceived as a creative and improvisational coordination of perception and action: as an itinerant movement along a way of life understood as path to be followed, rather than a corpus of rules and principles to be passed on. This path-following takes place not in an engagement between practitioners and the material world by way of the senses, but in the coupling of substantial flows and sensory awareness in a world of materials.

When the perplexed question of "what to do" surfaces in speech, in our minds, or at a point of no return, this act of "doing" could also be theorized as a factor of agency: as a process involving indexes and effects; that is, the mediation of agency by indexes, motivating inferences, responses, or interpretations. This logbook with its many entries will in turn become jetsam itself, not thrown into the water to lighten a distressed ship's load, but instead jettisoned into the current of our world to circulate a multitude of different modalities with the hope of it finding its way into other hands and other factors of agency. In *How To Do Things With Art*, Dorothea von Hantelmann traces the title of her book from John Langshaw Austin's discussion of the performative—or reality-producing—capacity of language, to the reality-producing dimension of art.[7] The performative dimension signifies art's possibilities and limits in generating and changing reality. In this book, this performative dimension is reflected in the many crew members' ways of tackling and producing meaning alongside, with, or against the conventions of their world, which in turn opens up the possibility of changing them—if not at this waypoint, then perhaps at the next, where the light is refocused in the right angles: the triangles of a fleeting geometry that yields to the shadow of the ocean waves. And then, unceasingly, lives again.

NOTES

1. Marguerite Duras, *The North China Lover* (London: Flamingo, 1992), 214.
2. See for example David Harvey, "Space as a Keyword," in *David Harvey: A Critical Reader*, eds. Noel Castree and Derek Gregory (Hoboken: Blackwell, 2006).
3. Ezra Pound, *ABC of Reading* (New York: New Directions, 1960), 43–44.
4. Slavoj Žižek, *The Sublime Object of Ideology* (London: Verso, 1989), 138.
5. Hannah Arendt, *The Human Condition* (Chicago: The University of Chicago Press, 1958), 184.
6. Mladen Dolar, *A Voice and Nothing More* (Cambridge, MA: MIT Press, 2006), 73.
7. Dorothea von Hantelmann, *How To Do Things With Art* (Zurich: JRP Ringier, 2010), 17.

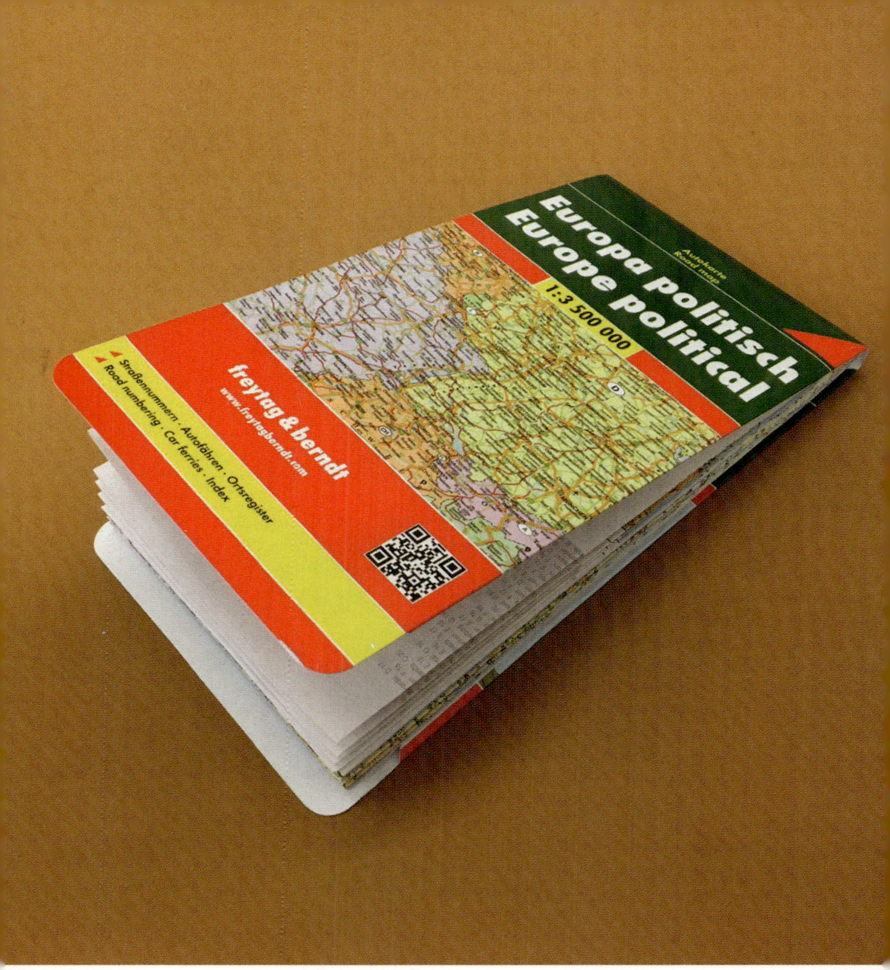
Europa politisch
Europe political
Autokarte
Road map
1:3 500 000
freytag & berndt
www.freytagberndt.com
Straßennummern · Autofähren · Ortsregister
Road numbering · Car ferries · Index

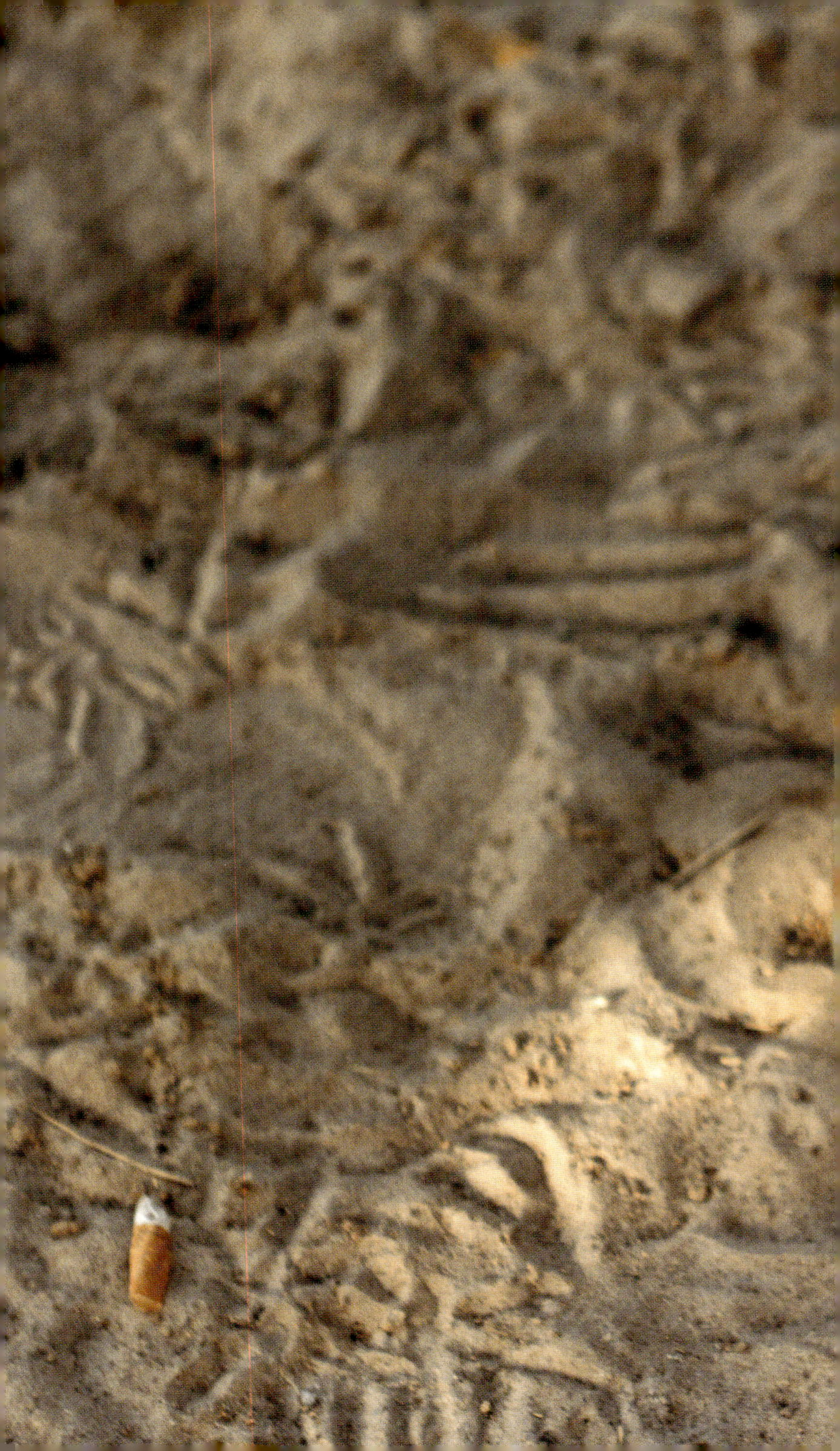

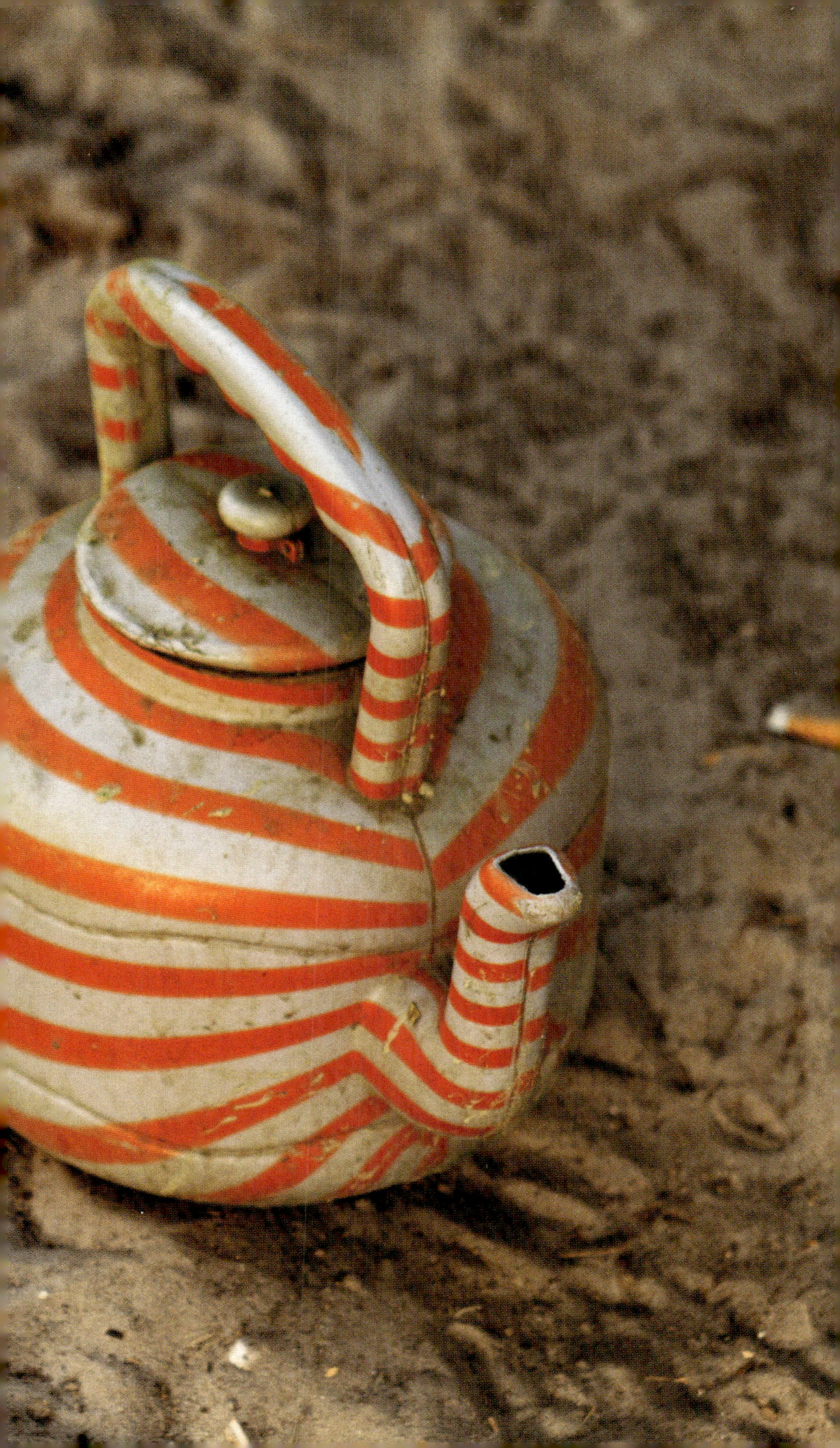

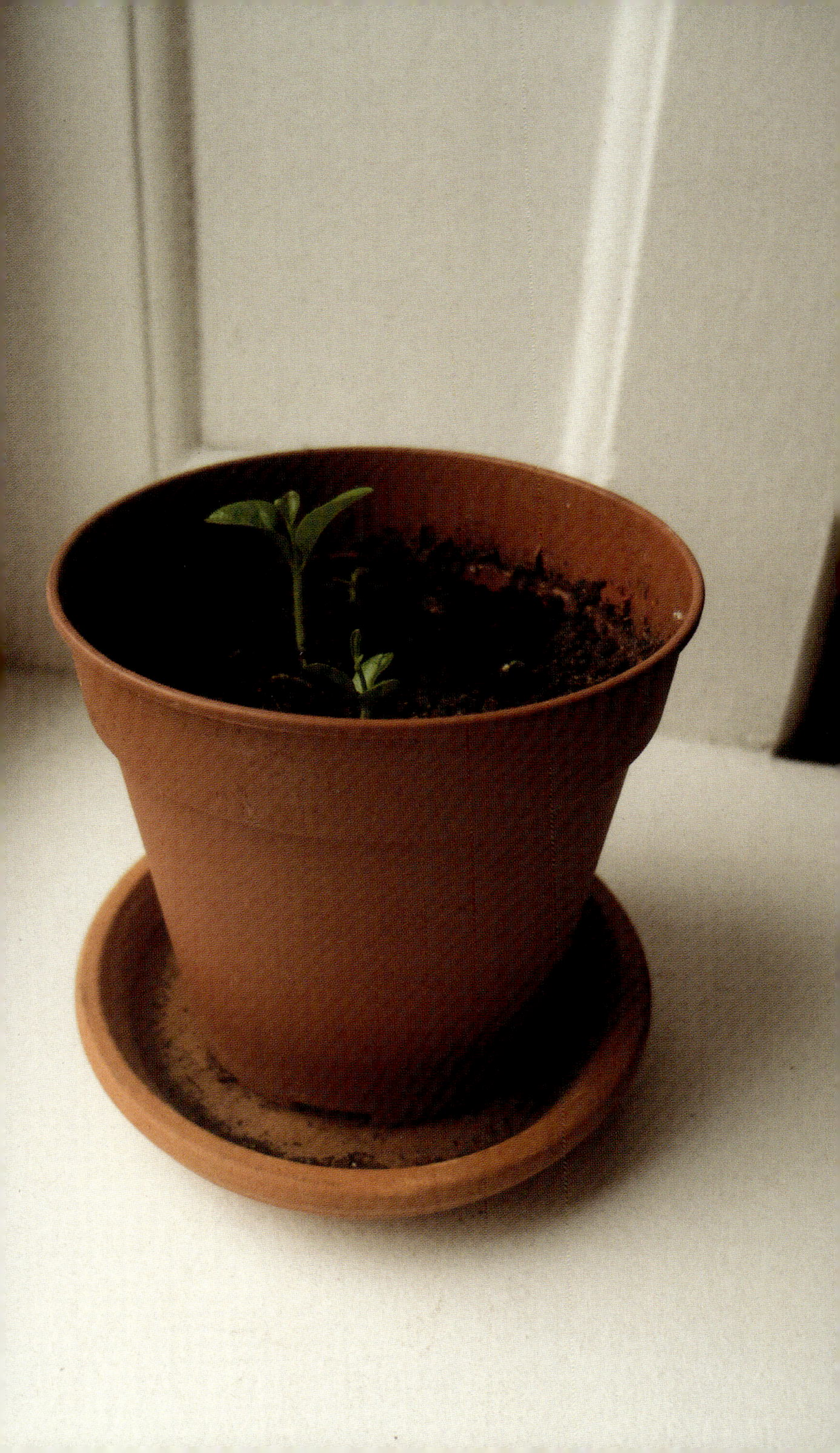

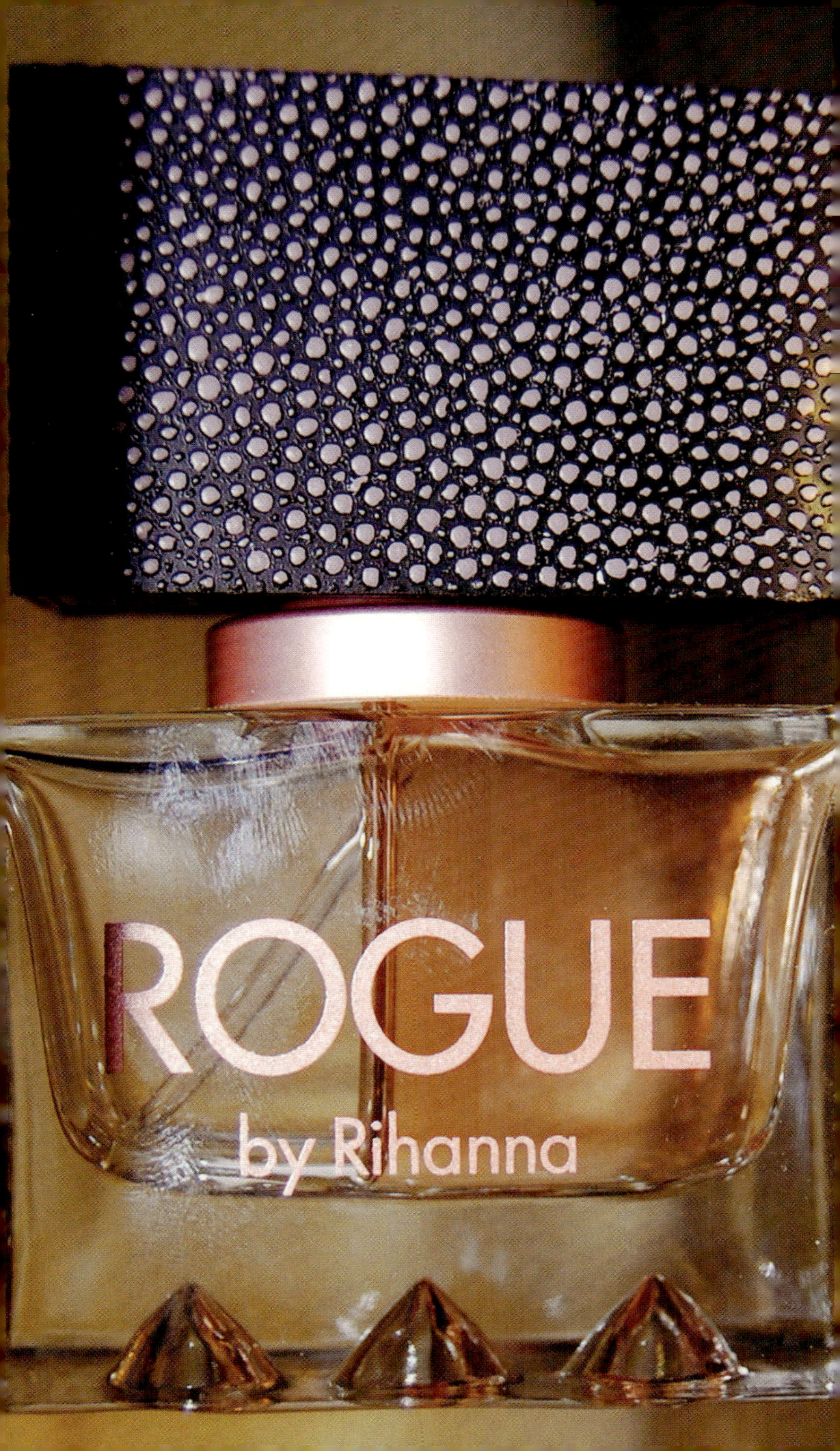
ROGUE
by Rihanna

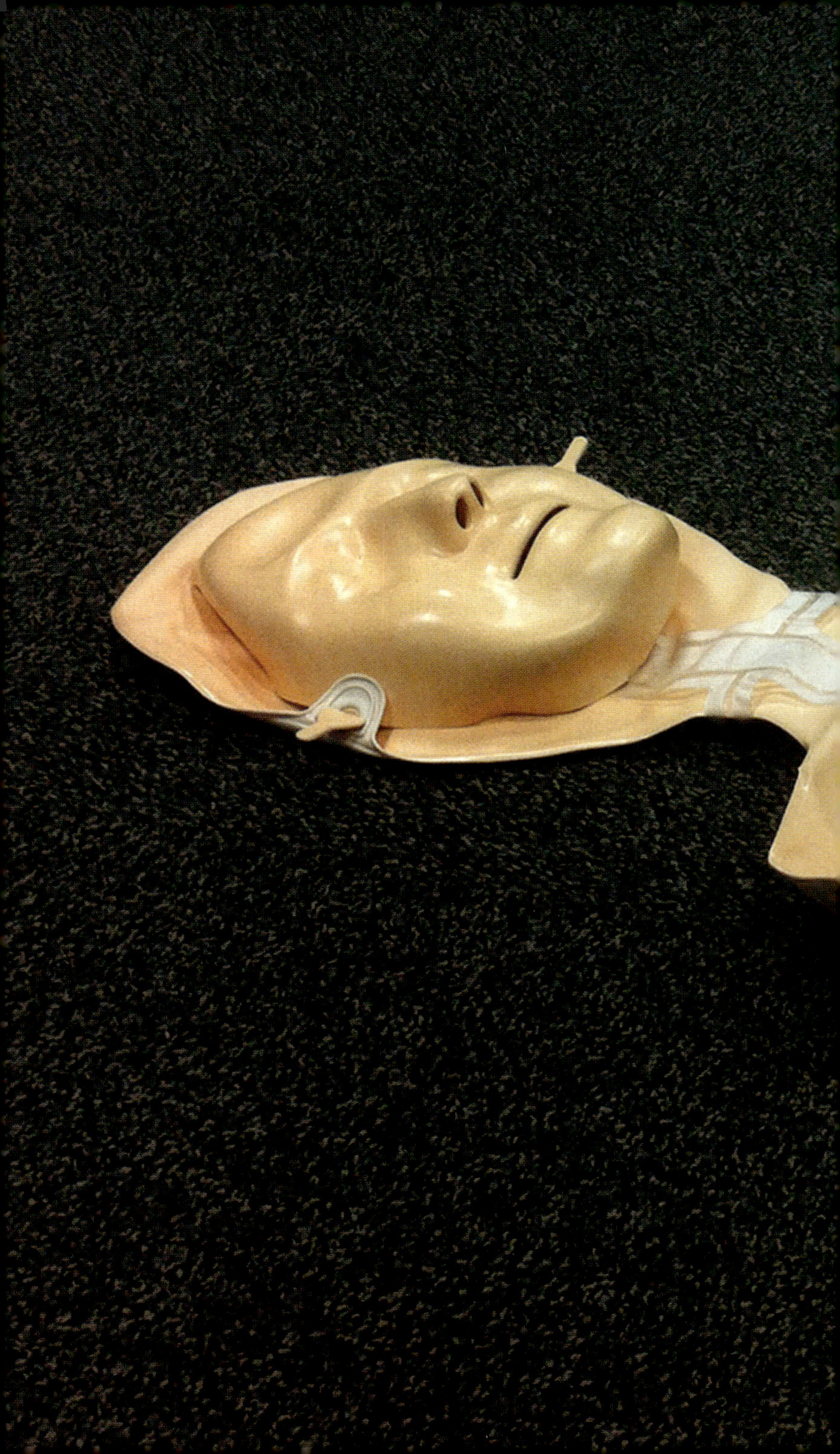

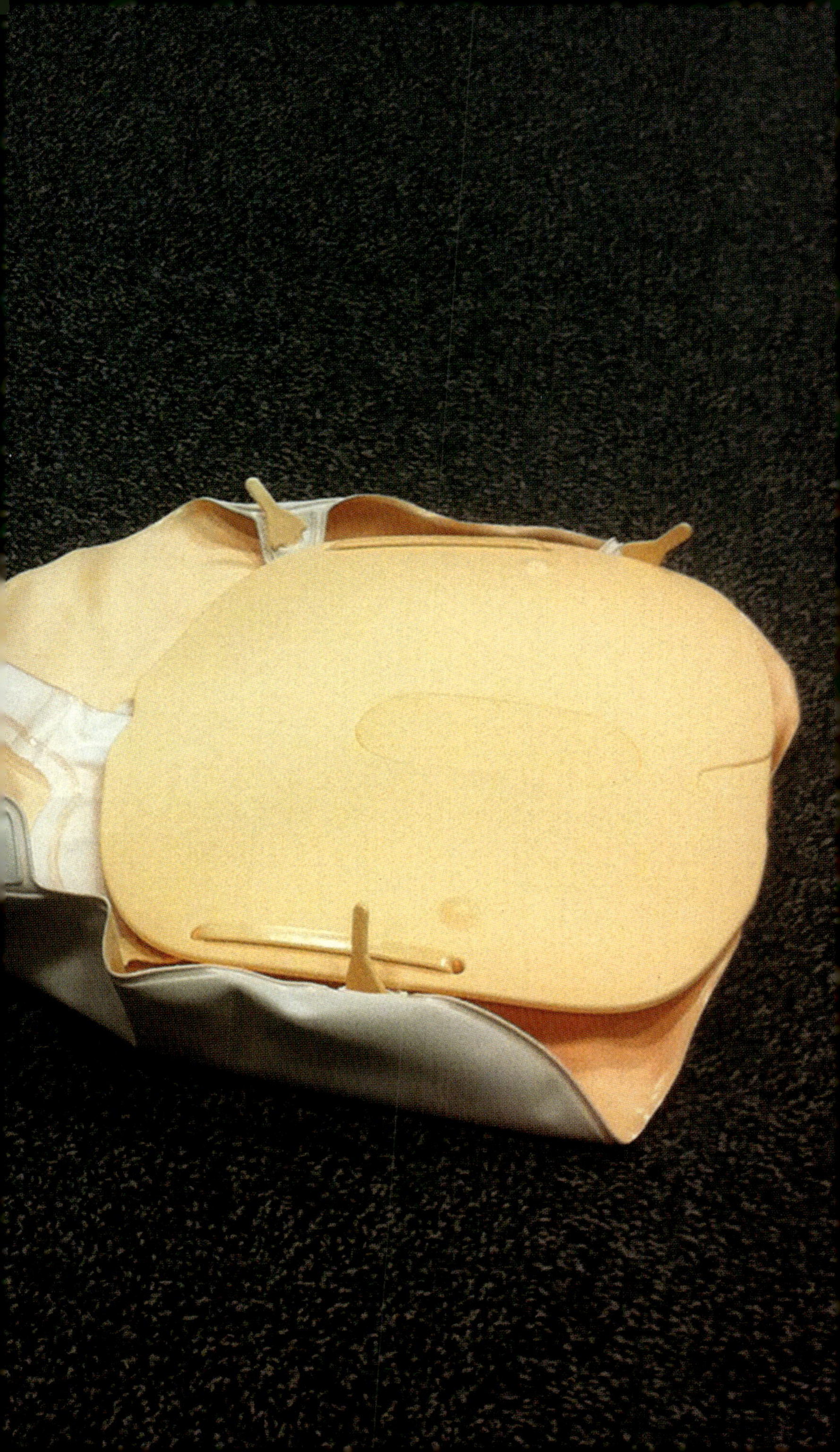

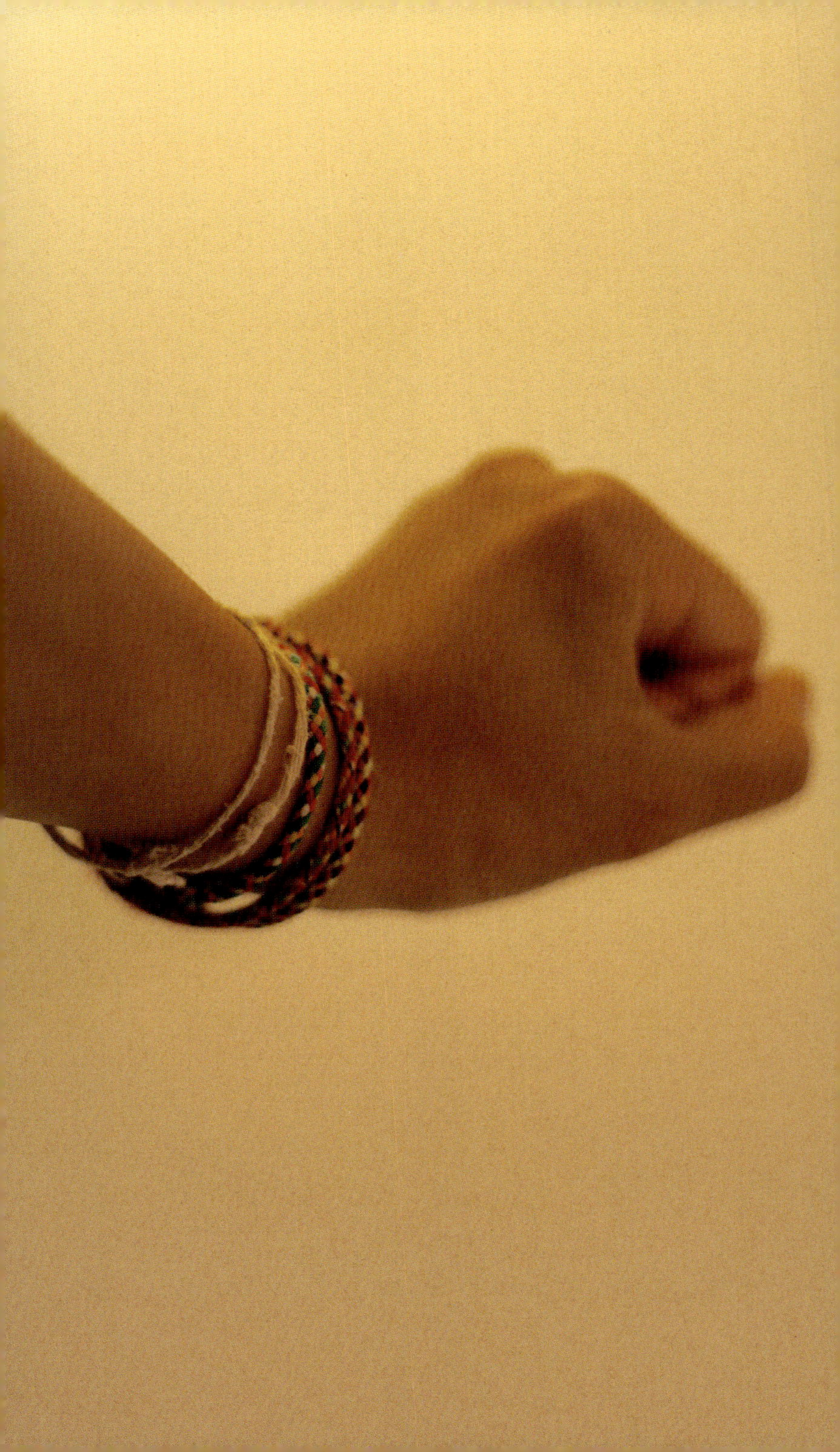

BIRD FLIGHT, STONE FLIGHT, A THOUSAND DESCRIBED ROUTES

Ellie Ga

On the Greek island of Lesbos, volunteers have fastened several pieces of laminated A4 paper to the metal gates of the port of Mytilene. The information is written in Arabic, Farsi, Pashto, and English:

> Keep your children in sight at all times. Warning: Crossing Bulgaria is extremely dangerous. You have the right to claim asylum in any country you enter. Fingerprints will be taken in many places...

My Arabic interpreter, Kate, and I have been in the port since dawn. We have just finished a day of interviews with women seeking asylum in Europe as they wait for the ferry to Athens.

We go to a restaurant and take a table next to an elderly man who is sitting alone eating his dinner. He seems at home, like he eats here every night. It's very smoky. Everyone still smokes in restaurants here. Kate complains to the waitress. It's December in Lesbos, and perhaps the old man, upon hearing us speaking English, correctly assumes that we're not here on holiday. Why would we be in Lesbos in the winter? Perhaps that's why he turns to us and says:

— In 1922, during the destruction of the city of Smyrna, my mother escaped to Lesbos on a small boat filled with people. Their tiny boats filled up with water. They tried scooping the water out of the boat with cups.

In 1922, hundreds—maybe even thousands—of refugees escaped the burning of the city of Smyrna, also referred to by its Turkish name of Izmir, by crossing the Aegean Sea on makeshift boats. Many of the people of Lesbos are either descendants of those who survived the perilous boat crossings during that week in September 1922, or of those who were uprooted during the mandatory population exchanges between Greece and Turkey that followed soon afterwards. Close to a million Greek Orthodox Christians in Turkey and a half million Muslims in Greece were forced from their ancestral homes and "exchanged," which is described as *Mübadele* in Turkish and Ανταλλαγή Πληθυσμών in Greek. In Greek, this period of time is referred to as Μικρασιατική Καταστροφή or "the Asia Minor Catastrophe."

Catastrophe (κατα + στρέφειν, or *kata-* + *stréphein*): Long before the word was used in the way we think of it today, catastrophe was a term used in ancient Greek drama to describe a reversal of what is expected, a turn of events. *Cata* meaning "downward" and *strophe*, "a turning."

— And you lost all your bags?

— Everything, we lost everything. Our clothes. Our phone. Our money.

— Was that the most difficult moment for you?

— No, it was the sea. We nearly drowned.

— A young man tried to empty the water out of the boat with his shoe.

— That was in the beginning?

— No, that was after 90 minutes. We drifted for two more hours after that.

— Were you able to see?

— Yes, but not far into the distance. People were praying, and I could not take any more pictures.

In that first week of December 2015, the majority of Syrian women that we spoke to made the perilous sea crossing from the area surrounding the coastal city of Izmir, sometimes still referred to by its Greek name, Smyrna. Hundreds—maybe even thousands—of refugee boats have been launched from this area in the hope of reaching Lesbos, Greece, and beyond.

I've been volunteering on Lesbos intermittently for almost a year, returning each time in a slightly different capacity, and each time European policies and local government attitudes have shifted. Lesbos has become a physical barometer of these shifts.

Now it is May 2016, and the laminated A4 sheets of advice were ripped down several months ago, not long after the EU-Turkey deal blocked the flow of asylum seekers into the EU. There are few visible traces of the so-called refugee crisis on the island that, during the peak period in the previous October, had experienced more than 2,000 asylum seekers arriving every day.

The collapsed wooden boats, deflated rubber dinghies, and mountains of life vests have been hauled to the garbage dump. The Arabic signs in the windows of travel agencies have been taken down and replaced by signs in English and Turkish. There is a hope that summer tourism will return, and that the "crisis" will be contained in the squalid detention centers that remain out of sight.

According to Evridiki Chyrsagi, an oceanographer at the University of Athens, the Aegean Sea is considered a "highly energetic region." The Aegean is semi-enclosed, its waters drifting across the almost-landlocked basin of the Eastern Mediterranean. And inside these waters there are countless islands, huddling in the space between land and sea. The combination of wind patterns and local currents is influenced by the shape of the shoreline and the constraints of the coast. On top of this, or underneath, are the inflows and outflows from the Black Sea, causing significant fluctuations in salinity and temperature.

All of this makes Evridiki's work on oil spill prediction far more difficult. If there is a spill in the Aegean, she will set her model in motion: predicting the speed of the spill and where it will go. But all this depends on the movement of the sea at a particular time and place.

— The Aegean is characterized by several gyres and eddies. Eddies are like gyres that move. They don't just stay in one place.

— Eddies are gyres that drift?

— They don't exactly drift.

— But for my amateur vocabulary?

— Yes, we can say that eddies are smaller gyres that drift.

Gyros, like *stréphein*, is another ancient Greek word for "turning." Like many before her, Evridiki tries to understand the turning of the sea.

On a beach in the north of Lesbos, a statue of Theophrastus overlooks the Aegean Sea in the fishing village where he was born. In Mytilene, the island's capital, a street is named in his honor. Its walls are scrawled with declarations of love, anti-austerity messages, and an anti-fascist slogan derived from a Greek pop song.

According to legend, it was Theophrastus who launched the first message in a bottle to learn about the flow of the Mediterranean. There is no proof of this, except that Theophrastus was a great naturalist, and that it seems to be an obvious experiment for someone who was born on Lesbos. As a young man, he left the island to study under Plato at the Academy in Athens. Theophrastus' botanical classifications were the most enduring of his scientific contributions, remaining almost unchanged until the work of Linnaeus, almost 2,000 years later.

We do not know what Theophrastus learned after launching his first message in a bottle, but in 1893 the Norwegian explorer Fridtjof Nansen took this experiment a step further. He designed a boat that could withstand the pressure of Arctic pack ice. This boat was called the *Fram*, or "forward" in Norwegian. With a crew of twelve people he then drifted on the ice for three years, crossing the uppermost reaches of the frozen Arctic Ocean.

Prior to Nansen's expedition, the prevailing scientific theory predicted that, if a boat could cross the Arctic pack ice, it would reach an open polar sea. Once on this sea, a boat could sail directly to the North Pole. This belief explains why so many expeditions ended tragically, why boats continued to sail into the ice, only to be surrounded and crushed. In fact, it was the debris of one of these ill-fated boats which provided Nansen with the evidence to support his theory. When the remains of the American polar schooner *Jeannette* ended up on the other side of the Arctic Ocean two years later—on an ice floe drifting off the southwest coast of Greenland—Nansen interpreted this debris as evidence that the frozen Arctic Ocean still moves via currents and gyres, like the rest of the world's oceans. How else could remains of the *Jeannette* have ended up on the other side of the Arctic Ocean? Surely the *Fram* could drift with the pack ice on the same current that carried the debris of the *Jeannette* over the top of the world.

The debris from the *Jeannette* drifted onto the shores of Greenland like a message in a bottle—speaking about, and across, distance. Nansen interpreted the debris as a call-to-act, which gave him the motivation to build a ship and prove a scientific theory that few people accepted at the time:

> Next we must choose a fitting place and moor the ship firmly between suitable ice floes, and then let the ice screw itself together as much as it likes—the more the better. The ship will simply be hoisted up and will ride safely and firmly. The current will be our motive power, while our ship, no longer a means of transport, will become a barrack, and we shall have ample time for scientific observations.

Nansen chose to lodge the *Fram* into the ice north of the New Siberian Islands, not far from where the *Jeannette* had been crushed. One hundred and ten years later, a two-masted sailboat named *Tara* was launched to catch the same current the *Fram* had used in order to drift through the Arctic Ocean. The *Tara* was also designed for the purpose of drifting in the ice: with the same sloping sides, retractable rudder, and shallow keel, but made from aluminum instead of greenheart wood.

Like the *Fram*, the *Tara* was designed to drift for years in the polar pack ice, allowing its crew to gather a constant flow of scientific data. Unlike Nansen's expedition, the *Tara* expedition had two changes of crew. Two scientists and I joined the expedition halfway through, thanks to a small plane that could land on the ice. The *Tara* traveled on the Transpolar Drift Stream, which was unknown, or at least unnamed, until Nansen's expedition. The *Fram* drifted for three years in the ice. The *Tara* drifted much faster, not quite two years—which has been attributed to the decreasing thickness of the pack ice. And like the *Fram*, we drifted over the top of the world, skirting, but not quite reaching the North Pole. Unlike the *Fram*, the ice released us in the middle of winter—in the middle of the polar night.

In the moments before the ice released us, the Norwegian carpenter, who trimmed and waxed his mustache in the style of Nansen, got on his knees at the prow of the boat and launched our message in a bottle:

> I feel as if such a bottle has fallen into my hands, the fulfillment of its mission assisted by the whole enormous element of the ocean.

The Russian poet Osip Mandelstam compared writing poems to launching messages in bottles into the sea. Somewhere, someone, will find the poem and read it. In his essay "On the Interlocutor," Mandelstam stresses that the poet must write to an unknown person, to an unknown addressee, that there must be some kind of distance to overcome by the act of writing a poem. Yet for the contemporary reader who knows of Mandelstam's fate, this text reads as a harbinger of events to come:

> The seafarer at a critical moment casts into the ocean a sealed bottle that contains his name and a description of his fate. Many years hence I find it in the sand while roaming in the dunes, read the letter, learn the date of the event

> and the last will of the deceased. I am within rights to do so. The letter sealed in the bottle is addressed to whoever finds it, being the finder I thereby am the mysterious addressee.

Mandelstam wrote "On the Interlocutor" early in his career, in 1913, years before he and his poetry were banished—before the act of writing would be a dangerous act—before his death in the Stalinist purges in 1938.

The poems that Mandelstam launched would travel in the minds and on the tongues of a committed group of friends and family. Years later, the poet Paul Celan would see himself as Mandelstam's mysterious addressee. For Celan, the kinship to Mandelstam was both poetic and biographical. Both were poets of Central European Jewish origin; both wrote poetry from a state of exile; both were accused of plagiarism. Mandelstam's poetry resulted in his banishment from society. Celan, unlike his parents, managed to survive the Second World War and was driven to radically deconstruct his mother tongue, German, in order to write poetry that could address the complexities of exile.

Celan published a French translation of "On the Interlocutor" in 1967. Mandelstam's essay about a bottle thrown into the sea makes its return 50 years later, in Celan's acceptance speech of a literature prize in Bremen:

> A letter in a bottle thrown out to sea with the—surely not always strong—hope that it may somehow wash up somewhere, perhaps on a

shoreline of the heart. In this way, too, poems are en route: they are headed toward.

Eric Kempson and his family live next to the beach in Eftalou, in northern Lesbos. Eric is a beachcomber. He earns his living by making crafts from the driftwood he finds on the beaches. While walking on the beach one spring morning in 2015, he finds, as he does on most mornings, the debris of a journey—made by people who undertook a clandestine crossing from Turkey to Lesbos in the middle of the night:

> — This is an adult life jacket here and next to it we have a small child's life jacket and another small child's life jacket. And here is a small doll that has been left by one of the children. You can see how small this doll is by the size of my hand and you can see how small this life jacket is when I put it next to the doll. Let's put it together. Look. Look how small the child must have been who was wearing this life jacket.

One hand shakily films the other hand putting the objects next to each other as Eric's off-camera voice thickens with grief, then anger.

> — Okay, I'll put this one on the Internet today.

That was Eric's first YouTube post, filming his encounter with an unintended message on the beach. That's the moment Eric and his family decided that they could no longer turn their backs on what was happening on the beach next to their home. You could say that the doll Eric found on the beach was a message, which he interpreted as a call to act. His video blog is a plea for help, which became a beacon for journalists, officials, and volunteers like myself.

During one of my rounds of volunteering on Lesbos, I learned about The Museum of the 1922 Refugee. I've come back to the island with my friend Eva, acting as my Greek interpreter, in the hopes of visiting the museum. We haven't been able to find a working phone number. We sent an email but never received a response. Perhaps it's not open during the off-season. It's May, and the tourist season hasn't quite begun.

We do one last search online and find another website for the museum, listing a mobile number. The man on the other end is not in Greece, but he gives us the phone number of the museum's cofounder. We call, and she agrees to open the museum for us in the late afternoon.

Driving to the southern tip of the island, the island tapers off into two divergent landmasses. The village of Skala Loutron sits on the bay, far from the bustling capital of Mytilene, and even further from the picturesque villages in the north where Eric and his family live and where the refugee boats were still arriving just a couple of months ago. The "refugee crisis" seems a world away from this quiet village with its half-demolished factory complex, a basketball court, and playground alongside a boarded-up café on the square with a sign written in English:

Rooms to rent.

Several men are repairing a fishing boat on the dock. We pull over and ask for directions, and one of them replies with a smile:

> — What business do you have at our museum?

We arrive as the museum-keeper, who is also the co-founder, is opening the gates. Sunlight pours into the former schoolhouse. A hand-painted map on the wall depicts what the Greeks have historically called Asia Minor, which includes most of modern-day Turkey.

The museum-keeper walks across the length of the map, which covers an entire wall, sweeping her arms over the breadth of the landmass painted in yellow ochre. As she gets to the shoreline, she starts saying the place names, touching them with her finger, and her finger lands where we are now:

> — This village was created by the Greek government to be inhabited by refugees from the city of Phocaea in Asia Minor.

The vitrines are filled with personal belongings—mostly ornately embroidered clothes, some jewelry. The jewelry isn't very valuable, the museum-keeper says. The most valuable things would have been used as currency upon arrival in Greece. She points to a vitrine containing a small doll alongside a folded blue and brown knitted blanket:

> — My neighbor used this to carry her two children across the sea. This was all she brought with her.

Some of the people who had more time to leave, like her family, managed to bring their sewing machines with them. She explains that this is what saved them from destitution. Above the sewing machine there are bar graphs, maps, and pie charts, detailing the population exchanges. Next to this is a group photograph, consisting primarily of women, children, and the elderly—the new arrivals—taken outside what is now the village café.

> This age is my age, is a beast, my beast.
> No one can look it in the eye, as none
>   would fix its vertebrae
> with his own blood as glue, the broken
>   backbones
> of two centuries.
>
> But any thing alive must drag its backbone
>   with it, so
> compelled, only as far as it can, as its short
>   life allows.
> The waves play and plash the lines of
>   spinal chords
> they can't see, nor we.

Mandelstam's poem ВЕК (translated into English as *The Age*) was written the same year this photograph was taken, in 1922. The same year that Mandelstam married Nadezhda, the person who would save his later poetry from the Stalinist purges by committing it to memory. Line by line. Stanza by stanza. Strophe by strophe. *Strophe*: a group of lines of poetry. Borrowed from *stréphein*, a turning. In ancient Greek drama, the word was used to denote the part of an ode sung by the chorus while turning in one direction.

> Tree buds will bulge again and sprouts
>   spray green.
> Still beautiful, my pitiable age, with your
>   broken back,
> spine splayed, smile senseless, you turn to
>   look over
> your shoulder in backward gaze, as a
>   beast, once supple,
> young and lithe, to see the tracks your
>   own paws made.

Celan translated век into German as *Meine Zeit* along with thirty-nine additional poems by Mandelstam. The translations were done between 1958 and 1959, during the same period that Celan's own collection of poems *Sprachgitter* (*Speech-Grille*, or *Language Mesh*) was published. I imagine the second stanza from Celan's poem *Allerseelen* (*All Souls*) as a caption for this group photograph of the new arrivals outside the village café, with nothing to turn to but "their own heavy centres"—and the camera:

> Bird flight, stone flight, a thousand
> described routes. Glances
> purloined and plucked. The sea,
> tasted away, drunk away, dreamed away.
>   An hour
> soul-eclipsed. The next, an autumn light,
> offered up to a blind

feeling which came that way. Others, many,
with no place but their own heavy centres:
        glimpsed and
avoided.
Foundling, stars,
black, full of language: named
after an oath which silence annulled.

Surrounding the group photograph are official documents, like the Nansen passport. In his later life, Fridtjof Nansen, the Arctic explorer who interpreted debris lodged in an ice floe as a call to test out his theory about drift, became the High Commissioner for Refugees for the League of Nations. The Nansen passport, first issued in 1922, was an internationally recognized form of identity for stateless people. Nansen and his office contributed to the institutionalization of the refugee. One can only wonder what was the catalyst for this work. Was it also the relic of the crushed boat, the *Jeanette*, reinterpreted years later as a call to use his power and influence for humanitarian causes during the last decades of his life?

Nansen was also one of the architects of the mandatory population exchanges between Turkey and Greece, which became law in 1923. Whether this was Nansen's idea is questionable. As a non-politician, and famous explorer, his name was reputable—it was useful promotion for a controversial policy. But whatever the extent of his personal contribution, Nansen nevertheless sustained a third career, beyond that of a scientist and explorer. The same year he won the Nobel Peace Prize for this work:

> To me … the Peace Prize is strange and incomprehensible; since I was forced by chance into this work, which was not mine at all … My scientific work has convinced me … that everything goes in cycles, in waves, it is my consolation, even if the periods of decay can be long, and the wave troughs deep; a crest comes again, if only one can wait …

Eva and I clean up the remnants of the coffee and cakes that the museum-keeper made. She insists we take the rest with us. We leave the museum and return to the harbor, the seemingly run-down village imbued with significance. In the middle of the square, there's a slab of white marble standing upright. We hadn't noticed it earlier. Eva translates the Greek inscription, and again I imagine Celan's words as a caption:

> From an "already-no-more" into a "still-here."

WORKS CITED

Paul Celan, "All Souls," *Poems of Paul Celan*, trans. Michael Hamburger (London: Anvil Press Poetry, 2007).

Paul Celan, "Bremen Speech," *Collected Prose*, trans. Rosmarie Waldrop (New York: Routledge, 2003).

Paul Celan, "The Meridian," *The Meridian: Final Version—Drafts—Materials*, trans. Pierre Joris (Stanford, CA: Stanford University Press, 2011).

Roland Huntford, *Nansen: The Explorer as Hero* (London: Duckworth, 1997).

Osip Mandelstam, "On The Interlocutor," trans. Philip Nikolayev, *Battersea Review*, http://thebatterseareview.com/poems/85-back-issue-content/154-on-the-interlocutor (accessed May 1, 2017).

Osip Mandelstam, "The Age," trans. Matvei Yankelevich (unpublished, 2016).

Fridtjof Nansen, *Farthest North: The Norwegian Polar Expedition 1893–1896* (New York: Skyhorse Publishing, 2008).

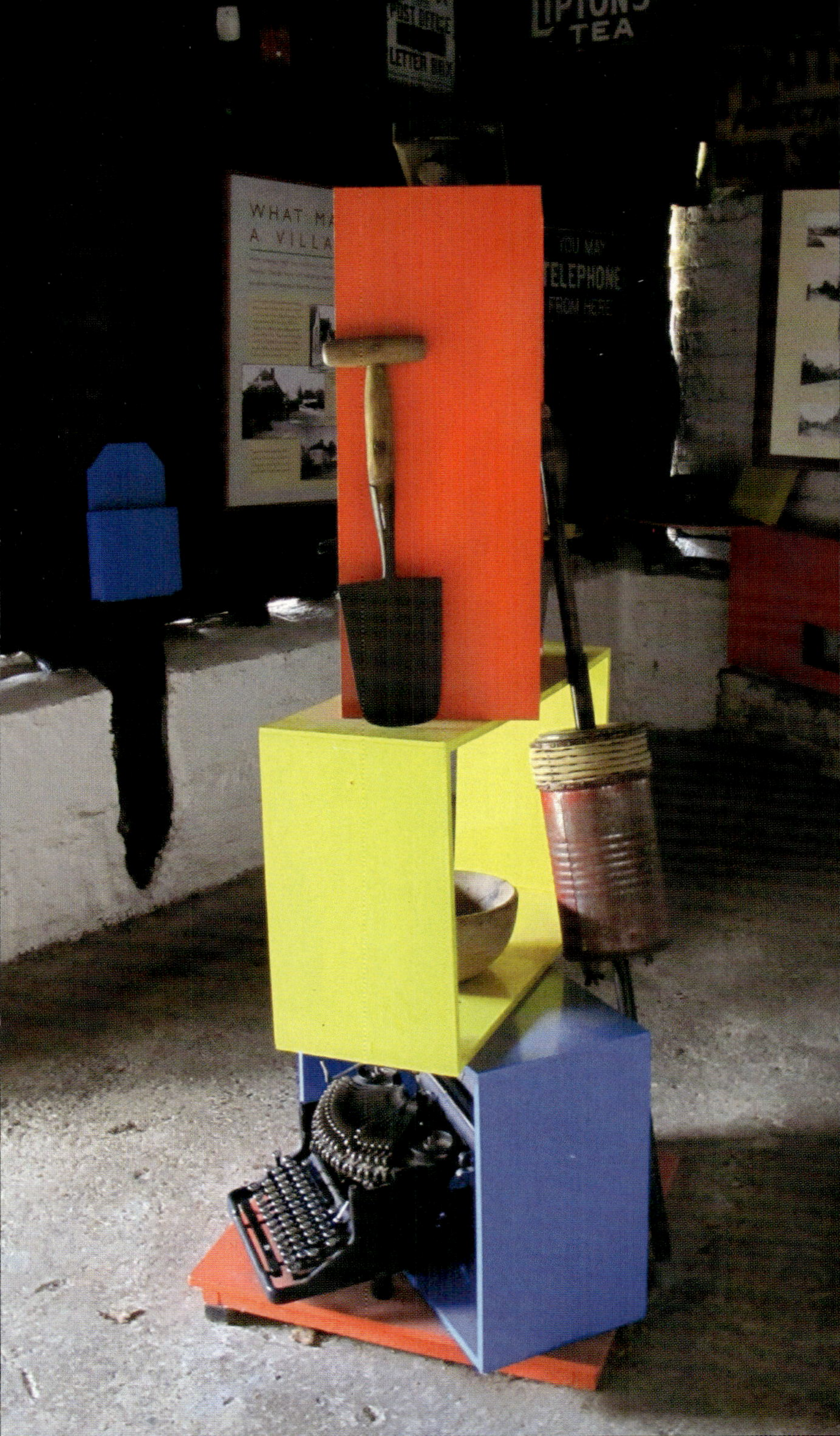
TEA
WHAT MA
A VILLA
YOU MAY
TELEPHONE
FROM HERE

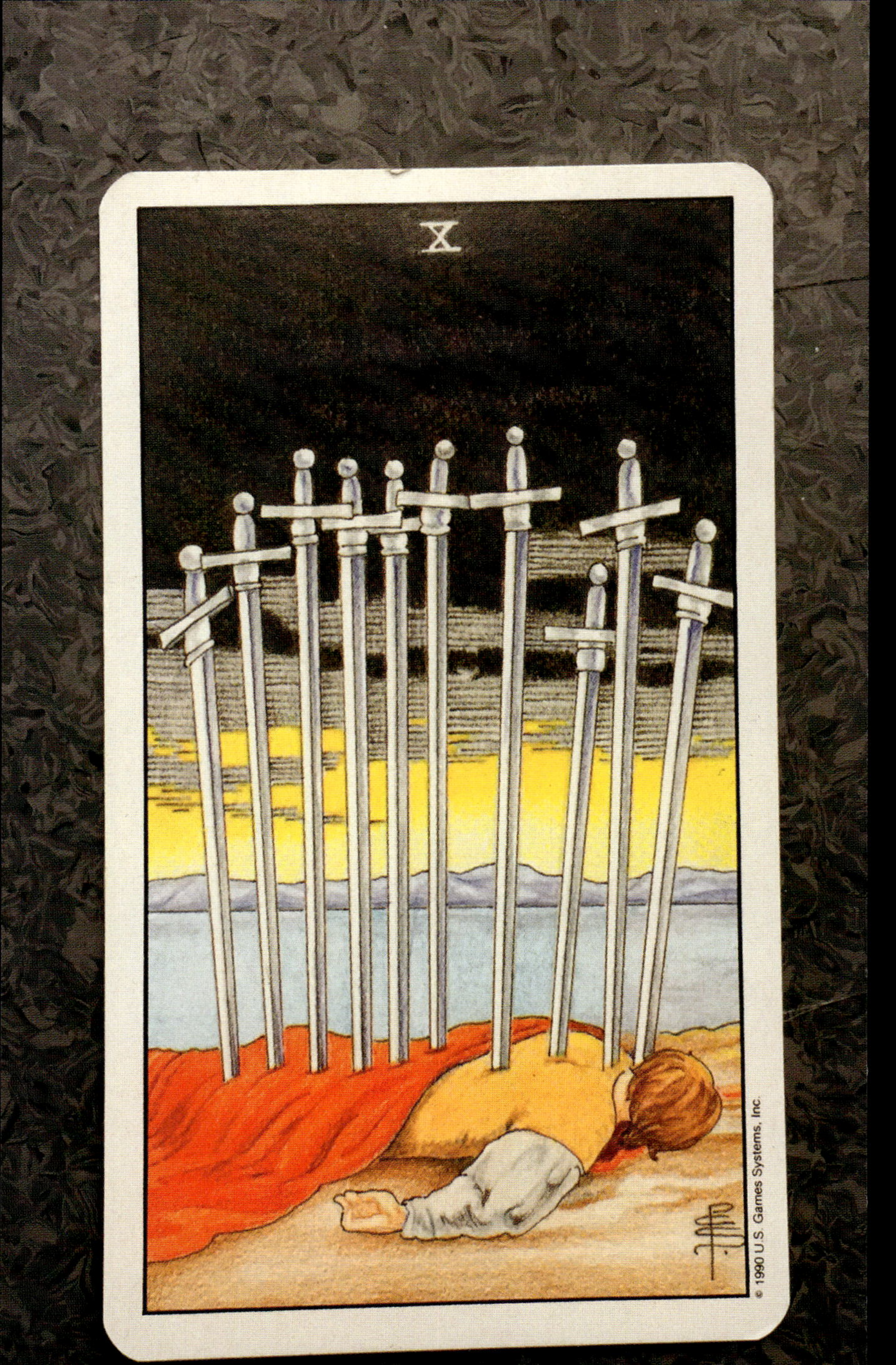
X
© 1990 U.S. Games Systems, Inc.

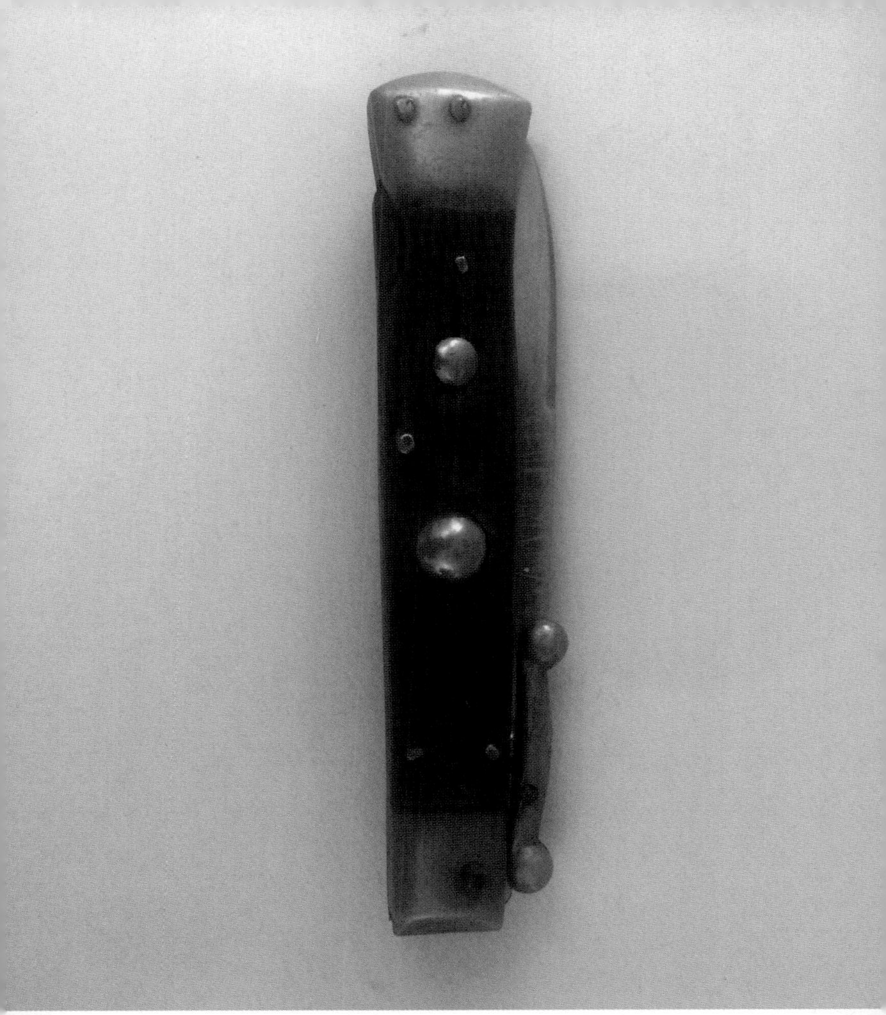

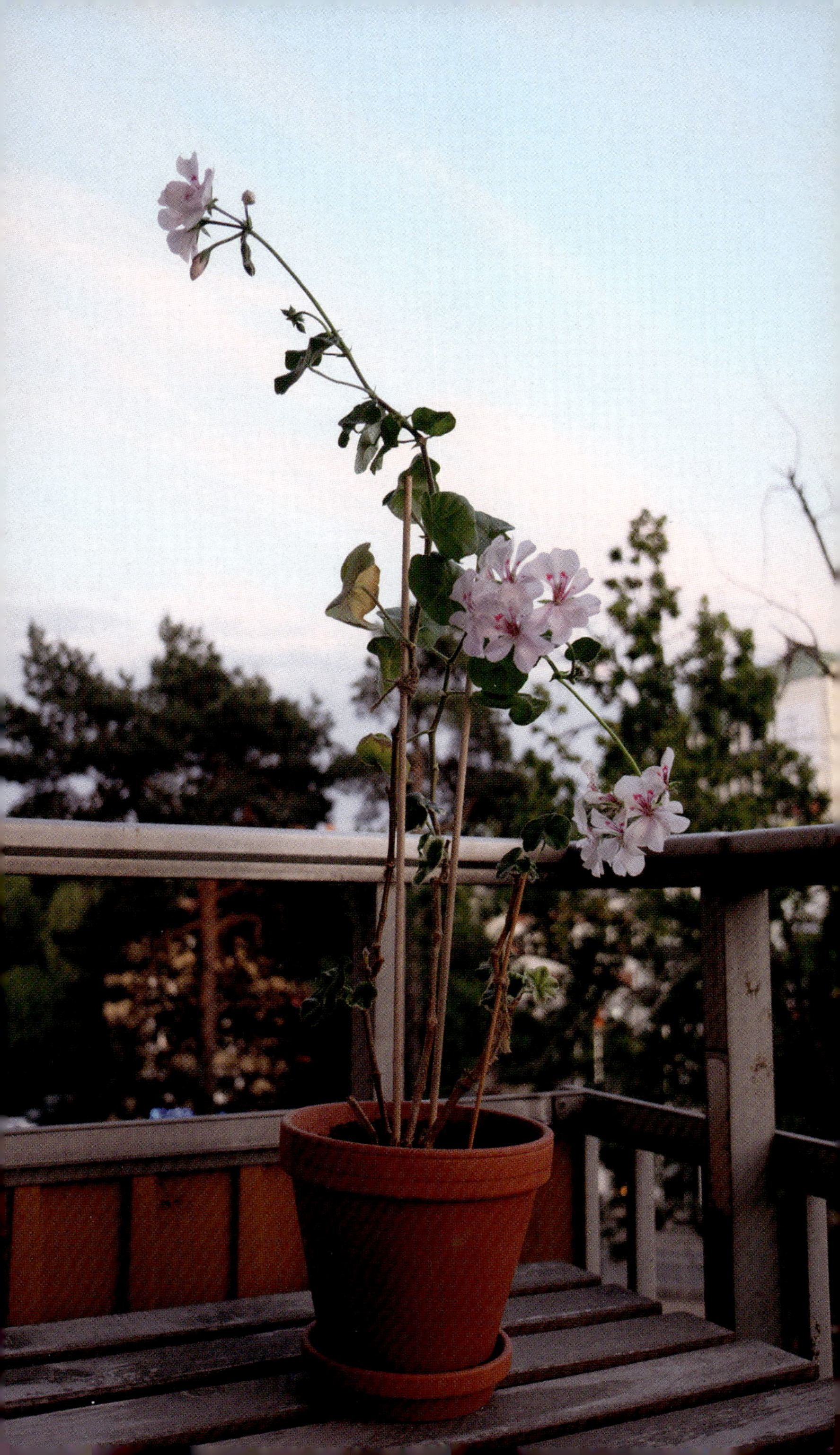

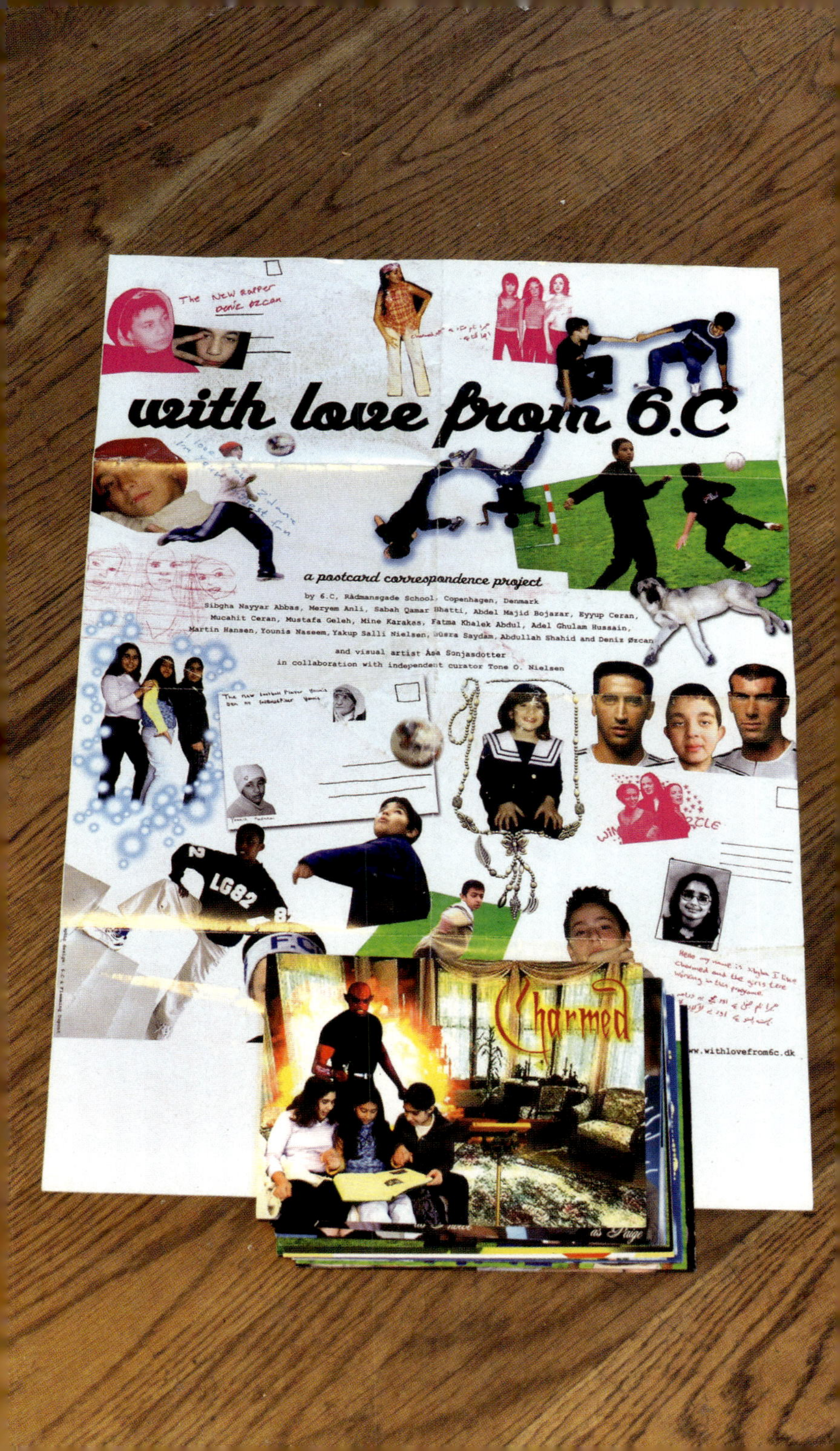
The New Rapper
Deniz Øzcan
with love from 6.C
a postcard correspondence project
by 6.C, Rådmansgade School, Copenhagen, Denmark
Sibgha Nayyar Abbas, Meryem Anli, Sabah Qamar Bhatti, Abdel Majid Bojazar, Eyyup Ceran,
Mucahit Ceran, Mustafa Geleh, Mine Karakas, Fatma Khalek Abdul, Adel Ghulam Hussain,
Martin Hansen, Younis Naseem, Yakup Salli Nielsen, Büsra Saydam, Abdullah Shahid and Deniz Øzcan
and visual artist Åsa Sonjasdotter
in collaboration with independent curator Tone O. Nielsen
LG82
Charmed
www.withlovefrom6c.dk

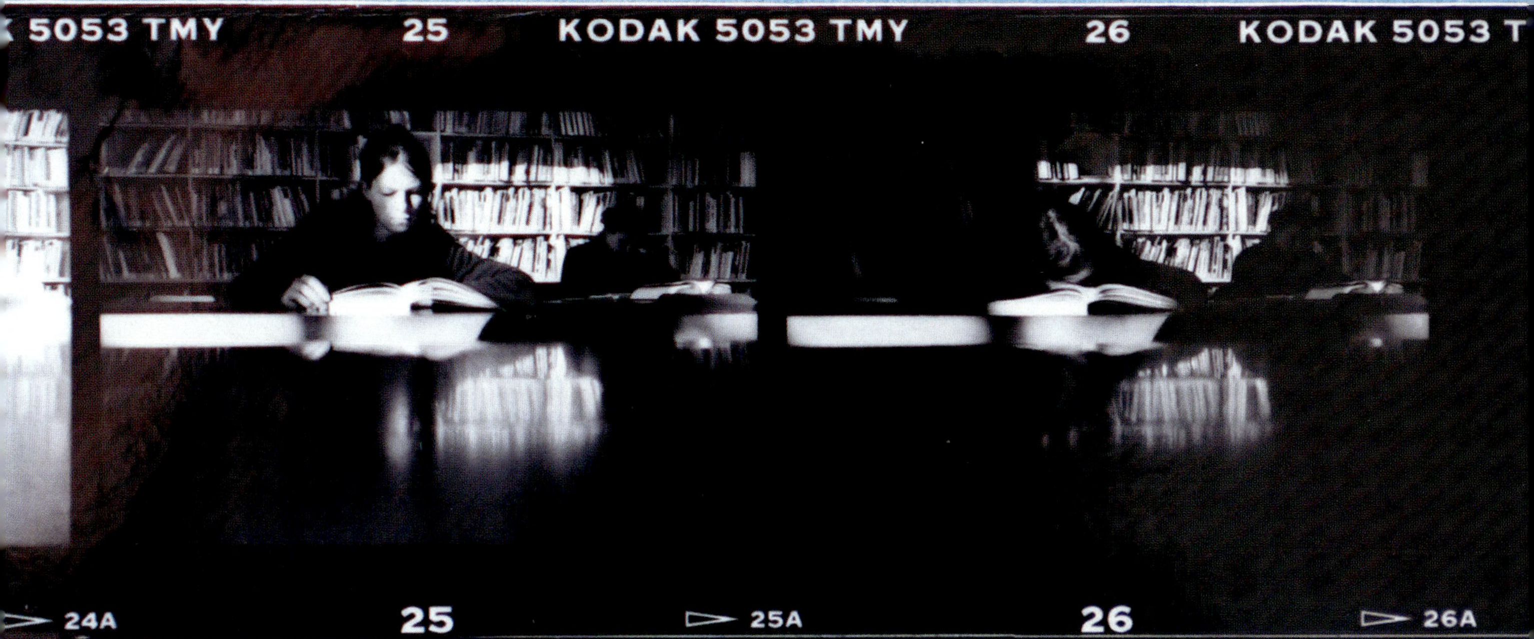
5053 TMY
25
KODAK 5053 TMY
26
KODAK 5053 T
24A
25
25A
26
26A

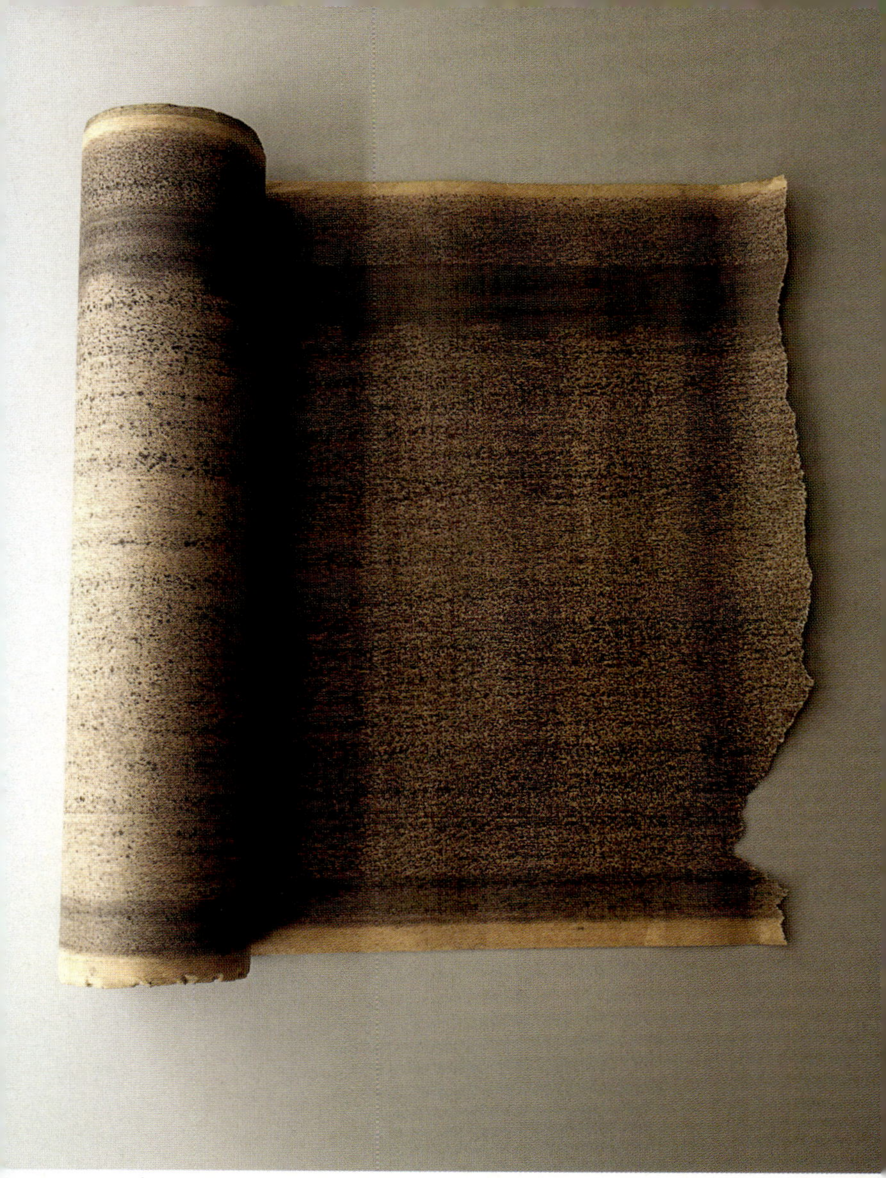

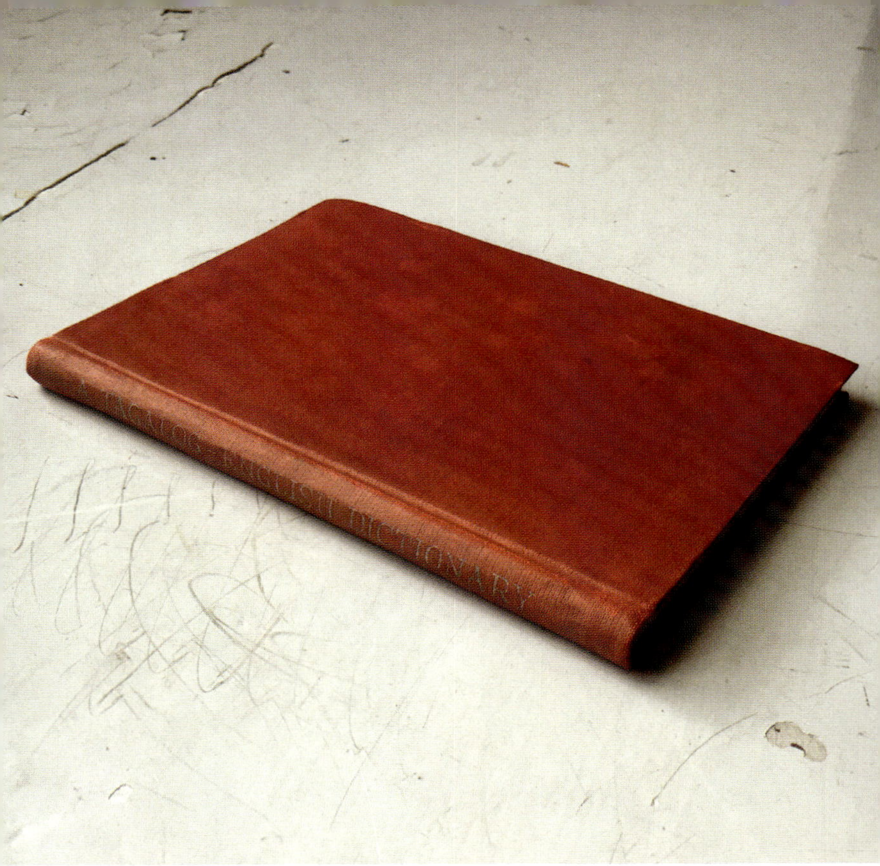
DICTIONARY

WAITING, WANDERING, AND WONDERING. "POST-CINEMATIC" SPACES IN THE MULTIPLE PRESENT

Robin Curtis

To navigate implies identifying and orienting oneself withing the relationship between self and the other and the relative locations of each in time and space. While road maps, signs, previously trodden pathways, as well as points of transition between discrete spatial entities such as those offered by bridges or border crossings all traditionally have been understood to stand at our disposal as visible markers to accomplish the task of navigation, electronic and digital media, apps as well as apparatuses, have increasingly come to embellish, modify, and question the manner in which the contours of space are outlined. They have thereby altered the act of passage, expanding and highlighting the interactions at work in such movements. More broadly conceived, the process of navigation thus suggests the interaction, imbrication, and flow of all objects within a given set of parameters, such as a certain cultural, urban, or even a media ecology.

Expanding Marshall McLuhan's hypothesis from *Understanding Media: The Extension of Man* (1964), Elaine Scarry argued in a technological and medially inclusive fashion in 1994, that: "If our artifacts do not act on us, there is no point in having made them. We make material artifacts in order to interiorize them. We make things so that they will in turn remake us, revising the interior of embodied consciousness."[1] With Scarry's long-term view of this matter in mind, one that allows for a complex intermingling of past, present, and future media and texts in our desires and projections, I would like to consider some contemporary encounters with media, mediatized environments, and other complex, multilayered aesthetic interactions. Specifically, I am interested in exploring how the overlapping of texts, media, technologies, and cues—and thus also the affordances of each—highlights the ways in which our past experiences can significantly shape and intermingle with present ones, highlighting the presence of networks of possibilities within each of those texts, media, technologies, cues, and affordances.

DISSOLVING ORIENTATION

Recently a number of media scholars have argued that our contemporary sense of space (and time) is increasingly represented through aesthetic strategies defined by "post-continuity."[2] Within this aesthetic paradigm, exemplified for instance by Michael Bay's explosive blockbusters (including the *Bad Boys* and *Transformers* franchises), narrative cohesion is not entirely disrupted. However, the cohesion of time and space certainly is. This latter cohesion was once considered a hallmark of continuity editing's "human" perspective on the world, guided by a particular conception of the manner in which attention operates.[3] A decisive shift has taken place that has done away with an overarching need for a cohesive spatio-temporal narrative thread to guide one's movement through cinematic space. According to Steven Shaviro's account of this shift:

> In classical continuity styles, space is a fixed and rigid container, which remains the same no matter what goes on in the narrative; and time flows linearly, and at a uniform rate, even when the film's chronology is scrambled by flashbacks. But in post-continuity films, this is not necessarily the case. We enter into the spacetime of modern physics; or better, into the "space of flows," and the time of microintervals and speed-of-light transformations, that are characteristic of globalized, high-tech financial capital.[4]

But clearly, as the box office receipts for Bay's blockbusters attest, we continue to assimilate these shifts in some fashion, despite the change to the "space of flows" cited by Shaviro, which is implied by this recent evolution away from editing strategies based on a classical continuity that privilege psychological and spatial coherence. Indeed, these new strategies have quickly become the template for spatial and temporal navigation, now as familiar as continuity editing was in the past.

But if, as Vivian Sobchack has argued, "cinematic and electronic screens differently solicit and shape our presence to the world, our representation in it, and our sensibilities and responsibilities about it,"[5] what effect does our increasing exposure to the digitally facilitated post-cinematic, post-continuity strategies of negotiation in time and space have on our movement through other environments, mediated or (ostensibly) unmediated?

Reminding us of the pertinence of Heidegger's point that "the essence of technology is nothing technological,"[6] Sobchack emphasizes the need for an examination of the complex parameters at play beyond the merely "technological" aspects of any phenomenon. Indeed the assumption and examination of a reciprocal relationship between technology and the human body is an absolutely central aspect of Vivian Sobchack's project. With Heidegger's postulation in mind, she highlights precisely this readily neglected reciprocity, which occurs due to the contextual qualities of technologies in use and thus counters the inclination to understand technology as a static force exerting unilateral influence on a human body. She describes technology as:

> historically informed not only by its materiality but also by its political, economic, and social context, and thus it both co-constitutes and expresses not merely technological value but always also cultural values. Correlatively, technology is never merely used, never simply instrumental. It is always also incorporated and lived by the human beings who create and engage it within a structure of meanings and metaphors in which subject-object relations are not only cooperative and co-constitutive but are also dynamic and reversible.[7]

Sobchack has taken care throughout her body of work to offer thorough examinations of very specific examples of media texts and situations and their particular affordances. A key part of her project is underscoring that there are reciprocal processes[8] at work in those technologies of representation simultaneously serving as technologies of perception (such as photography, film, television, videotapes, DVDs, cell phones, and computers):

> a qualitatively new techno-logic begins to alter our perceptual orientation in and toward the world, ourselves, and others. Furthermore, as this new techno-logic becomes culturally pervasive and normative, it can come to inform and affect profoundly the socio-logic, psycho-logic, axio-logic, and even the bio-logic by which we daily live our lives.[9]

Examinations of the rise of hybrid space and spatial experience typically see the proliferation of mobile technologies and digital media as the source of that rise. The 1990s are generally identified as the decisive decade of shift, during which the borders between physical, material space, and the space of information became blurred.

Concerned primarily with the manner in which social relationships and avenues of communication function and have evolved, key contributions to this field, such as sociologist Manuel Castells' expansive study of the monumental changes in social space in recent decades,[10] often have shown less interest in the specific effects of aesthetic experience upon the way in which we as individuals navigate through space—actively and passively, decisively or thoughtfully, consciously or on impulse—than in more everyday informational phenomena. It was Castells who articulated the distinction between what he termed the "space of material places and locations," (anchored in local memory and tradition) and the increasingly significant "space of flows" (the space of information, communication, and capital, which is ahistorical, location-free, and continuous). In accounts such as Castells', digitization has allowed for the augmentation of human perceptual channels via increasingly smaller and/or larger apparatuses that enable access to proliferating dynamic data through various channels and that confound the distinction between absence and presence.

But is it really a simple matter to distinguish between physical, virtual, or what Lev Manovich has called "augmented"[11] space—solely on the basis of the insertion of a technology which acts as an interface for experience and mediates between a real environment, augmented reality, augmented virtuality, and a virtual environment? Manovich defines augmented space as "the physical space overlaid with dynamically changing information. This information is likely to be in multimedia form and is often localized for each user."[12] Crucially he then wonders: "Do these layers [defined by form as well as spatial and informational layers] add up to a single phenomenological gestalt or are they processed as separate layers?"[13] Another important question is whether one can easily differentiate between the operations of intertextuality, intermediality, and the effects of hybrid space?

The following text focuses on the relationship between space and time, our physical situation, and our movement through space and time as generated through such complex layering: How can the spatial effects of such a navigation be isolated from a notion of time postulating a layered, hybrid, or multiple present, which is rendered by the various kinds of templates and experiential layers at play at any given moment? What role does recollection or projection play in the experience of the multiple present? Whereas we are clearly becoming rapidly accustomed to the integration and indeed imbrication of digital media into everyday routines—to the extent that we barely register their presence or influence—do contemporary forms of aesthetic experience train and shape experience in the material, unmediated world through a similar practice of layering? I argue that they do—by virtue of choice and trajectory. A feature which guided my selection of the phenomena in question is the particular aesthetic sensibility of immersion or immersive experience that has become a particularly potent trope of our time (albeit one with extremely unstable meaning). The media discussed here, immersive theater, an augmented reality game, and 4-D cinema, invite one to inhabit a fictional/digital/augmented space. In doing so, they highlight a number of inconsistencies and productive paradoxes implied by that inhabitation and navigation. I consider the paradoxes of location and situation made available by these phenomena productive, in that they make the density of affordances at work in these phenomena palpable, and they thus force us to consider Lev Manovich's question regarding the nature of augmented space more attentively: Namely, do such paradoxes add up to a single phenomenological gestalt, or are they processed as separate layers? Through an immersive engagement with these individual phenomena (albeit sporadic, oscillating between absorption and critical reflection, engagement and amused consternation) we are offered the opportunity to turn our attention away from a hermeneutically driven interaction in favor of an observation of the "separate layers" at work.

KALEIDOSCOPIC (IMMERSIVE) THEATER

Upon entering at the ground floor door to the six-story building, which had long served as a warehouse in New York's Chelsea district, (and after being obliged to turn over your cell phone, bag, coat, and ticket to attendants) you find yourself in a series of hallways shaped by black-painted pressboard walls—much like a traditional funhouse such as those still in operation at the Prater in Vienna. Although these hallways suggest the jagged-edged trajectories of a maze (or alternately the interiors of a Daniel Libeskind building or Gregor Schneider's *Haus Ur*), there are still no choices to be made yet. They lead to a single destination (thus operating according to the principles of a uni- rather than multicursal maze):[14] the "Hotel McKittrick," which is, according to your ticket, the name given to this ensemble of rooms. It is from there that the multicursal pathways of this experience open themselves to you.

In the immersive theater experience *Sleep No More*, which has been running continually since 2011 at this location in New York, you are confronted first and foremost by the vastness of the space available and second by the task of negotiating this space consisting of over 100,000 square feet, covering six floors, and divided into more than 100 rooms.[15] These have been meticulously set-decorated with a mixture of props, period furniture, and fixed detritus to suggest a combination of the precise attention to detail of an art installation (or the equally peculiar contemporary *Wunderkammer* that is the "Museum of Jurassic Technology" in Los Angeles) and the look of a video game (eerily reminiscent of the scenography of early interactive adventure games such as *The Seventh Guest* or the later horror game series *Silent Hill*).

And yet much of what has been written thus far about this wildly popular immersive theater experience succumbs to focusing on the structuring power of the dramatic text that ostensibly provides the basis for the *Sleep No More* experience, namely Shakespeare's *Macbeth*. W.B. Worthen's examination of the significance of character in *Sleep No More* is a compelling and detailed analysis of the encounter with the space. I consider this as a *pars pro toto* example of large body of recent theater scholarship addressing this work.[16] By choosing to summarize *Sleep No More* as "a meditation on *Macbeth* and a response to the function of Shakespeare in contemporary performance culture,"[17] Worthen situates the experience squarely within a single frame of reference, to which other experiences might perhaps be peripherally *and secondarily* added. However, just as Games Studies has struggled to position itself in relation to the demands of ludology and narratology in developing a fitting methodological strategy for revealing the specifics of the gaming experience,[18] any account of immersive theater necessarily struggles with the pluralities of space and time made available via this aesthetic form. Why *must* you seek out the threads that link the wanderings and wonderings of your allotted stay in the *Sleep No More* environment to *Macbeth*, or its human performers? Why would you not wander and wonder, as *World of Warcraft* players have often been wont to do as they pass through expansive digital landscapes, chatting online with the fellow travelers/gamers in digital space (although you are obliged by the "rules of the game" to remain silent in *Sleep No More*)? Why not simply check out the space itself, without undertaking any tasks or actions at all?

Despite the obvious relevance here of the multimedial implications accompanying Hans-Thies Lehmann's influential *Postdramatic Theatre* (2006)—which highlights the mid to late twentieth-century shift in theater away from a textual to mediatized image and sound culture and the apparent automatism of "immersion" through the removal of the fourth wall in a theatrical setting—the kaleidoscopic specifics of the particular experience of make-believe[19] made available through *Sleep No More* can be easily excised from any written account of the experience via the insertion of an overarching narrative (*Macbeth*).[20] Upon arrival in the space of the performance, you might indeed choose to trot after the performers through the space as best you can, along with the rest of the crowd, while using the links to the narrative of Shakespeare's drama like Ariadne's ball of thread.[21] Such reliance on the *Macbeth* narrative, however, threatens to either rule your experience or, *ex post facto*, your account of that experience, of the navigation, the encounters, the juxtapositions, and the choices you make during your roughly three-hour inhabitation of the space afforded by virtue of the roughly $100 ticket you have purchased. The reliance on such a narrative thread carries an economic advantage: you can thus be assured of having seen a performance of *Macbeth* (a middlebrow to perhaps highbrow activity) and not just visited an expensive funhouse (a lowbrow activity).

However, you might prefer not to follow but instead to wait, wander, wonder, and appreciate the silent eeriness of the many, many heavily decorated rooms that you encounter (empty of any human presence other than your own), while asking yourself what are the peculiarities of the experience of space on offer here. Upon arrival, for instance, you are greeted with the actorly lasciviousness of a young woman dressed for a night out in the 1930s (as are all the performers) and are then led from the "Manderley Bar" (the name of Maxim de Winter's estate in Hitchcock's *Rebecca*) of the "Hotel McKittrick" (familiar from Hitchcock's *Vertigo*), in which you are obliged to gather with other participants before being led toward and then released into the spaces that are part of the show. The general ambiance of the "Manderley Bar" is reminiscent of an amalgamation of David Lynch's films, due to the sense of temporal dislocation that is effected by the collection of signifiers at work in the bar (an experience also typically evoked by Lynch's oeuvre). What effect do all these signifiers (even if fictional) of multiple situations in time, space, and diegesis have upon the experience of space that is to come, when presented to the theatergoer upon entry to the *Sleep No More* venue?

I would argue the effect goes beyond a simple case of having other forms of intertextual reference superimposed onto the *Macbeth* narrative. Instead, we experience *Sleep No More* as an ergodic[22] encounter with a cybertext, which questions our ability to easily distinguish between the visual epistemes of presence discussed by Sobchack. Moreover, the merging of different sound references (audible are excerpts of Bernard Herrmann's scores from Hitchcock films, suggesting that we may actually be dealing with audiovisual epistemes) with an array of other verbal and visual fictional deictic markers places us functionally within the frame of reference of contemporary digital media experience, even though *Sleep No More* employs no electronic screens. We simply carry the neural pathways already formed by post-continuity with us.

DEIXIS IN THE 4-D CINEMA

In the autumn of 2016 a single 4-D cinema opened in Canada, in the Cineplex Odeon complex in downtown Toronto. At present these cinemas are quite rare, with only four in the US and eight in the UK.[23] In addition to the accoutrements of a regular 3-D cinema, these cinemas feature seat movement, fog, scents, rain, wind, bubbles, ticklers, snow, lightning, and directed blasts of air, all of which are timed to suggest a particular placement of the viewer within the diegesis of the fictional film on the screen. However, this is not as simple an undertaking as it might sound, since it involves and seeks to engage with both the signification processes of an individual film and the location of the material body of the viewer in time and space.

In his 1934 study entitled *Theories of Language*,[24] psychologist Karl Bühler first identified the significance of deictic markers in speech, which anchor utterances to the situation of the human body in a specific situation in time and space through the use of words that show or demonstrate (and are therefore dependent on usage in a particular spatio-temporal situation for their meaning). In terms of deictic utterances, Bühler coined the term "origo" as the point of origin; it is the "I-here-now," or "tactile body image" which enables the spatio-temporal situation of the material human body and thus makes such utterances possible. The question central to this research was how the materiality of the human body makes itself felt within the symbolic system of language, or indeed in other semiotic systems? In the 1980s, two film scholars working on the elaboration of film semiotics, Francesco Cassetti and Christian Metz, each considered the way in which a similar kind of encounter with spatio-temporal situations was performed by narrative film, albeit with only minimal interest in the viewer's body (and a great deal more attention to the filmic text).[25]

Narrative films do indeed often bid us—not only through sound effects but also through narrative devices—to question our "safe" situation as viewers in the time and space of the cinema and locate it instead within the diegesis of the film, oftentimes a frightening proposition. What becomes clear through the specific navigations made by the viewer as directed by 4-D cinema is that we, as film viewers in standard 2-D cinemas, are particularly adept at navigating a wide range of transpositions that allow an empathetic form of mimicry to take place in relation to all manner of characters, inanimate objects, atmospheres, and situations.[26] This we do while watching a film without particularly taking note of it—practically all the time.

However, in a completely disconcerting way, 4-D cinema directs us to leap from one specific cinematic space to another, from falling rain on one side of a shot-counter-shot construction to the snapping of rats' tails against our legs on the other side. This utterly disturbs our individual navigation of empathetic investment by attempting to situate us concretely within the space of each individual shot. In fact, our own capacities for alignment and mimicry far transcend the series of placements on offer in the 4-D cinema, which are fixed via the specific transpositions of place made plastic through the series of effects used. In other words, only when we watch a film in a 4-D cinema, does it become clear that we—as imaginatively mobile viewers fanaticizing a vast array of shifting allegiances—far outstrip the orchestrations of the 4-D apparatus that seeks to situate us momentarily and discretely, here, and then here, and then here, within the film's diegesis. Furthermore, by the effects of the 4-D cinema we sometimes feel emphatically reminded that we are situated in the space of the cinema itself.

In each of these first two examples, in the immersive theater and the 4-D cinema, the forms of aesthetic experience made available are—despite the expansive qualities of the presentations on offer—temporally and spatially contained and framed. The viewer is allotted a certain amount of time (and no more) within the room or rooms in question and is held (voluntarily, of course) within the confines of that particular theatrical space. A third example moves beyond such containment, however, in that it passes all decisions regarding the time and space of its appearance to its user, who is in control of the on/off switch of the app.

AUGMENTED REALITY MAPS THE CITY

The manner in which props for imagination are coopted by or integrated with deictic processes in a multilayered present[27]—via the interaction of imagination and perception—becomes immanently clear when one plays *Pokémon Go*, a location-based augmented reality game for smartphone. By combining the GPS function of a smartphone that localizes the user on a map of her particular surroundings with the phone camera's ability to offer a representation of that location in real time, this augmented reality game invites the user to engage with an array of fantasy creatures in the "space of material places and locations," to return to Castells' paradigm. By quite literally superimposing the Pokémon creatures that you collect and play with onto the image of the street or building made visible through your cell phone's camera lens, *Pokémon Go* layers its own props onto your physical space. It thus also adds additional layers of tasks to the everyday act of navigating city streets. In the weeks and months following its July 2016 release, the game reached a remarkable degree of saturation, with players of all ages engaging visibly (and sociably) with the augmented reality game in public.[28]

Kendall Walton's *Mimesis as Make Believe* (1993) offers an important contemporary intervention into the philosophical discussion of aesthetic experience and the widespread implications of make-believe.[29] His central thesis is that aesthetic experience (or rather fiction, as he terms it) creates a prop, such as a film, a novel, a painting, or a sculpture etc., that we use in "games" of make-believe played while engaging with these props, which in turn affect us physiologically. For Walton, a prop is the entirety of the aesthetic object rather than a particular feature of that object. Walton seeks to describe the form of "participation" that adults are willing to engage in when occupied with aesthetic experiences in general, even if the particular form of engagement is not as obviously mediated by a technological apparatus as is the case with augmented reality games. In a contemporaneous review of Walton's book, the neo-formalist film scholar Noel Carroll located the usefulness of such fictions in facilitating our "gaining a sense of playing new roles and of learning about ourselves and our responses when we confront imagined situations."[30] However, he also wondered why it is that such props sometimes don't function. In other words, why is it that we are often not moved by fictions (for example, by horror movies that fail to scare)? To my mind, this critique is analogous to the interpretive framework often imposed upon *Sleep No More*, creating the expectation that it constitutes either a skilled or failed performance of *Macbeth*. It is important to consider the enormously complex function of props, which should not only be seen as tools that serve in the operation of predetermined genres or narratives, or as signposts on the way to a feeling of "horror" or "anxiety." Instead, props such as the interaction with Pokémon on the streets of our cities (or the décor and players of *Sleep No More* and the entirety of the stimulants of the 4-D cinema) also do a variety of things simultaneously. Walton himself highlighted the social nature of make-believe and the manner in which props take on their meaning in a social setting:

> Props generate fictional truths independently of what anyone does or does not imagine. But they do not do so entirely on their own, apart from any (actual or potential) imaginers. Props function only in a social, or at least human, setting.[31]

With this in mind, it is important to not overlook the creative and social implications of *Pokémon Go* as a prop for collective make-believe.

What is striking to me about the *Pokémon Go* experience is the manner in which the augmentation of props, such as the Pokémon themselves, via the mediated image (and the screen of the cell phone) showing the streetscape in which you yourself stand, effects and highlights a curious kind of erasure, even as it encourages participation in a collective game of make-believe. *Pokémon Go* enables an encounter with, an oscillation between, and thus an awareness of Castells' "space of material places and locations," which relies on memory and local knowledge and tradition, and of his so-called space of flows (the space of information, communication, and capital, which is thus ahistorical, location-free, continuous). Typically we follow habitual paths through a familiar city, but *Pokémon Go* sometimes leads us in idiosyncratic and unexpected directions, off our own beaten paths (something that Google Maps or Apple Maps does not typically require us to consider doing), and thus we are encouraged to potentially encounter new spaces by following unfamiliar pathways through the city (even to the extent that the game might compel us to cross to the other side of the road before we normally would). Through playing *Pokémon Go* we can equally easily be induced to cease looking at the faces of others, their dress, and at the storefronts or streets as we pass, as we are so engrossed by the capture of the Pokémon on our screens, which ultimately belong in every way to the space of flows.

WAITING, WANDERING, AND WONDERING

Both analog and digital media function in cooperation with the texts, interfaces, or images that they make tangible to us as embodied users; these complex medial assemblages are in turn processed and thus form overlapping impressions within our perceptual systems. The complex "props" for aesthetic experience made available via the media discussed here (the immersive theater experience of *Sleep No More*, the experience of the 4-D cinema, or the gameplay of *Pokémon Go*) highlight the density of our investment in our experience of time and space: *Sleep No More*, 4-D cinema, and *Pokémon Go* each provoke a mingling of the "space of material places and locations," attuned to local memory and tradition, and the "space of flows," a space of information, communication, and capital, thus also a space that is ahistorical, location-free, and continuous. In each of these experiences, this mingling takes place to a different extent and more or less effectively at various moments in time during the experience.

Goal-oriented motion presumes that a clearly formed narrative or teleology is always in place that guides our present-moment experience and decision-making, suggesting that we are simply following a straightforward path. Waiting and wandering, on the other hand, disrupt more goal-oriented trajectories. The contrast between ludological and narratological perspectives on experience—as examined within the context of Games Studies—

is a reminder of the fact that for many forms of experience (not only aesthetic experience) it is not always helpful to presume that we are guided by a relentless goal-orientation or an interpretive framework. Motion (and motivation) are marked by hesitations and detours as well as "aimless" wanderings.[32]

Indeed, an increasing respect for these less goal-oriented trajectories is at the heart of what has become known as the slow scholarship movement. Slow scholarship embraces waiting, wandering, and wondering by rejecting the contemporary and increasingly neoliberal academic world's conceptualization of thought and scientific discovery in terms of a straightforward narrative, a kind of predictable mode of "rapid-transit system" that envisions a starting point and a destination in clearly foreseeable and calculable terms. But discovery is not always foreseeable and can seldom be described in terms of a trajectory through a previously mapped out space. Instead, discovery is characterized by, and here I concur most emphatically with Sobchack, increased attention to the specifics of a passage through the unknown.

The three case studies discussed here each provide very different forms of orientation to the user or viewer. The particular example of immersive theater offered by the vast performance space of *Sleep No More* is both contained and framed by the notion of the theatrical performance, which generally has the particular temporal constraints defined by what constitutes "an evening out," and thus, as in this case, is designed to last up to three hours, to permit a visit to the bar before and/or after the encounter with the performance space. The 4-D cinema similarly contains and frames the experience by virtue of the temporal and spatial constraints of a cinema, with a single screening lasting from roughly ninety to one-hundred-and-eighty minutes and the space of the cinema defined by its own entrance and exit. However the affordances of *Pokémon Go* differ significantly from the first two, in that the user moves at will through the space of the city, engaging similarly with the device and/or the city. And yet the possibilities are not endless, since our ability to engage meaningfully with the game is increasingly curtailed the further we move from the center of a big city, as the density of PokéStops and the opportunities for encounters with Pokémon characters decreases exponentially. In short, our specific trajectories through space profoundly affect the concrete affordances of this particular game, which does not engage equally everywhere, although it is always available.

The degree to which we engage with media and the manner in which we situate ourselves within overlapping spaces has everything to do with the training afforded by our past engagements with media, which in turn helps to determine the affordances of the media we engage with at any present moment. These past engagements themselves resurface in us to work like Ariadne's ball of thread guiding us not to seek an overarching narrative but rather to traverse idiosyncratic pathways in our encounters with the particular audio-visual episteme of presence made available through contemporary media. The passages and forms of presence I have been describing here are clearly occupied with something other than interpretation as a perspective on the interactions with other objects put into play, pointing to a broader question. Media ecology typically concerns itself with information networks and other large-scale structures, the macro perspectives that by virtue of their scale in relation to our perceptual systems reassuringly seem to escape anthropocentrism and human interpretive intentions. But the densities of the overlapping and competing informational systems that are part and parcel of the objects I have examined indicate that noninterpretive micro perspectives on media can also offer insights into small-scale "spaces of flows" such as these.

The very interminglings afforded us by virtue of various forms of engagement with objects in the world, such as the many described here, point to the need for a better understanding of such encounters on the "micro" level, within what has been termed the nonhuman turn. One of the most prominent proponents of an object-oriented ontology, Jane Bennett, calls for just such an analysis: "It makes sense to try to do justice both to systems and things—to acknowledge the stubborn reality of individuation *and* the essentially distributive quality of their affectivity."[33] She herself offers a written text, or a "text-body" as she calls it, as an example of an object in the world that gestures toward something more, as "a function of a *distributive network* of bodies: words on the page, words in the reader's imagination, sounds of words, sounds and smells in the reading room, and so on, and so on—all these bodies co-acting are what do the job."[34] To what end do we engage with such bodies as these? What future interminglings are suggested to us by way of these engagements? To this Bennett answers that "texts"—to which I would add, not only augmented reality games but also 4-D cinemas and immersive theater events—"are bodies that can light up, by rendering human perception more acute, those bodies whose favored vehicle of affectivity is less wordy: plants, animals, blades of grass, household objects, trash."[35] In other words, these aesthetic engagements make contemporary philosophical perspectives on the world palpable, such as nonhuman or object-orientation, which recognize the potential equality of objects amongst one another. These are matters of vital importance for our future.

NOTES

1. Elaine Scarry, "The Merging of Bodies and Artifacts in the Social Contract," in *Culture on the Brink: Ideologies of Technology*, eds. Gretchen Bender and Timothy Druckrey (Seattle: Bay, 1994), 97.
2. See Steven Shaviro, *Post Cinematic Affect* (Winchester: Zero, 2010); and Shane Denson, "Crazy Cameras, Discorrelated Images, and the Post-Perceptual Mediation of Post-Cinematic Affect," in *Post-Cinema: Theorizing 21st-Century Film*, eds. Shane Denson and Julia Leyda (Falmer: Reframe Books, 2016), 193–234.
3. From Hugo Münsterberg to Christian Metz, that is from the 1910s to the 1960s, classical film theory was long occupied with revealing the psychological logic of classical forms of film narration. See particularly Hugo Münsterberg, *The Photoplay: A Psychological Study and Other Writings* (New York: Routledge, 2002) and Christian Metz, *The Imaginary Signifier: Psychoanalysis and the Cinema* (Bloomington: Indiana University Press, 1986).
4. Steven Shaviro, "Post-Continuity: An Introduction," in *Post-Cinema* (see note 2), 60.
5. This very early text by Vivian Sobchack first appeared in a hugely influential volume *Materialities of Communication* edited by the German scholars Hans Ulrich Gumbrecht and K. Ludwig Pfeiffer, which was simultaneously published in English and German in 1988 by Stanford University Press in the US and Suhrkamp Verlag (as *Materialität der Kommunikation*) in Germany. The volume is a collection of writings by almost all figures from various interdisciplinary branches of German media theory and *Bildwissenschaft* who would become influential in the following two decades. Sobchack's text has since been reprinted multiple times, including in the author's own book: "The Scene of the Screen: Envisioning Photographic, Cinematic, and Electronic 'Presence,'" in *Carnal Thoughts: Embodiment and Moving Image Culture* (Berkeley: University of California Press, 2004), 136.
6. Ibid., 137. For the original citation, see "The Question Concerning Technology," in *Martin Heidegger Basic Writings*, ed. David Farrell Krell (New York: Harper, 1977), 317.
7. Ibid., 137.
8. Ibid., 137.
9. Ibid., 137.
10. See Manuel Castells' three-part study *The Information Age* (1996–98) and in particular the first volume *The Rise of the Network Society* (Oxford: Blackwell, 1996).
11. Lev Manovich, "The Poetics of Augmented Space," *Visual Communication*, vol. 5, no. 2 (2006), 219–240.
12. Ibid., 220.
13. Ibid., 219–220.
14. In his book *Cybertext*, Espen Aarseth revisits the notion of the labyrinth and points to the usefulness of Penelope Reed Doob's research from the 1990s, which identified the two distinct models of the labyrinth that may be found in classical and medieval culture, one of which has since been forgotten. While the multicursal labyrinth has dominated more modern conceptualizations of the searching pathway, the unicursal mode was a significant part of earlier physical and metaphorical notions of what a labyrinth is and does. Aarseth argues, this other notion can be very helpful in the conceptualization of the reading and experiencing processes enabled through cybertexts. See Espen Aarseth, *Cybertext: Perspectives on Ergodic Literature* (Baltimore: John Hopkins University Press, 1997).

15. For a series of photos of these rooms and information regarding the size of the space, see Wendy Goodman, *New York Magazine* (March 1, 2011), http://nymag.com/homedesign/features/sleep-no-more-2011-3 (accessed August 1, 2017).
16. See W.B. Worthen, "*Sleep No More* and the Space of Character," *Theatre Journal*, vol. 64, no. 1 (March 2012), 79–97. It is notable that Worthen's text announces on its first page that it "is part of a current project on Shakespeare performance studies."
17. Ibid., 82.
18. For a very succinct introduction to this debate, see Janet Murray's response to Espen Aarseth on her blog *Janet H. Murray: Humanistic Design for an Emerging Medium* entitled "The Last Word on Ludology vs. Narratology" (June 18, 2003), http://inventingthemedium.com/2013/06/28/the-last-word-on-ludology-v-narratology-2005 (accessed August 2, 2017).
19. I will return later to the significance of Kendall Walton's examination of make-believe as a key feature of aesthetic experience in his *Mimesis as Make-Believe* (1990).
20. See Hans-Thies Lehmann, *Postdramatic Theatre* [German, 1999], trans. Karen Jürs-Munby (London: Routledge, 2006). Interestingly, in his assessment of the role of audiovisual media in the concept of postdramatic theater Lehmann also references an early version of Vivian Sobchack's "The Scene of the Screen: Envisioning Photographic, Cinematic, and Electronic 'Presence,'" (which was familiar to a German audience through its inclusion in the Suhrkamp publication in 1988) in describing the effects of multimodality and (digital) intermediality on contemporary theater.
21. It is important to note that the performances in *Sleep No More* remain entirely wordless throughout, and the performers move into and out of view through doorways that are often rendered inaccessible to the audience.
22. The "ergodic" is a key term in Aarseth's study of cybertextual strategies employed by a wide variety of media. The word "ergodic" is a neologism of his own creation, derived from an amalgamation of the Greek *ergon* or "work" and *hodos* or "path." It describes how texts such as those under study require non-trivial work on the part of the reader or user, in order to actively construct a "pathway" into and through the aesthetic experience.
23. For details of the screening configuration and attractions see the Cineplex website: http://cineplex.com/Theatres/4DX. For locations worldwide see http://cj4dx.com.
24. Karl Bühler, *Sprachtheorie* [1934] (Stuttgart: UTB, 1999). In English translation: *Theory of Language: The Representational Function of Language*, trans. Donald Fraser Goodwin and Achim Esch (Amsterdam: John Benjamins, 1990).
25. See Francesco Casetti, "Face to Face," in *The Film Spectator: From Sign to Mind*, ed. Warren Buckland (Amsterdam: University of Amsterdam, 1995).
26. See Robin Curtis, "*Einfühlung* and Abstraction in the Moving Image: Historical and Contemporary Reflections," *Science in Context*, vol. 25, no. 3 (September 2012), 425–446.
27. For a more detailed examination of the manner in which deixis functions while viewing or using audiovisual media, see Robin Curtis, "Deixis, Imagination und Perzeption: Bestandteile einer performativen Theorie des Films," in *Deixis und Evidenz*, eds. Horst Wenzel and Judwig Jäger (Freiburg: Rombach, 2008), 241–260; and Robin Curtis, "Deixis and the Origo of Time-Based Media: Blurring the 'here and now' from the *Dickson Experimental Sound Film* of 1894 to Janet Cardiff's Installation *Ghost Machine*," in *Möglichkeitsräume: Zur Performativität von sensorischer Wahrnehmung*, eds. Christina Lechtermann, Kirsten Wagner, and Horst Wenzel (Berlin: Ernst Schmidt, 2007), 255–266.
28. See, for instance, James Parker, "When the World is an Arcade: The Psychogeography of Pokémon Go," *The Atlantic* (November 2016); or Franz Mäyrä, "Entering the Ludic Society: Pokémon Go," *Mobile Media and Communication*, 1–4 (2016), http://doi.org/10.1177/2050157916678270 (accessed August 2, 2017).
29. Kendall Walton, *Mimesis as Make-Believe* (Cambridge, MA: Harvard University Press, 1990).
30. See Noel Carroll, "On Kendall Walton's *Mimesis as Make-Believe*," *Philosophy and Phenomenological Research*, vol. 51, no. 2 (June 1991), 385.
31. Walton, *Mimesis as Make-Believe* (see note 29), 38.
32. See, for instance, Alison Mountz, Anne Bonds, Becky Mansfield, Jenna Loyd, Jennifer Hyndman, Margaret Walton-Roberts, Ranu Basu, Risa Whitson, Roberta Hawkins, Trina Hamilton, and Winifred Curran, "For Slow Scholarship: A Feminist Politics of Resistance through Collective Action in the Neoliberal University," *ACME: An International Journal for Critical Geographies* [Online], 14.4 (2015), 1235–1259, http://142.207.145.31/index.php/acme/article/view/1058 (accessed February 26, 2017).
33. Jane Bennett, "Systems and Things: On Vital Materialism and Object-Oriented Philosophy," in *The Nonhuman Turn*, ed. Richard Grusin (Minneapolis: University of Minnesota Press, 2015), 229. This text is a revised version of Bennett's response to Graham Harman and Timothy Morton originally published in *New Literary History*, vol. 43, no. 2 (Spring 2012), 225–233.
34. Ibid., 234.
35. Ibid., 235.

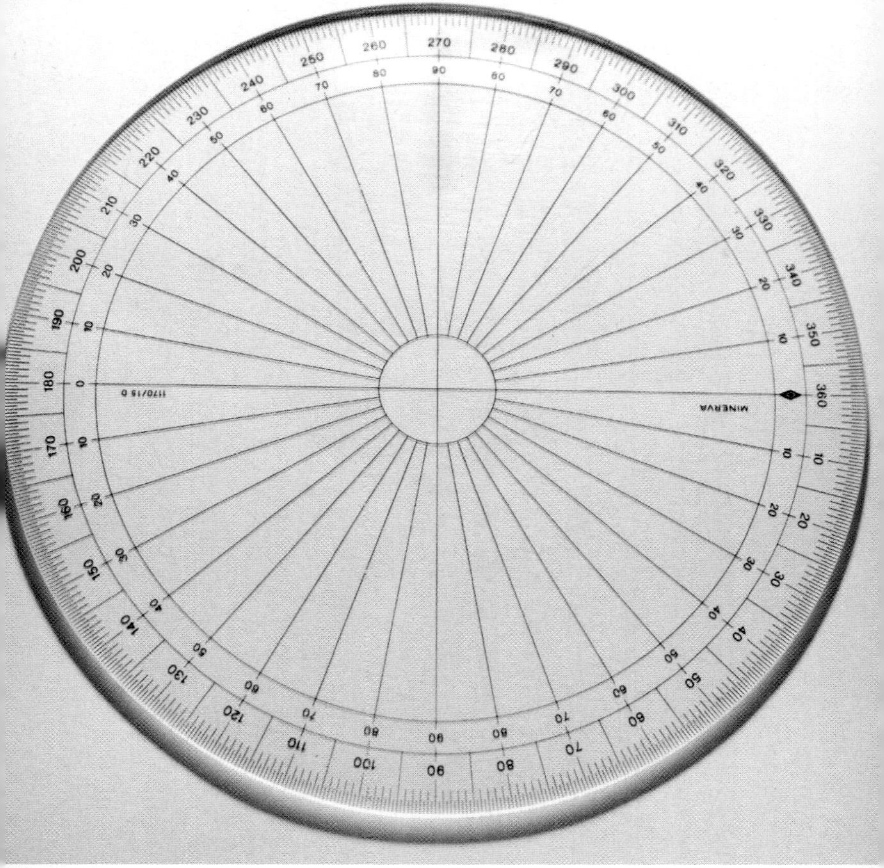
MINERVA
1170/15 D

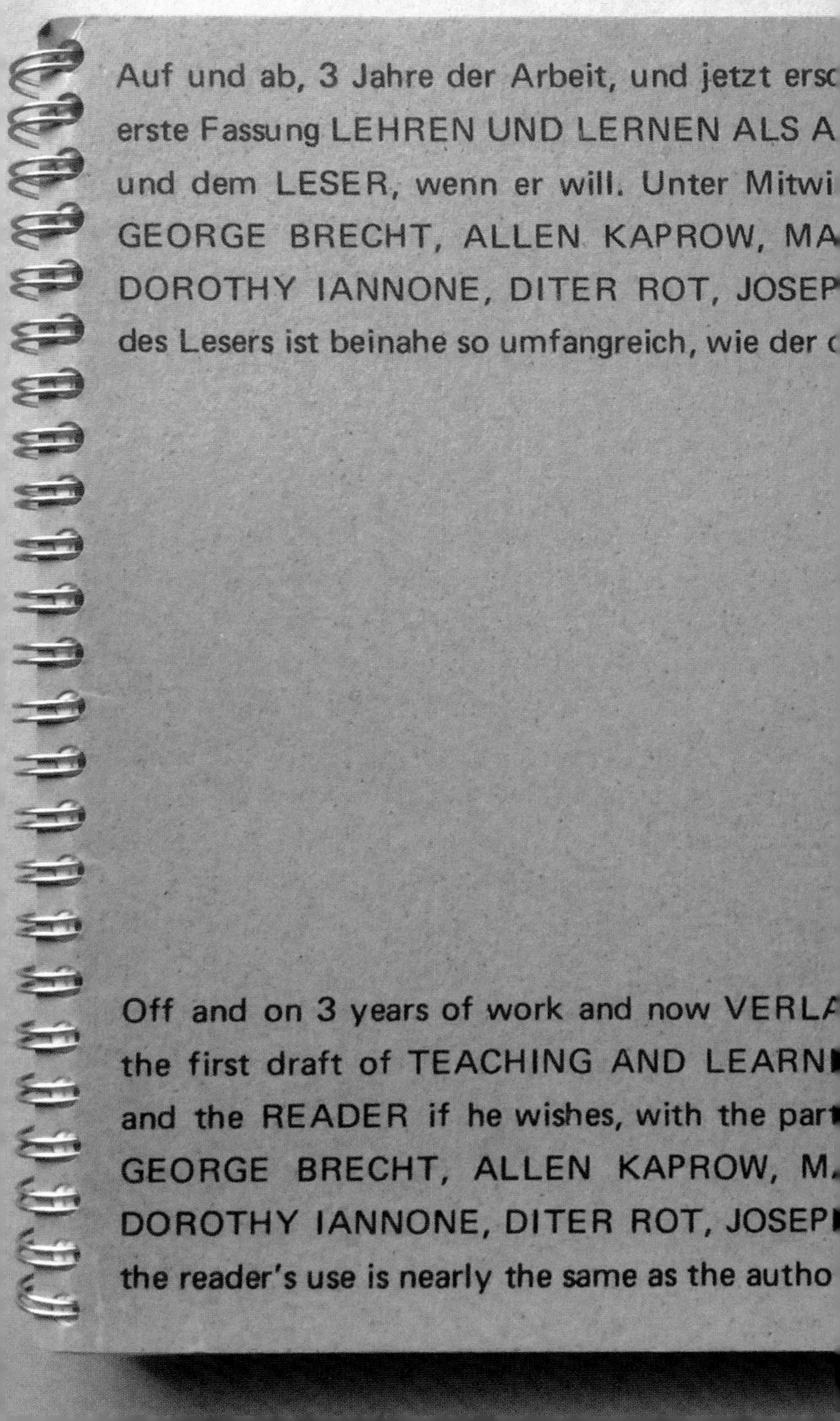
Auf und ab, 3 Jahre der Arbeit, und jetzt ersc
erste Fassung LEHREN UND LERNEN ALS A
und dem LESER, wenn er will. Unter Mitwi
GEORGE BRECHT, ALLEN KAPROW, MA
DOROTHY IANNONE, DITER ROT, JOSEP
des Lesers ist beinahe so umfangreich, wie der
Off and on 3 years of work and now VERLA
the first draft of TEACHING AND LEARN
and the READER if he wishes, with the par
GEORGE BRECHT, ALLEN KAPROW, M
DOROTHY IANNONE, DITER ROT, JOSEP
the reader's use is nearly the same as the autho

im Verlag Gebr. König, Köln - New York, die
EHRUNGSKUENSTE von ROBERT FILLIOU
von JOHN CAGE, BENJAMIN PATTERSON,
LE, VERA und BJOESSI und KARL ROT,
JYS. Dies ist ein Multibuch. Der Schreibraum
ors.

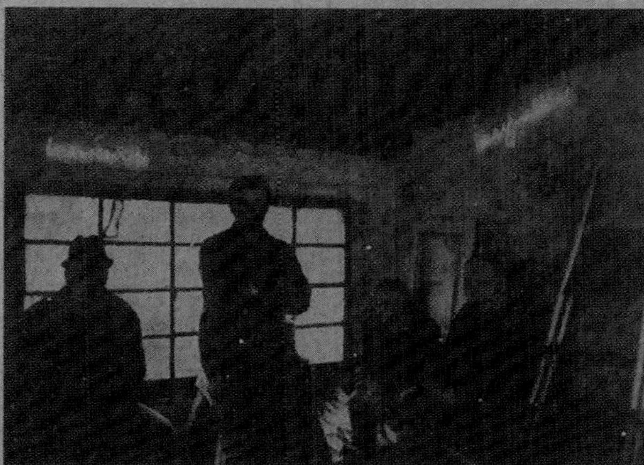

BR. KOENIG, KOELN - NEW YORK publishes
S PERFORMING ARTS by ROBERT FILLIOU
on of JOHN CAGE, BENJAMIN PATTERSON,
LLE, VERA and BJOESSI and KARL ROT,
YS. It is a Multi - book. The space provided for
.

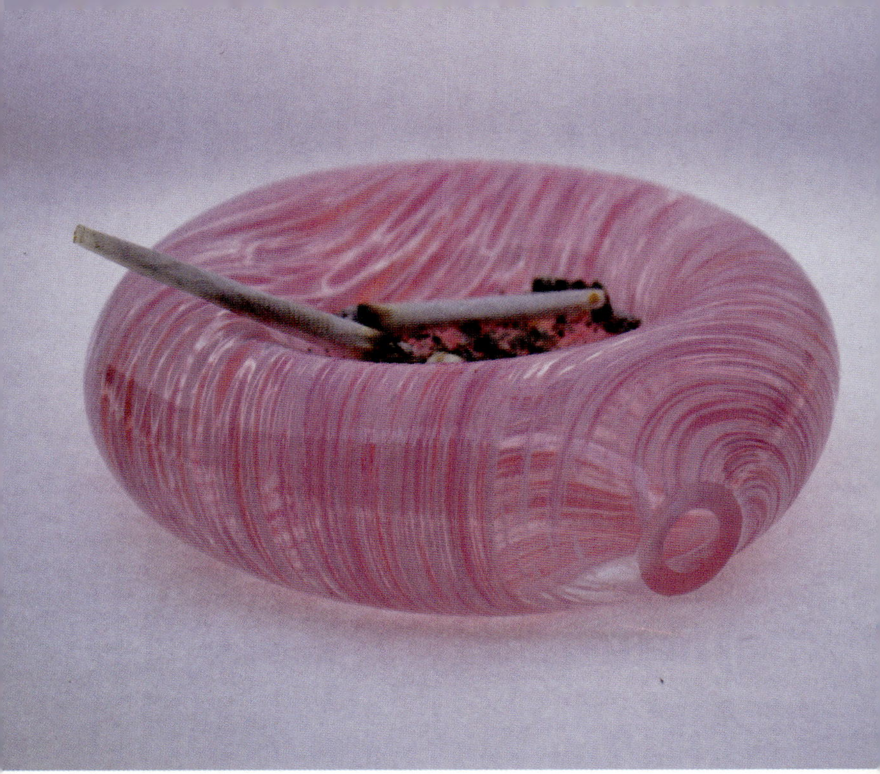

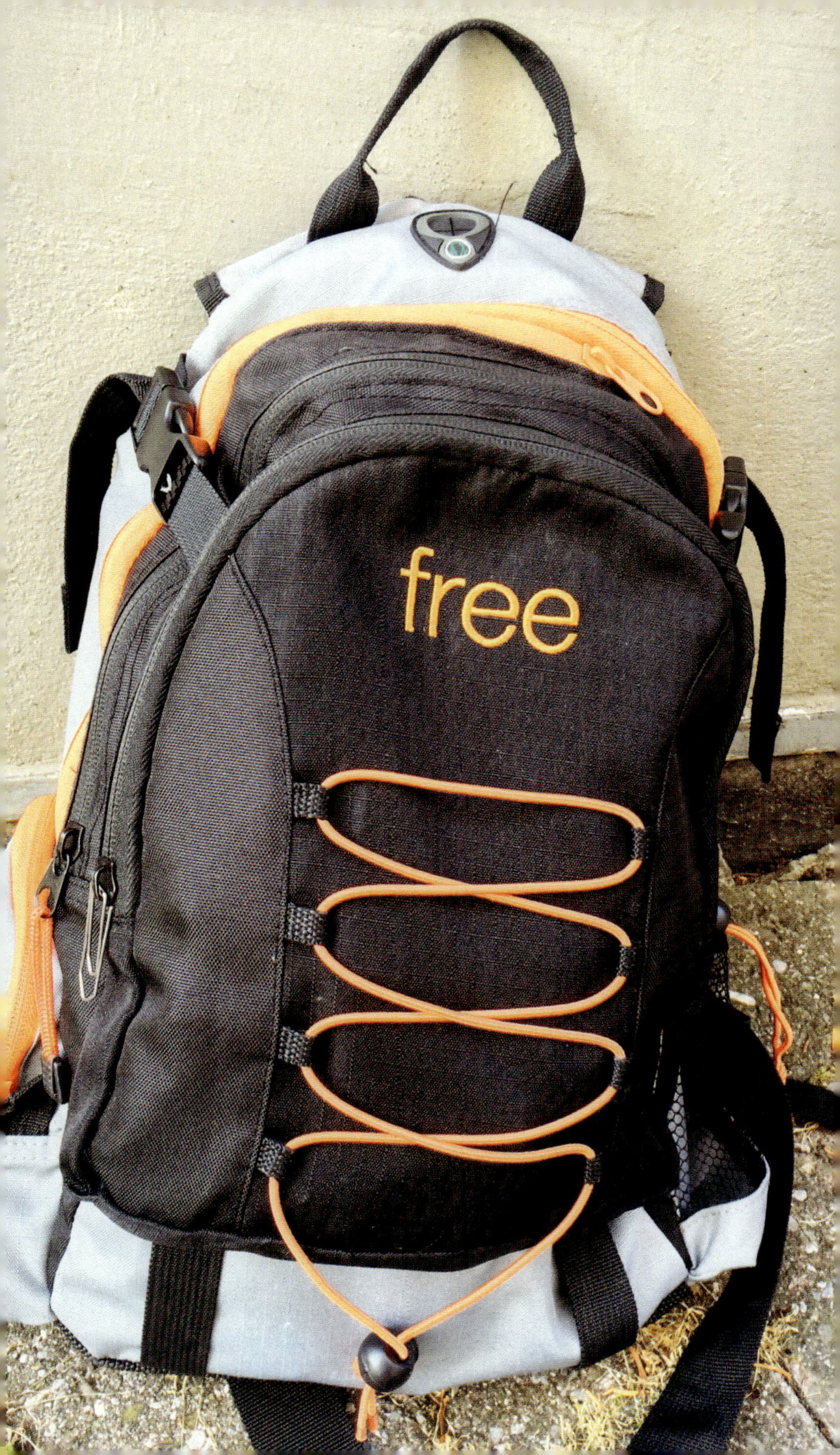
free

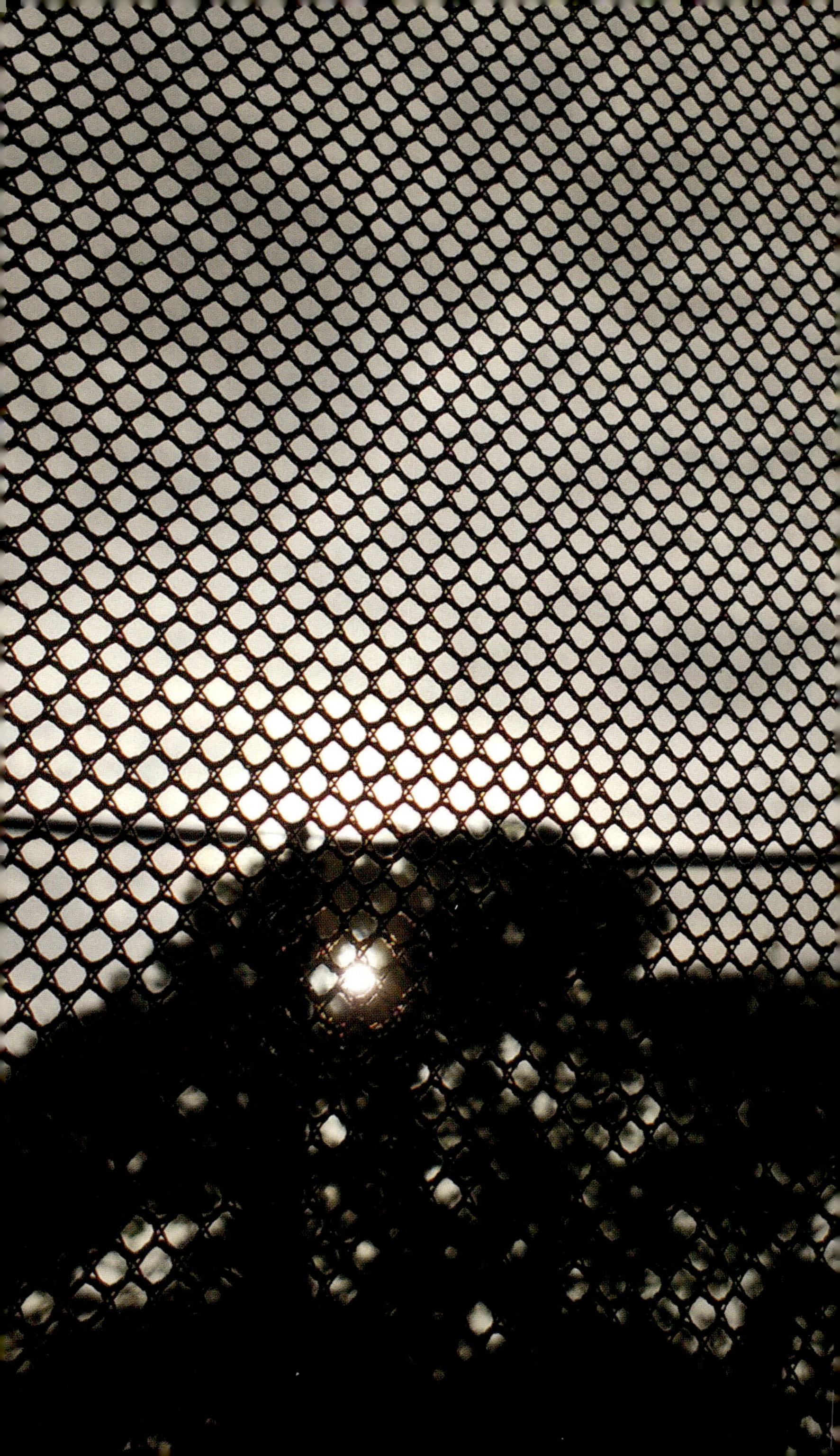

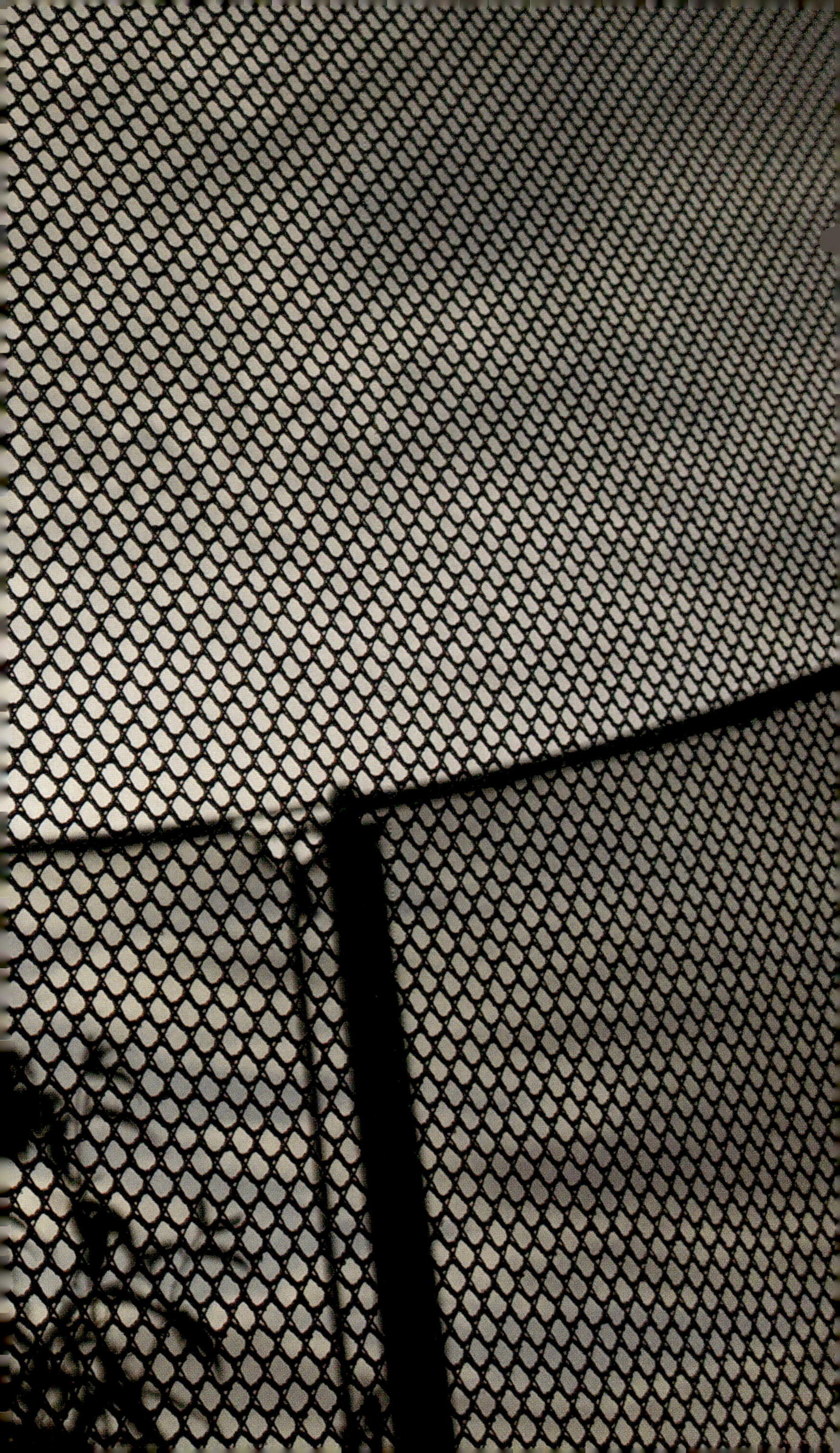

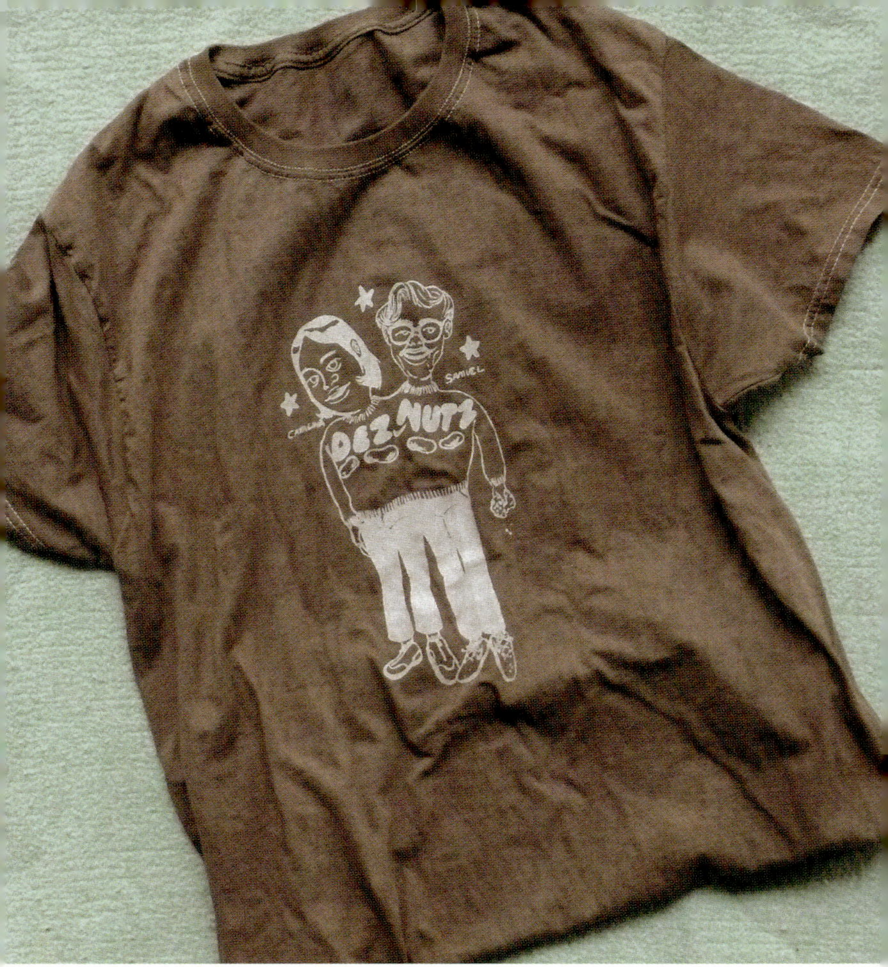
SAMUEL
DEZ NUTZ

THE NAME OF THE ROSE

Lili von Wallenstein

> But certainly for the present age,
> which prefers the sign to the thing
> signified, the copy to the original,
> representation to reality, the appearance
> to the essence ... *illusion* only is sacred,
> *truth* profane. Nay, sacredness is held
> to be enhanced in proportion as truth
> decreases and illusion increases, so that
> the highest degree of illusion comes to
> be the highest degree of sacredness.
> — Ludwig Feuerbach[1]

KEYWORDS

Emptiness, extremism, intersections, online radicalization, terrorism.

PROLOGUE

> Surely We brought man into being
> out of dry ringing clay which was
> wrought from black mud, while We
> had brought the jinn into being before
> out of blazing fire.
> — The Quran[2]

Colleen. Colleen LaRose.

I sound out the name in the passport, reading my birth details, looking at the numbers that state my height. So many years. So few inches. So meaningless.

Next, I cross out ~~Colleen~~. After that: LaRose. ~~Colleen LaRose~~. That name is no longer mine. That life is no longer mine either.

I get up from the couch, thinking to myself that it would all have been a bit better if the room had been big enough to move around in, to suffer and pace back and forth in. I rummage through the beer cans, cigarette butts and bottles on the table, but I no longer find anything there: I find nothing. If there was any kind of happiness to be found in this "house," I suppose I would have tried. If I could have been born as somebody else, I suppose I would have chosen that.

I've never been able to make sense of the windowpanes in my home. I'm standing by a window, but I can't see the other hovels outside, I can't see any of the dereliction that surrounds me. Hovels, shacks, sheds. Homes? All I can see is my own reflection. Under my T-shirt, I see the mounds of my breasts: several hundred grams of silicone stuffed in underneath the skin. Just think, a few months ago I believed they were the finest thing any man had ever given me. I see my face: straight, unassuming nose, green eyes, blonde hair that's beginning to show gray, all of the things that will help me "blend in with people ... to achieve what is in my heart." That's more or less what I wrote to him the other week. I was hoping he'd write something about my eyes, or at least about my fearless soul and my big heart, but he never did.

Men. Why are they always there? Why can't a single story take place, evolve without including them? Avoid them, Dad between my little girl's thighs, Jim during my teenage years, John, Tom, and Bart. Dead, disappeared, or just gone—I don't know. All that remains are fragments of memories and impressions: the scent of my father, the scent of bodylotion. His face, distorted, completely concentrated, yet completely absent at the same time. I thought it was just what dads and girls did together.

Later on, I'd realize that I had been wrong, that HE was wrong. Later on. Later on I'd do a bunch of stupid things—because of what he did, and because my mother did nothing to help me. Because I hated him. Because I hated ~~Colleen LaRose~~, and everything that was in any way connected to her. ~~Colleen LaRose~~.

The smell of the years on the street, of that pale purple T-shirt that I never washed, of my feet when I finally made my way inside. Exhausted. The smell of tears and stale beer and my sweat and my helplessness when I was in the car getting ready to drive to my death, or at least drive away from everything. All of it: all of these things caused by men. Men, or maybe love. Because it was love that made me take care of them, of the house, of Kurt's sick father (he never thanked me, nobody ever thanked me for anything). That made me drink, that made me want to die. It's love that makes me keep trying. Love, or maybe fear, fear of being completely alone, of life turning out to be exactly as meaningless as it seems.

I remember the man in the bar that night in Amsterdam when Kurt and I had fought, and all I wanted was something to make me forget that the only time we ever went on holiday abroad together was a disaster. I remember Kurt—like a faded photograph, even though I still live with him, and even though I see him almost every day. It doesn't mean a thing. Just like the others, he's dead to me. They're all just as absent, gone, insignificant, and as dead as ~~Colleen~~.

FACTS ABOUT COLLEEN LAROSE, A.K.A. "FATIMA LAROSE," "JIHAD JANE," "SISTER OF TERROR"

On January 6, 2014, ~~Colleen R. LaRose~~ (born 1963)—a.k.a. "Fatima LaRose," "Jihad Jane," "Sister of Terror,"—a resident of Montgomery County, Pennsylvania was sentenced to ten years in prison by a US court. Her crime: plotting the assassination of Swedish artist Lars Vilks.[3]

How did it all start? On June 20, 2008, ~~LaRose~~ published a comment on YouTube, in which she stated that she "desperately wants to help" Muslims. The message was signed "Jihad Jane." On December 9 of the same year, ~~LaRose~~ wrote to one of her contacts online and explained that she wanted to become a martyr. On February 20 of the following year, ~~LaRose~~ emphasized how advantageous her appearance would be, in that it would allow her to blend in and succeed in her mission: an attack on a target that by all accounts had yet to be selected. On March 7, a man writes to ~~LaRose~~ asking her to marry him "from within Europe." ~~LaRose~~ replies that she will try to get a residence permit in Europe and then marry him. Three days later she sends a request to the Swedish embassy. The request concerned a residence permit for Sweden.

The man who asked for her hand writes to ~~LaRose~~ again, asking her to travel to Sweden, where she is to locate Lars Vilks and kill him. On the same day, March 22, 2009, ~~LaRose~~ responds that she will do what he asks her to. It will be her singular goal until she "succeeds or dies." The man replies that she is to kill Vilks "in a way that will frighten all infidels."

THE VARIETIES OF TERROR

> The term "abnormal behavior," like terror, has continually defied satisfactory definition. Still, it is clear that those who attempt bizarre, ostensibly political actions with uncertain or irrational outward motivations do so for what are internal, personal reasons. American

society has recently witnessed several examples of a particular variant of deviant behavior, that of the psychotic assassin. While the assassin's profile is well known—he or she is usually the product of a broken home, has serious sexual problems, has a history of frequent unemployment, and is incapable of establishing effective personal relationships—it is all too common to be of any practical use.[4]

I BECAME A TERRORIST FOR LOVE

My computer beeps at me. Despite all this time in front of the computer's pale blue, anxious, yet soothing glare, I still haven't learned what all the different noises and symbols mean. First, I read the sender's name: Eagleeye. Then, I read the message aloud, slowly. He writes that he wants us to get married. He writes about pride, idolatry, and swine. His English is better than mine, or rather his language skills in general are better than mine. I chew my lower lip while I struggle to compose a response.
I already know how I will end my reply: Best Regards, Jihad Jane.

Will I go through with what I've been asked to do? If somebody were to ask me why, I'd tell them that there are many reasons, and many justifications. I don't know why (yes I do: I want something more than lovelessness, poverty, and addiction).

There are many explanations, but the simplest one is that I'm doing it out of love. I mean, we'd spent so much time talking, and we'd gotten to know each other, and I feel that they are my brothers—I *do* feel it—and I feel that they need me in a way that I've never been needed before. When they say something, I listen, and consider what I'm being told. When they ask me for something, I can't say no. I don't want to say no. Because I love them (and my love is pure, strong, and self-sacrificing; it is odorless). And just imagine: if the US were invaded by enemy powers, if we'd been bombed and killed, and forced to leave our homes… Well, I can't stop thinking about it.

> Feuerbach starts out from the fact of religious self-alienation, of the duplication of the world into a religious world and a secular one. His work consists in

resolving the religious world into its secular basis. But that the secular basis detaches itself from itself and establishes itself as an independent realm in the clouds can only be explained by the cleavages and self-contradictions within this secular basis. The latter must, therefore, in itself be both understood in its contradiction and revolutionized in practice. Thus, for instance, after the earthly family is discovered to be the secret of the holy family, the former must then itself be destroyed in theory and in practice.
— Karl Marx[5]

FACTS

Let's stick to the facts. In late August 2009, ~~LaRose~~ removes the hard disk from her desktop computer and steals her life partner Kurt Gorman's passport. She plans to hand the passport over to her "brothers." ~~LaRose~~ travels to Ireland where she intends to live and train with jihadis. On September 8, she becomes a member of Vilks' online community and becomes a citizen of his "artist's enclave" in Sweden.

She continues to write messages to her contacts all over the world, and they continue to write to the woman who goes by the online aliases of "Sister of Terror" and "Jihad Jane." She continues to discuss jihad on various extremist online forums as well as trade in bloody video clips with other users on YouTube. On September 30, 2009, ~~LaRose~~ writes to her contact Eagleeye that it is "an honor and a pleasure" to die or kill on his behalf. She also writes that only death can "stop me now that I am so close to the target!" On that same day, she has a conversation with a man from Saudi Arabia in an online forum and takes this opportunity to convert to Islam: "I bear witness / that there is no god / but God / and I bear witness / that Muhammad is the messenger of God."

EMPTY NAMES

Dear Eagleeye,

Since our last chat I have been thinking a lot: thinking about you, me, and the future. I've been through so much, and I've survived so many things that could have killed the strongest of people. I've always found consolation in the thought that there must be some purpose to my life. When my eyes were opened to Islam, and I got to know you, when I got to know all of us, I thought that this was what I was meant to do—this was the reason why I'd lived through all those things. Eventually, I found a place where I sort of belonged. [...]

Nothing has changed. I'm still sure this is the right thing to do. I'm not afraid. I'm not afraid to die. It will be an honor to die for the Ummah.[6] I don't know what else to write. Words are not enough to describe my feelings, my preparedness, my gratefulness.

Love,
Jihad Jane

THE CONVERT

After converting, ~~Colleen LaRose~~ takes the name Fatima. Perhaps this act transforms her into another person, and perhaps it doesn't. Regardless of her (possibly) new self, her experiences in Ireland don't seem to match up with her hopes and expectations. The man she has traveled to visit, who is supposed to act as her spiritual guide—an Algerian who is not to be confused with Eagleeye—hardly corresponds to the more or less established stereotypes of a successful jihadi. On the contrary: Ali Damache is an ex-salesman who has lost his job and spends his days in an apartment, in a building marked for demolition (a loser, in the same way that she's a loser). On top of that, he marries another woman while she's there. ~~LaRose~~ is disappointed. ~~LaRose~~ is alone. Or: whether or not ~~Colleen LaRose~~ or Fatima or Jihad Jane actually was those things, or felt that she was, is something we can never know, of course. Her loneliness and disappointment are thus merely assumed. Perhaps her loneliness and disappointment were what made the whole thing possible in the first place? *It is all too common to be of any practical use* [my emphasis].

SISTER OF TERROR, SISTER OF NEED

Suppose they were to distribute images of me in newspapers and on television. Suppose they were to write about me. Suppose then, that they asked me why I did it.

"Weeell," I'd say, "weeell, so, all I can say is that I did it for love—for love of my friends, love of the Prophet, love for the man I've never met, love and longing for...

I don't know what for." My voice would be strong and convicted, principled and powerful. Somewhere, beyond the obvious (only perceptible to people who have suffered as I have), my voice would also bear witness to the grief and longing within me.

I wouldn't say I did it because life seemed so awfully hopeless and dull, because I had nothing else to do: nobody likes a loser.

"It was a way of surviving, one way among a number of possible and imaginable ways." Is that a good answer, or a bad one? I don't know. (Or was it really all just about a way of dying?)

"It was just another attempt to be loved, yet another attempt to fill my life with meaning." This is a bad answer, inasmuch as it is emotional and unclear. Nobody likes a lovesick woman, especially not one that's unhealthy and weak. (Also: being loved and finding some meaning with everything—aren't they really one and the same? I don't know.)

If somebody were to ask me why I always signed my messages with those names, naturally, I'd answer that I did it because I liked the sound of them, and because the names inspired terror, interest, and respect (all of the things that the name ~~Colleen LaRose~~ could never do).

PROBLEM STATEMENT

What makes us human? All of those emotions that we carry around inside. All of that cheap, tear-drenched mess of love, emptiness, longing, and grief. And: under the T-shirts, and under the cheap lacy underwear, and under the piles of blue eye-shadow, and under the bad skin, and under the just about adequately tied head cloth there is hatred, like a black, ugly diamond that's been squeezed into being over millennia.

What makes us human? Maybe this: that we write, communicate, that we try to express to others how we'd like our world and our lives to be arranged. This way, we can become somebody, and become something. All the names, all the words, and all the images and videos that I share on YouTube and Myspace create and recreate me: Sister of Terror.

SUMMARY

Let's stick to the facts. After a few weeks, she leaves Ireland and returns to the US.

The purpose of her journey is unfulfilled: she has neither killed nor found love or the meaning of her life. Before she leaves, she emails the FBI and asks them for money for her ticket back. The FBI denies this request but they arrest her when she arrives at the airport in Philadelphia.

When one of the men (tall, discreet, and handsome in a tailored suit) approached her, she thought that this could possibly be the beginning of something beautiful: a new love, a new life—but the end followed.

And this is the end: when ~~Colleen LaRose~~, without her burqa, with her hair unkempt, and the old jean-shorts she'd spilled something on, was led away in handcuffs—as always, led and controlled by some man, his name unknown or irrelevant or just too holy. She probably wasn't thinking of anything in particular, well: perhaps she wondered if they had arrested ~~Colleen LaRose~~ or Fatima or Jihad Jane, and if it really mattered. At the moment, all those nouns, all those identities seemed of no use at all. Perhaps she was thinking that she was going to be locked up, rephrased, and recreated yet again, in some way or other; a new load of paperwork to fill out, new sequences of letters and numbers, new names, new men, new ways of trying to get close to another human being.

NOTES

1. Quoted from Guy Debord, *The Society of the Spectacle*, trans. Donald Nicholson-Smith (New York: Zero Books, 1994), 11.
2. The Quran 15:26–27.
3. In 2007, conceptual artist and art theorist Lars Vilks (born 1946) found fame thanks to his drawings of Muhammad, in which the prophet of Islam is depicted as a dog. The drawings were intended to be shown in an exhibition planned for the same year. The exhibition was cancelled and instead the pictures were published in *Nerikes Allehanda* as illustrations for an article about freedom of speech. After their publication, Vilks received several death threats, and al-Qaida put a price on the artist's head to the tune of $100,000. In May of 2010—the same year that LaRose was accused of involvement in the plot to assassinate the Swedish artist—Vilks was assaulted at a lecture where the film *Allah ho Gaybar* (2007) by Iranian-Dutch artist Sooreh Hera was screened. The film shows men in erotic poses, wearing masks that depict the prophet. A few days after the lecture, Vilks' house in Skåne was the target of arson, a crime for which two men would later be convicted. In December of the same year a bombing occurred in central Stockholm. The perpetrator—who was the only person to die in the attack—had sent letters to the Swedish Security Service and the TT news agency, explaining that the deed was a reaction to Vilks' drawings and the silence with which the people of Sweden had responded to them. Vilks has been living under constant police protection since 2010.
4. J. Bowyer Bell, *Transnational Terror* (Washington: American Enterprise Institute for Public Policy Research, 1975), 10.
5. Karl Marx, "Concerning Feuerbach," in *Karl Marx: Early Writing*, trans. Rodney Livingstone and Gregor Benton (London: Penguin Books, 1992), 422.
6. An Arabic word meaning community.

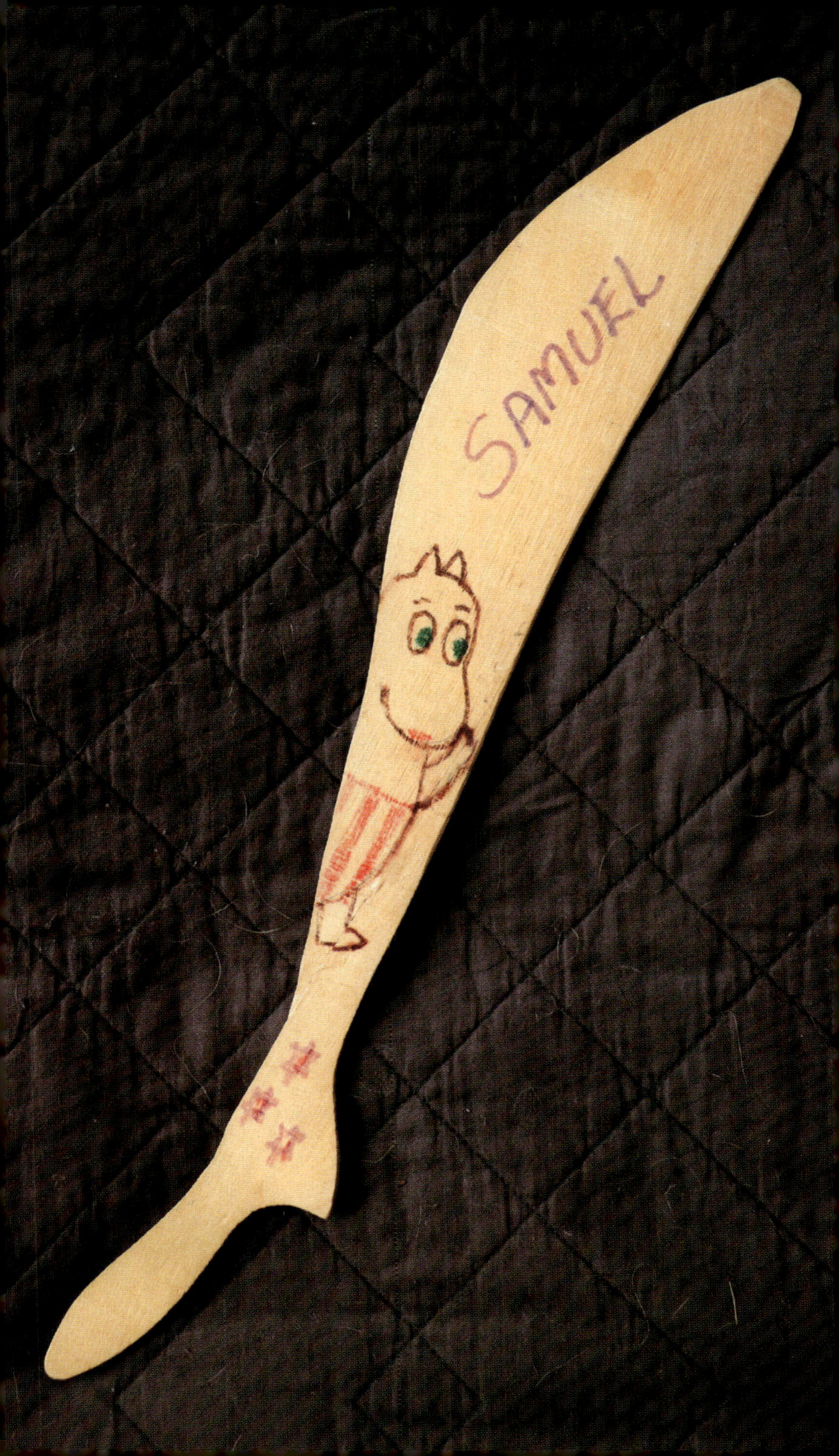
SAMUEL

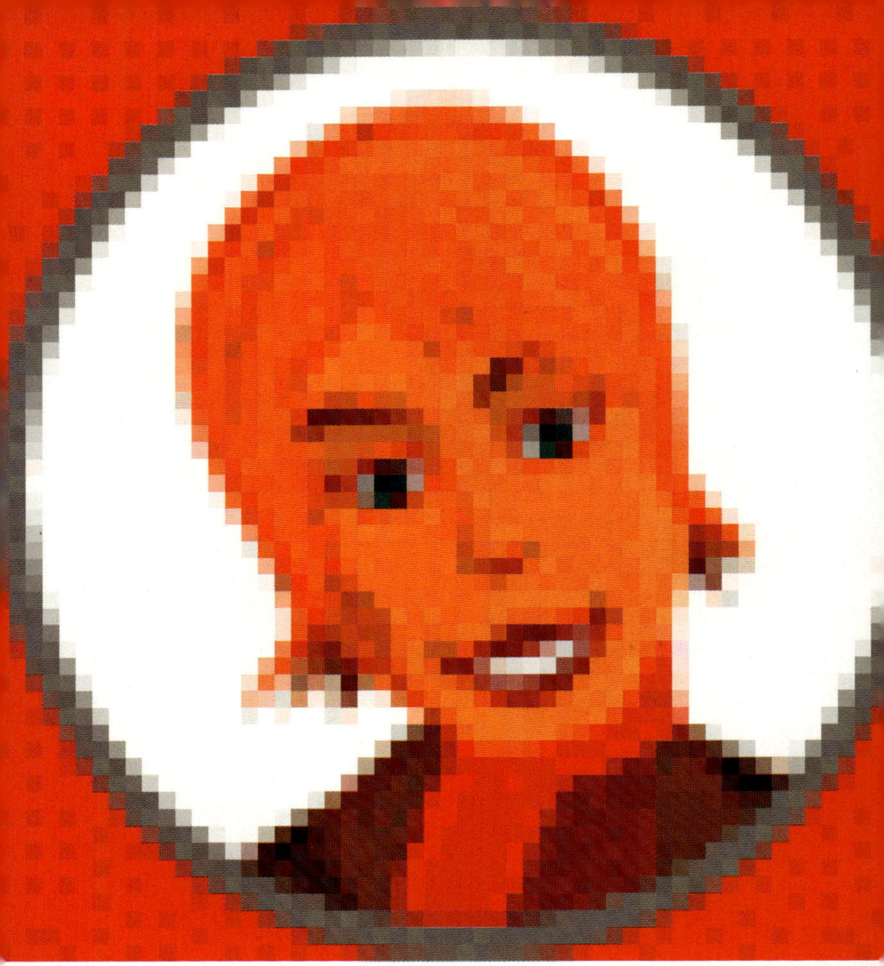

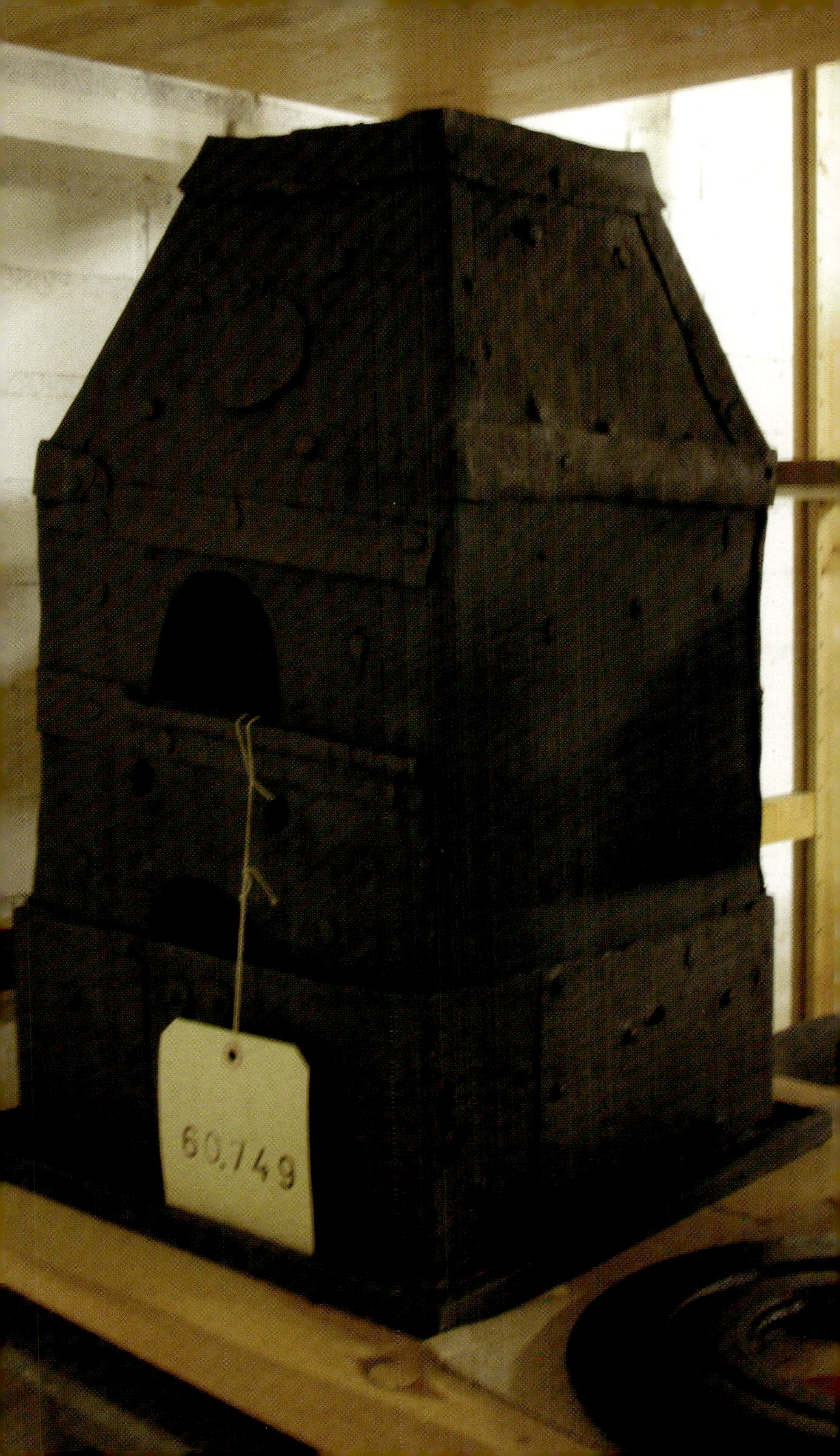
60.749

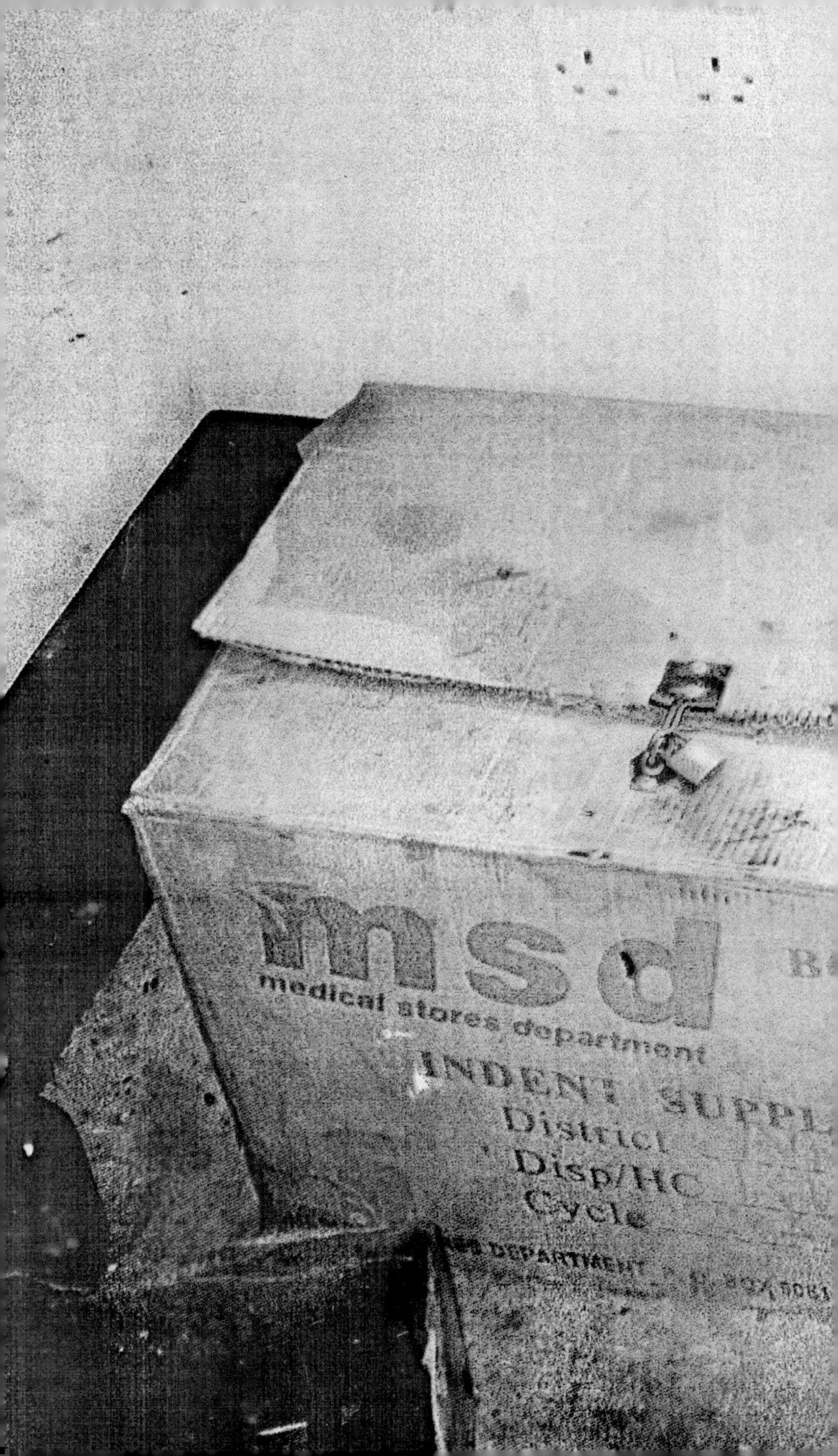
msd
medical stores department
INDENT SUPPL
District
Disp/HC
Cycle
DEPARTMENT

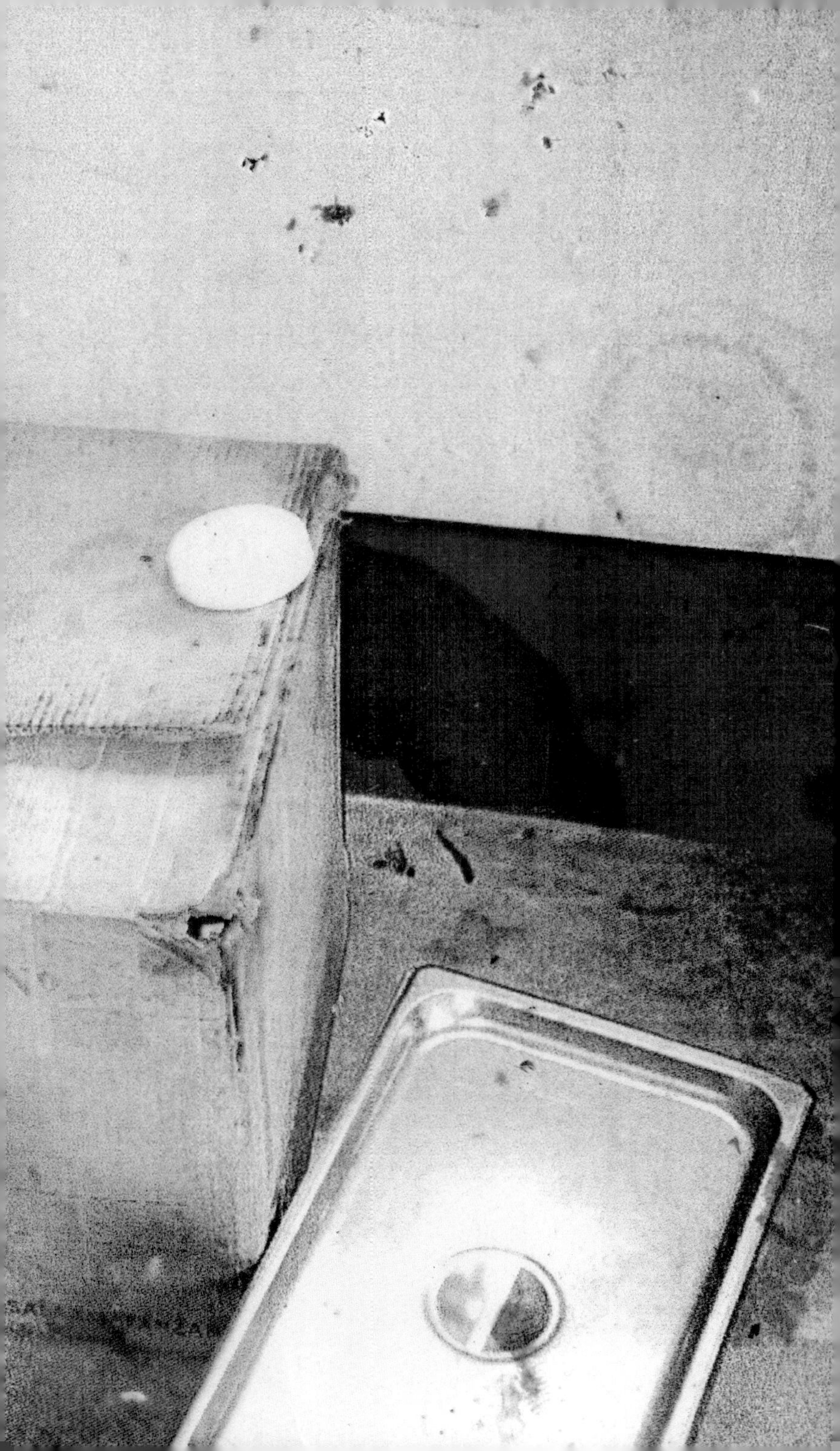

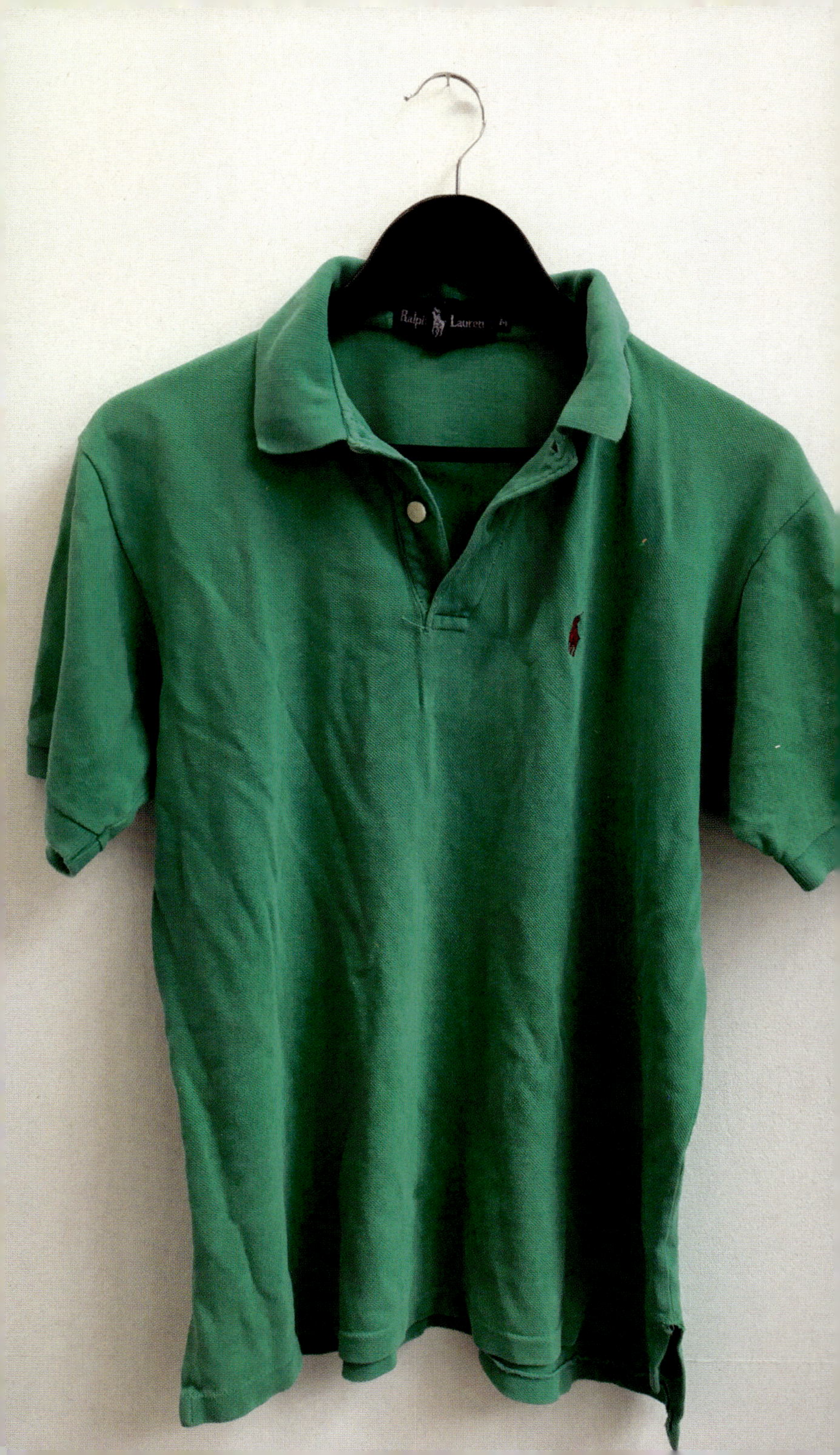
Ralph Lauren M

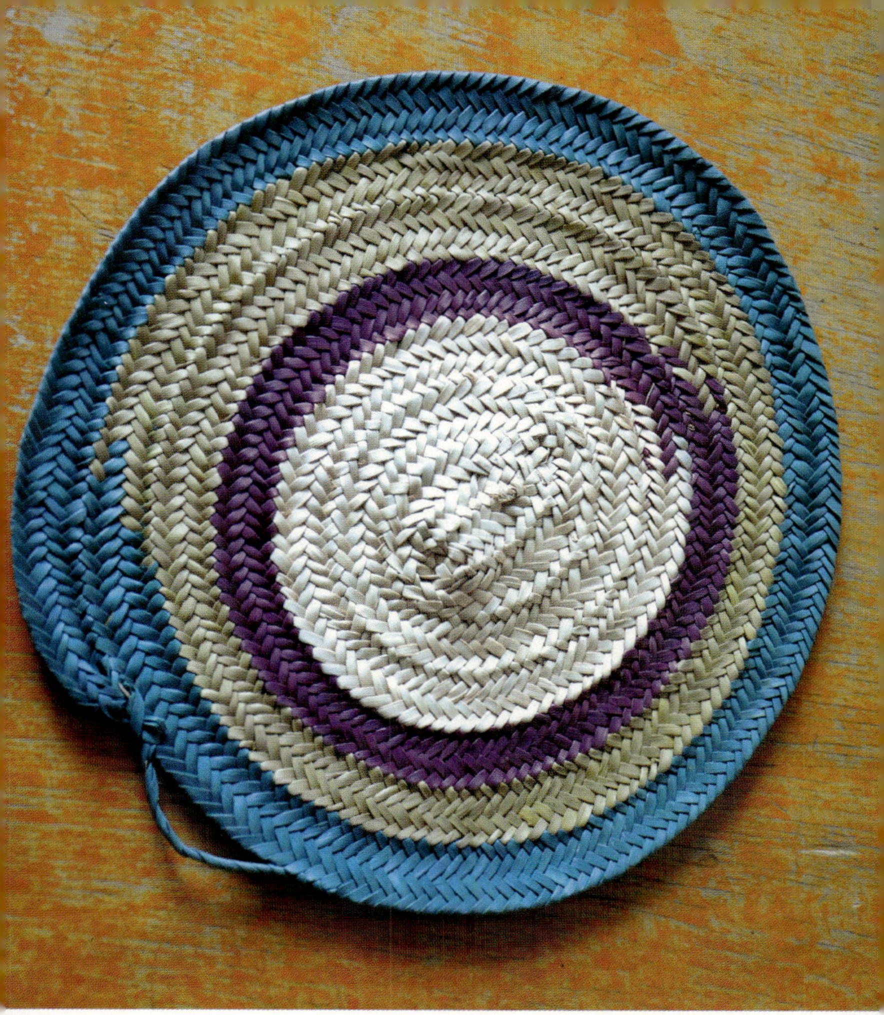

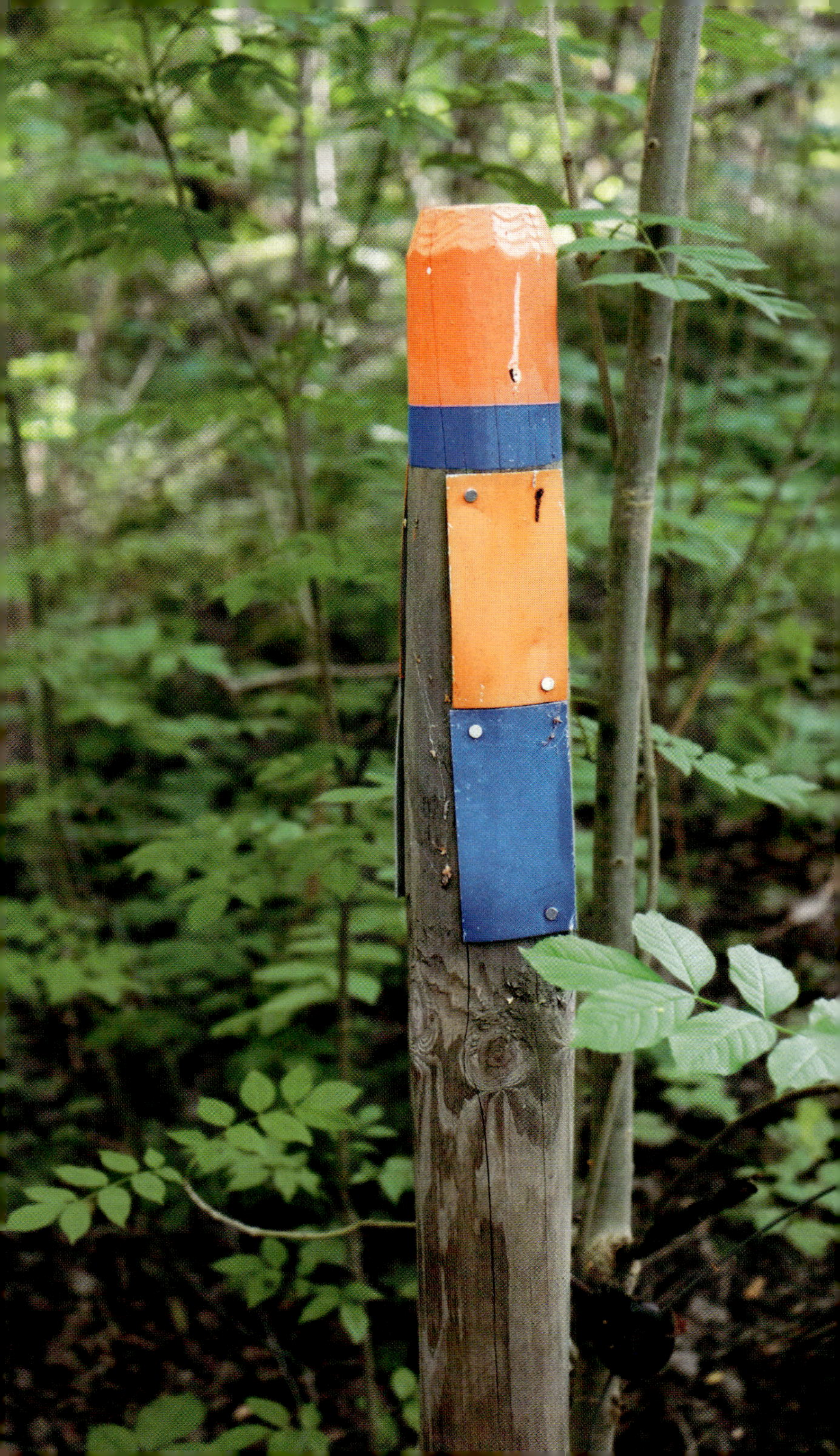

SOMEWHERE ELSE AND OTHER PLACES

Hana Jaber

For Michel Péraldi

TWO SCENES

I am looking at two images on a screen. The first is a still image: a young boy cast up from the sea after the capsizing of the inflatable boat on which he had embarked together with his family. Lying on the sand of the Turkish shore, in a red T-shirt and blue shorts, he seems to be sleeping on a deserted beach. The second is an image of motion: a scene of thousands of women, men, and children breaking through the Greek-Turkish border and rushing forward to reach European soil no matter what. In the first case, the three-year-old child was a victim that Europe, or Canada, was unable to save from the barbarisms of history. In the second, the flood of humanity wiped out borders and tore down the wall of a dominating civilization—an invasion by barbarians. The two images, however, show the same migrants. The first embodies the guilty conscience of humanity and its missed chance for redemption. The second reactivates a specter long erased from Europe's collective memory: the return of something horrible that was believed to have been left behind.

EPOCHÉ

The urgent necessity to rethink otherness and human mobility no longer needs to be demonstrated. I write these words and suddenly stop, once again, poised on the edge of an *epoché*—a state of suspension of judgment—a time that is just as impossible as it is necessary… Through my kitchen window near Paris, I see the neglected garden, while sensing an urge: "the time has come to change civilization," as Edgar Morin puts it. Navigating a neglected garden, all thoughts interrupted. How did we get there?

LONG-AWAITED SPRING

January 2011 and the following months. The Arab Spring had just erupted: Tunisia-Egypt-Libya-Bahrain-Yemen-Syria. Heated discussions with colleagues and friends. Very few fully grasped the impact of the tidal wave the spring to the south and east of the Mediterranean had triggered; not only in Arab societies but also far beyond. I understood that what I experienced—as lively discussion, as a topic of intelligent conversation, or even as a golden opportunity on a CV—was actually the founding moment of a new era. Take action, say yes, and then leave. Television, internet, newspapers, etc. A virtual world taking the place of reality. The Arab Spring brought the idea of a reversible past back to me, of a "somewhere else" within the screen.

BUT SYRIA

The Syrian nightmare. The demonstrations, the tanks, the ground-to-ground missiles, the militarization of the revolt, the aerial bombings. The chemical weapons, the appalling photographs in the Caesar Report, the increased significance of the IS and the paralysis of the UN. Groups of men and women, growing larger and larger, crossing the frontiers of Jordan, Turkey, Lebanon. The shipwrecks in the Mediterranean, the forced border crossings to Europe, the contingents of people coming from God knows where, the photo of Alan Kurdi thrown by the sea onto the shore, the image of the young Omran Daqneesh taken dazed from the rubble, and all the others… The "founding moment" had given birth to a monstrosity that is still continuing to take form.

TRANSIT

February 2015, Paris, one evening at around 10 pm. A woman and her three boys of about the same age as my son have arrived, unannounced, at our house to stay for "one or two nights." They had come from Syria. Paris was one stage of their European exile. Disordered hustle and bustle predominate. On television, the polemics—ad infinitum—around the massacre at Charlie Hebdo competed for acoustic space with the chatter and laughter of the adolescents. The mother was having a telephone conversation with her "contact" who, from abroad, was in charge of the continuation of the route: "Norway, you say, why?... Why not... But, in that case, why not Germany, or Belgium, that would be closer wouldn't it? I'll think about it and call you back." Discussions, reflections, hesitations, asking for advice, clarification; the mother called her "contact" back: "I have thought about it... Let's stick to the terms of our first agreement. Sweden is the country I want to go to. I have a close friend there; it would be much easier for me." I remarked to my young son that he was experiencing a moment he should remember; a moment when the destiny of a family, in the middle of a great voyage and still unsure of its final destination, was being decided by the flip of a coin.

1996, the camp for Palestinian refugees in Wihdat, Jordan. Semi-structured meetings with refugee families from 1948. The exodus and the wound that has never healed. History lives there in parenthesis, waiting for a return that seems like a magician's smoke-and-mirrors trick. Memory of the loss and the humiliation of having been deceived. The memory of an old woman, who has since died and whose name I no longer remember, with clear features and a prettily tattooed chin. She told me that she did not want her children to lose the accent of the village they came from near Hebron: "Like that, when we return, it will be as if we had never left." This other old woman, who has also passed away, told me in minute detail that if they hadn't "left," her husband would not have taken a second wife … And that gentlemen, with sunken cheeks lined with a dense network of wrinkles, was repeatedly dismissed from his work for "insubordination" toward his employers, who made him perform high-risk work. He had lost everything "except my life."

THE OTHER

1989, in Paris for almost a year. Château d'Eau quarter. Discussion about otherness organized by my flatmate, a young German man. Who was the audience at the home of the person who had instigated this debate? Capricious amnesia, volatile memory. The quarter, "colorfully African" and still Parisian at the same time, labeled as a *coupe-gorge* no-go area and one that I had just discovered for myself, had taken hold of me. In the Senegalese restaurant on the rue du Nord where we ate (who were "we"?) the strange recollection that, sitting around the table, the *Andere*, was me. But how was I the other?

THE IMPULSE TO LEAVE

October 10, 1981, Middle East Airlines' Beirut-Paris flight. My first plane trip. Hard to understand the reason for the seat belt, the tray in the back of the seat in front of me, the buttons on the armrest. The unpleasant feeling of being put to the test. The feeling of being laid down on cotton wool, floating in a strange equilibrium with reality, the image of the plane following its path, seemingly immobile above a carpet of clouds. Setting foot on the tarmac of the Nice-Côte-d'Azur airport in the late afternoon in autumn, I still did not know that the young high-school student I was had just outlined a radical alterity, an irrevocable past. How to reinterpret, *a posteriori*, such an impulse to leave; the search for somewhere else—the petit-bourgeois, confused longing to be different, but not only that.

THE MIGRANT, A CHANGED NOMAD?

On the one hand, the nomads of Manchuria, the Arabian Desert, and Western Sahara whose geography, history, and identity were shaped until recently by wandering. On the other hand, the foreign seasonal workers, Moroccans in Spain and Filipinos in Japan, whose

mobility is now governed by the constraints of ever-accelerating capitalism. The first world almost disappeared to the advantage of the second, in favor of state frontiers and the imperatives of globalization. Is the migrant the nomad of the twenty-first century as some like to suggest? If so, this would be a nomad changed by the weight of history. Changed in the sense of altering the components, of becoming other.
A panoply of migratory realities exists, and there are similarly many words to describe alterity, opening up identities in the process of redefinition.

THE UN AND CO.

The key to these redefinitions lies in the hands of international and national organizations, political or purely administrative authorities. They were created in the wake of the Second World War, a period that saw the redrawing of state frontiers in Europe and decolonization of empires in favor of sovereign, independent nation-states. A comprehensive legal system, embodied by the UN and its battery of connected agencies, considers itself the guarantor of a universal human condition. A semantic with a wealth of nuances was constructed to designate mobility both within and between nations. In the aftermath of the Second World War, migration—inherent to the dynamics of societies—became regulated by a juridical and lexical arsenal deployed with the claim of giving order to the dawn of a new era.

SEDENTARY HABITUS

The semantics of mobility relates, *a contrario*, to how the habitus of contemporary humanity is defined and is subsequently kept within the bounds of territoriality and sedentariness. The sedentary habitus, sanctioned as an indicator of progress and synonym for civilization in all the hermeneutic ambiguities of the term, is crowned by the citizen person. By leaving, the migrant becomes a potentially deficient being. His/her presence refers to the alteration of the relationship to the place and the link. The markers of sedentariness are called on to overcome this deficiency: who is this individual, where does this person come from, where is he/she going, why and for how long.

SOMEWHERE ELSE AND OTHER PLACES

Once "somewhere else," the migrant is obligated to have a story to tell. His/her intentions are evaluated according to categories of perception drawn up, *a priori*, in the repertory of the institutions. This traveler is neither the tourist nor the student and differs from the expatriate. This traveler is not to be confused with the immigrant and is distinct from the refugee—who in turn is classified as a political, climatic, humanitarian, and possibly even regular or clandestine refugee—etc. Fuelled over the past decades by the input from the global economy, conflicts and catastrophes, these categories go hand in hand with the varying treatments of such travelers, subject to the whim of political contexts and representations. Therefore, potentially, the traveler in transit will be ignored, the tourist pampered, the businessperson flattered, the expatriate coveted, the seasonal worker disdained, the immigrant despised, the refugee suspected, and the person without papers sent back.

THE "METAMORPHOSIS" OF THE MODEL MIGRANT

Caught up in terms of intentionality, the migrant becomes the "stranger" within a national group, the object of an institutional assignation that wipes out other dimensions of his/her biography and progressively infiltrates the sphere of identity that he/she is constructing through a "somewhere else." The migrating individual is forced to internalize this institutional variable, and his/her "metamorphosis" thus becomes even more effective, if it leads him/her to blend in with the crowd. But the human influx is intensifying, and cultural and religious origins are becoming more diversified. The required process of "invisibilization" cannot occur by migrants falling in with a uniform society. Today's national landscapes are revealed as heterogeneous. The cultural, linguistic, and social divergences that exist are characterized by the aspiration to achieve legitimacy in the spaces they occupy and to offer the migrant anonymity through diversity as well as invisibility. The inscription of heterogeneity as a norm enables a change in the identity of the migrant, and also in that of the respective national mindscape, effecting a convergence through a process of reciprocal "pacification" and mutual acceptance.

ALTERITY, HETEROGENEITY

Today, more than ever before, heterogeneity, as a political norm for integration, has become a necessity, a quasi-imperative for the continuity of the social contract in different countries. But this is not possible, unless the initiative to explore others is grasped. Overcoming the respective fantasies that have worn thin but that still preside over dominant/dominated relationships is essential. This reciprocal exploration and overcoming can only transpire through a form of reification—at the very core of politics—of a value that seems to have become obsolete: the value of hospitality.

HOSPITALITY AND THE SOCIAL CONTRACT

Hospitality is a major ethical dimension in the relationship with the other. It is founded on the notion of obligation as a moral value and on the fundamental principle of parity and linguistic understanding between both parties, in keeping with an agreed code that simultaneously preserves and links them.* Reconciling the parity implicit in hospitality with the intrinsic deficit of citizenship in the notion of the migrant might seem to be contradictory, at least in appearance. The paradox is first and foremost ideological. Claimed as the supreme expression of the political individual, citizenship comprises, in addition to the postulate of the migrant's strangeness, a substrate of subordination.

* In French, the word *hôte* refers both to the person who gives and receives hospitality.

Moreover, the same paradox refers to the initial level of cohesion of the social pact in the host country. Of course, hosting the migrant is presented as an institutional affair. However, the interaction that enables the migrant to explore this "otherness" and to tell his/her migratory story is precisely what makes hospitality an issue for society.

THE INNER DEPTHS OF HISTORY

What is the link between my experience as a migrant high-school student, Palestinian refugees in a camp in Jordan, a Syrian seeking asylum in Sweden, and the Afro-Parisian quarter of Château d'Eau? If there were one, it would be the intense nature of the moments punctuating the individual stories. They are preserved and kept from being forgotten, invested with a cathartic mission, and—by simultaneously being set aside—refer to phenomena that are massive and anonymous. The texture of the migratory act does not make it possible to isolate the individual component of

migration from its mimetic and collective elements. The search for constants in regards to a potential systematic interpretation constantly collides with variables that invalidate such constants.
In the foregoing lines—deliberately planted firmly in a European perspective on migration—we cannot ignore that globalization is transforming the concept of civilization and culture. It interferes with the landmarks traced by national territories, hardening some and smashing others. It transports us somewhere else and brings multiple others to our doorstep, with their procession of pasts, presents, and futures that make history. Today, the inner depths of this history seem to be composed of hidden injustices, of contemptible vendettas, of hatred outliving its cause, of the stormy return of atavist pasts that take hold of the present like a delirium.

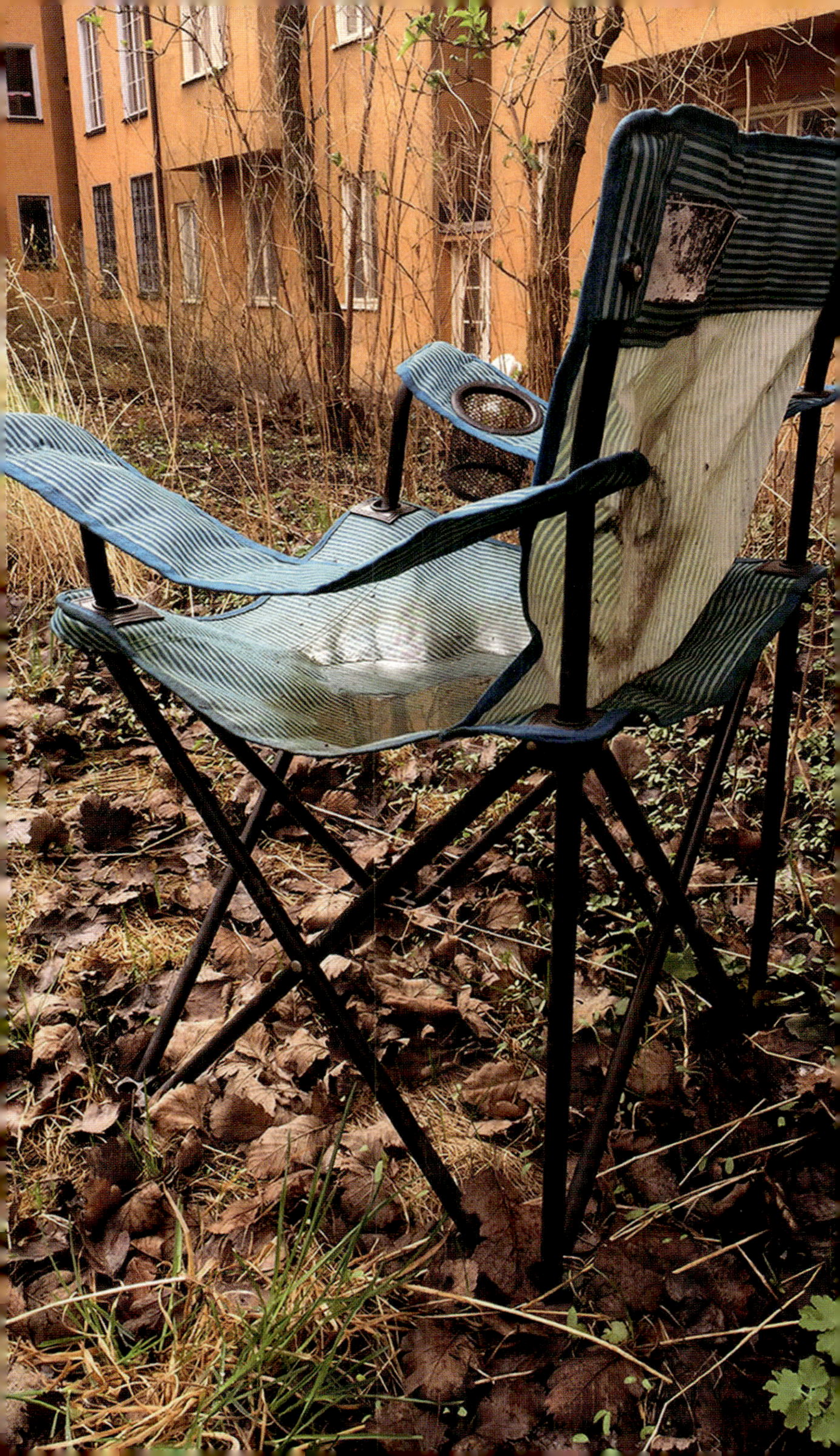

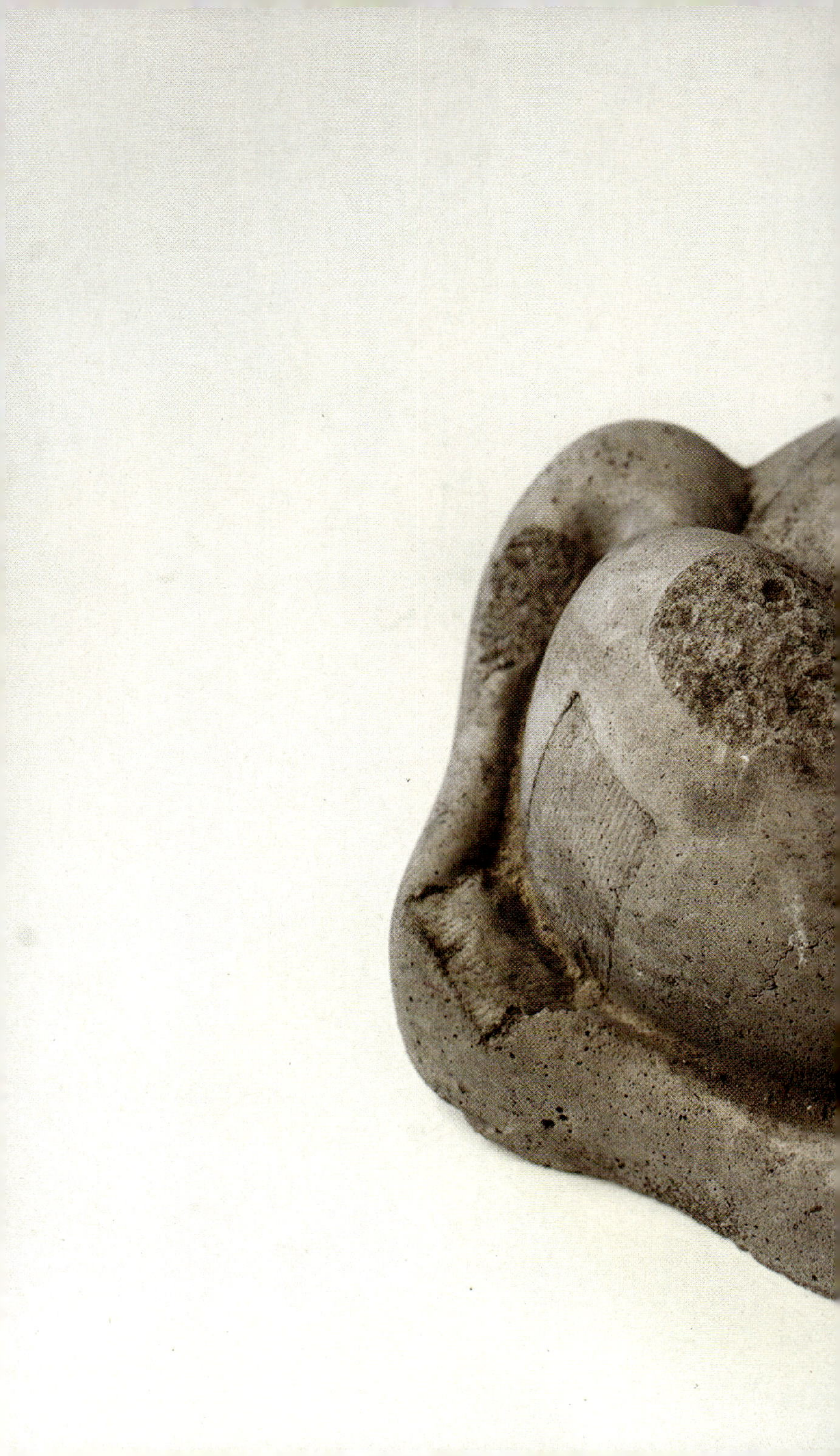

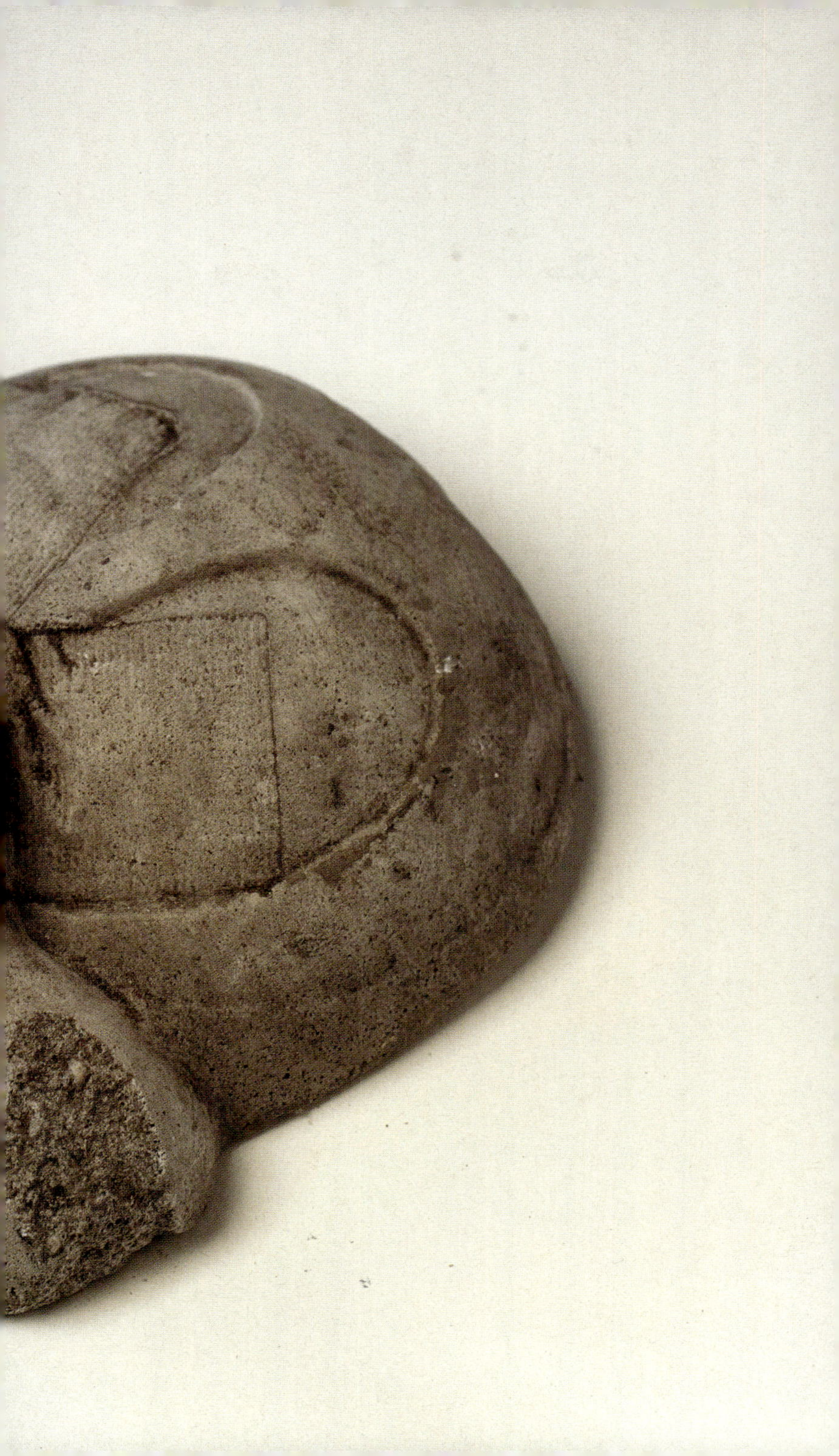

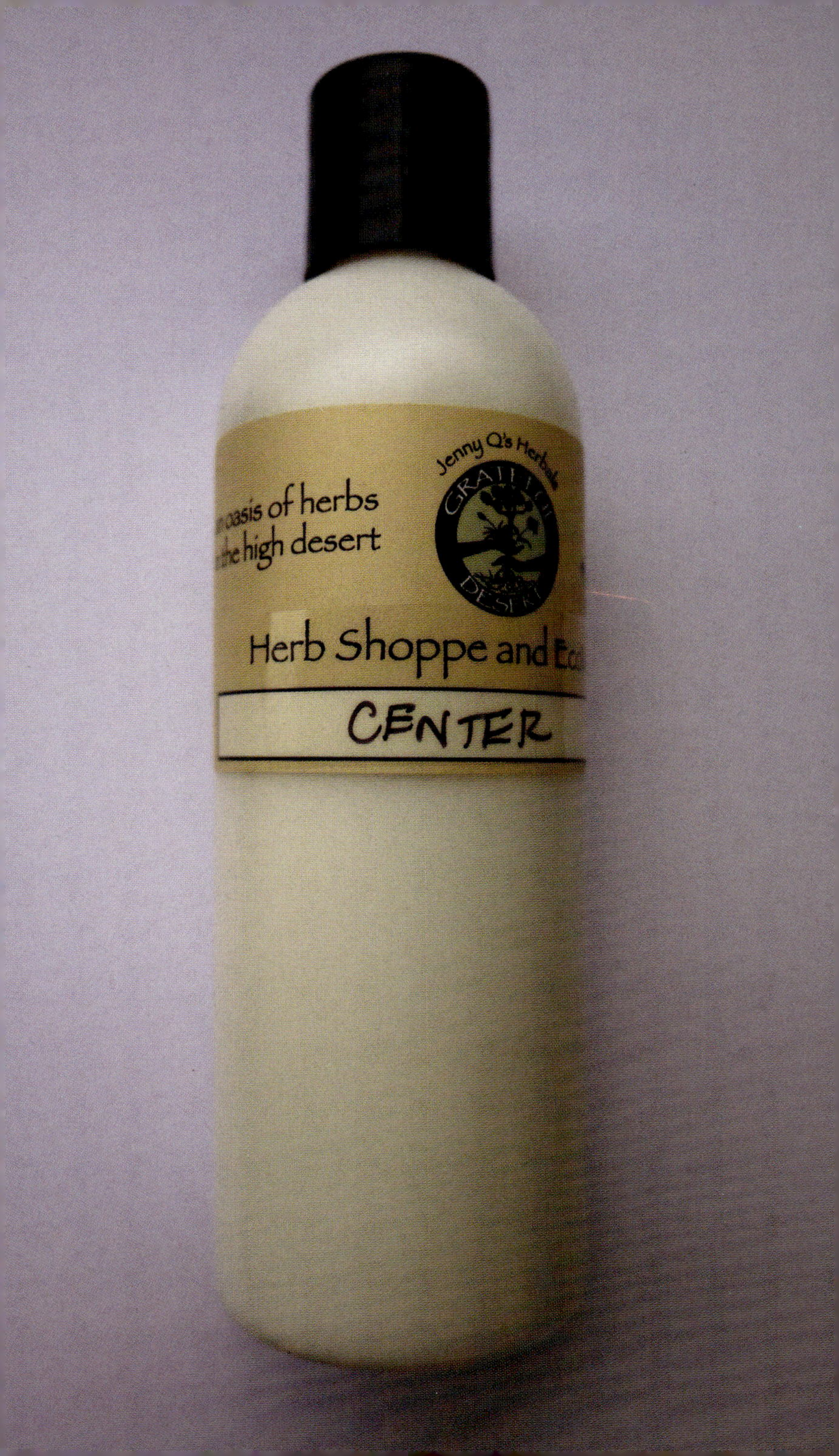
oasis of herbs
the high desert
Jenny Q's
Herb Shoppe and
CENTER

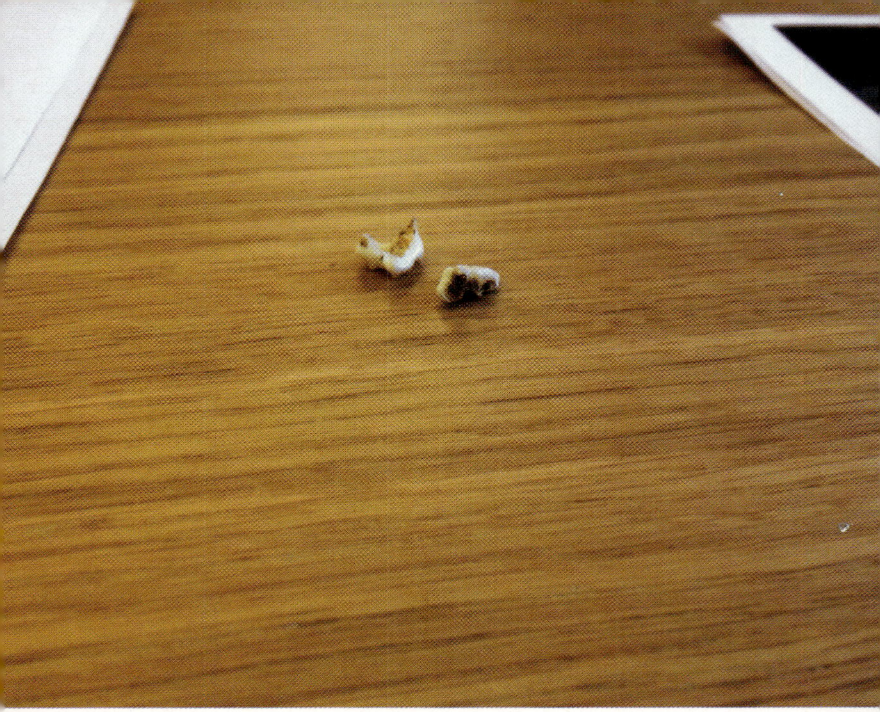

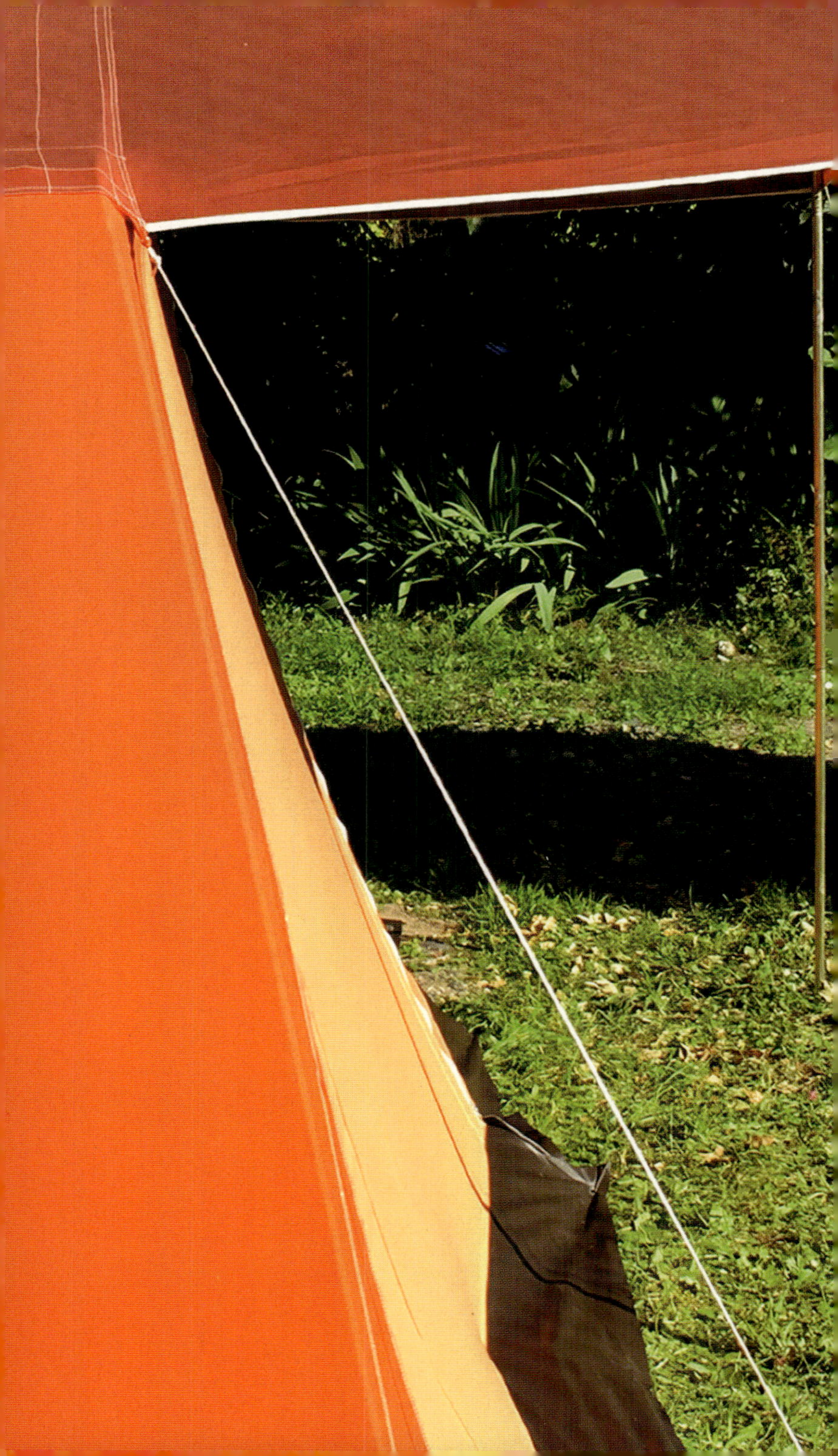

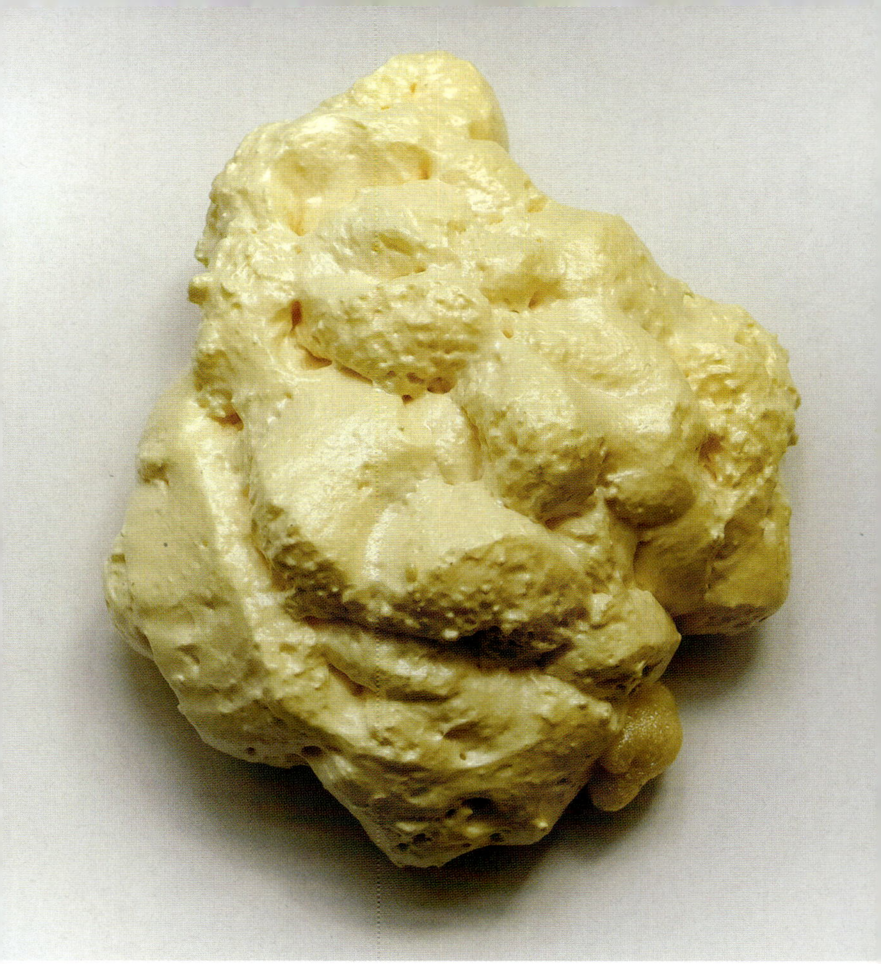

THE LONG MARCH THROUGH THE INSTITUTIONS. A STRATEGY FOR TODAY?

Mikkel Bolt Rasmussen

"The revolution is not a quick act that takes place once and transforms everything right away. The revolution is a long, complex process [...] Two years ago we were just a bunch of small esoteric groups believing we were the world spirit. Today the movement is thousands of people. But the transformation process will be what I have termed a long march through the existing institutions."[1] Thus spoke Rudi Dutschke in 1967 in a debate in Hamburg on the nature of the West German student movement. Borrowing the term of the "Long March" used by Mao to describe the 9,000-kilometer retreat and regrouping of the Red Army of the Communist Party of China in 1935, Dutschke affirmed his belief in a revolutionary transformation of capitalist society. Dutschke was not alone in developing an idea of a progressive use of the institutions of capitalist society at that time. In the late 1960s both the anti-authoritarian New Left as well as parts of the artistic avant-garde shared a belief in the need to transform society through the existing institutions.

In retrospect, many concepts and ideas from the late 1960s often appear problematic and difficult to put into practice today, now that the heyday of agitated critique has waned and has been replaced by repression, depression, or new neoliberal modes of being. But the idea of a long march through the institutions does not seem completely out of date. Ideas like cultural revolution or workers' self-management carry their historical weight in a more obvious manner than the idea of a long march through the institutions. The promises and failures of ideas like cultural revolution and self-management seem to have destined them to oblivion. But not so for the concept of the long march through the institutions. In recent years the idea has resurfaced both explicitly and indirectly in politics and art. We find it in *The Kilburn Manifesto* written by Stuart Hall. We find versions of it in the work of cultural theorists like Mark Fisher, who contemplates taking over cultural institutions. It is also present in accelerationism, and the idea of a progressive use of the institutions of capitalist society, and it is of course to be found in political phenomena such as Syriza in Greece and Podemos in Spain.

The following text is a brief discussion of the question of the notion of the institution and the limits of a progressive use of it. I would like to start out by asking whether Dutschke's notion of a long march though the institutions can help us in the present situation? What did Dutschke mean by "the long march through the institutions," and what are possible parallels between the recent discussion of a return to or critical use of the institution, for artistic and political purposes, and the ideas espoused by Dutschke?

Looking at Dutschke, we are immediately confronted by a historical paradox, because while most contemporary theorists use the term of the "long march" as a description of a progressive but, as I argue, largely *reformist* political project, Dutschke was describing a *revolutionary* process. His goal was a communist revolution: nothing less than a complete overhaul of capitalist society. Dutschke was an anti-authoritarian communist active in the West German student opposition movement in the late 1960s. After joining the German SDS (Sozialistischer Deutscher Studentenbund) in 1965, Dutschke soon became its most prominent voice and quickly came to play a central role in the mobilization of the West German youth against the Vietnam War in the late 1960s.[2] Referring to Herbert Marcuse's analysis of the one-dimensional society and, of course, also Marx's critique of the political economy and analysis of the capitalist mode of production—which had created an independent and alienating power running society without any consideration for human needs—Dutschke criticized not only a repressive West German state unable to come to terms with its Nazi past but also the booming postwar capitalist society and the new forms of control and submission it had created.

The phrase of "the long march" was used by Dutschke to conceptualize the revolution as a large and long-lasting project, not simply consisting of a quick overhaul, a state coup in which the revolution was a quick fix taking place from one day to the next; the revolution was a much more encompassing and complex process, he argued—thus the idea of a long march. As Dutschke stated in a television interview with Günter Gaus in 1967: "The difference between past revolutions is, among other things, that our revolutionary process will take a long time. It will be a very long march."[3] According to Dutschke it was not possible to reform the existing institutions, including the West German Parliament. The point was thus not to reform the institutions but to use them in the revolutionary struggle and somehow make them obsolete from within. The institutions had to be overthrown through a sustained, internally differentiated revolutionary process that consisted of a hostile take-over of the institutions and illegal activities outside. It was never just a question of running the institutions but always a question of creating something different.

Dutschke's vision of "the long march through the institutions" was based on a firm belief in the possibility of radical historical change. His notion was part of a larger rediscovery of earlier revolutions that had taken place in the years from the mid 1960s to the early 1970s, in which militants, workers, and students looked back and reconnected with the great proletarian offensive from 1917 to 1921 that effectively shook capitalist society. Dutschke, for his part, not only discovered Georg Lukàcs and Lenin but also drew on Dutch and German council communists, like Anton Pannekoek and Karl Korsch. He also read Amadeo Bordiga, coming up with plans for the creation of an autonomous Berlin Commune based on the lessons of the Paris Commune of 1871 as well as the short-lived Bavarian Council Republic in Munich in 1919.[4]

As we all know, Dutschke's project did not succeed. He abandoned activism and had to leave Germany, settling in Aarhus in Denmark and writing a dissertation that critiqued Lenin's understanding of the relationship between Russia's semi-Asiatic mode of production and its capitalist development. Western European protest movements fell apart quickly after the explosive events of 1968, except in a few countries like Italy and Portugal, where the movements were able to continue the struggle for a number of years before finally being swept aside by a counter-revolutionary offensive, which included substantial state violence and repression in the early 1970s. This paved the way for a dramatic restructuring of not only the global economy but also everyday life. The sites of the most militant European workers were closed down and the deindustrialization of Western Europe and the US began to take place on a large scale. Over the course of this process, workers in the centers of accumulation were replaced by much cheaper Chinese workers. This development—the emergence of neoliberal globalization—began to take place on an everyday level. In this context elements of the 1968 movement's critique of boring Fordist work were replaced by a new, individualized and hedonistic discourse of consumption and creativity. This effectively produced what Luc Boltanski and Ève Chiapello have termed a new capitalist spirit, in which components and fragments of revolutionary demands are transformed into nonthreatening neoliberal substitutes.[5]

This development also took place on a more individual level, in which the long march through the institutions turned out to be a somewhat different project than the one conceptualized by Dutschke: revolutionary critique was replaced by careerism. The later development is perhaps best personified by figures such as Daniel Cohn-Bendit and Joschka

Fischer. Cohn-Bendit was the infamous German-born student leader in Paris who was expelled from France by the authorities, an act that prompted a wave of Parisian students to take to the streets shouting "We are all German Jews!" in defiance of the attempt to cut off the head of the protest movement.[6] After being active in the radical left-wing scene in Frankfurt in the early 1970s, Cohn-Bendit joined the environmental movement before becoming a member of the German Green Party in 1984, ending up as an influential member of the European Parliament and a staunch defender of the EU. Cohn-Bendit's friend Fischer was part of the same ultra-leftist milieu in Frankfurt, heading a small militant street fighting group called Putzgruppe. Fischer, however, later became the leader of the Green Party and Foreign Minister from 1998 to 2005 as part of Gerhard Schröder's Social Democratic government that enacted a number of neoliberal policies, most notably the "Hartz IV" welfare reforms.

BREAK OR COMPLICIT CRITIQUE

Of course, also within art there was a partial rediscovery of previous revolutionary projects, in which the so-called neo-avant-garde revisited movements dating from the interwar period with a particular focus on the critique and ridicule of the institutional status of art and the interest in lending art a function beyond the confines of the art institution. Avant-garde groups like the Situationist International sought not only to continue the projects of Dada and Surrealism but to give them a more pronounced and explicitly revolutionary dimension. This resulted in the dispute of 1962 about the redundancy of art (both in the narrow sense of artistic media but also in terms of the art institution in general) as a means for revolutionary critique—especially in a capitalist society that increasingly depended on the production and circulation of images of a pleasant life filled with commodities and the representation of the threat of nuclear extension. The fraction of the Situationist group led by Guy Debord sought to leave the art institution behind and propagated engaging in what they termed "a revolutionary art of war." This was to be achieved not only by analyzing the society of the spectacle and its image-based forms of domination but also by practising subversive behavior on the margins of society, living the revolution within a hostile and occupied environment. Although their radicality and all-out avant-garde attack on art were unique, the Situationists were not alone in trying to move beyond the institutional framework of art. Artists active within the Fluxus and Happening movements likewise sought to put art to use outside the frameworks of the institution and the market.[7]

A different approach was presented by artistic practices that came to be known as institutional critique. Instead of trying to leave the institution, artists like Daniel Buren, Hans Haacke, and Michael Asher all sought to expose the institutional framework and aesthetic norms of modern art from within—working from the assumption that it was impossible to completely exit the institution. The Situationists were forced to leave art behind in favor of what they hoped would be revolutionary activities, while the artists associated with institutional critique stayed behind and practiced subtle displacements within the institution, not believing that it was possible to occupy a "free" realm outside art, beyond recuperation.

Peter Bürger's 1974 classic, *Theorie der Avantgarde* (Theory of the Avant-Garde) thus retrospectively can be described as a contemporary literary and historical account of the emergence of institutional critique, which analyzes the recuperation of the historical avant-garde by the postwar neo-avant-garde, Fluxus, pop, etc. Bürger argues that these groups and movements only managed to stage and represent *within the institution* the once radical gestures aimed at challenging the institutional status of art. Essentially, the avant-garde was now safely included in the very institution it had orginally called into question.[8] Bürger's book was written in 1973–74, at a time when the revolutionary energies of the 1960s were rapidly dissipating in West Germany and most other places. When Bürger published his book on French surrealism in 1969, *Der französische Surrealismus* (French Surrealism), the situation was different; in this text he explicitly linked Surrealism with May 1968 and the student movement. By 1974 the situation had changed, and Bürger choose to condemn the neo-avant-garde, implicitly identifying the Marxist historian, i.e. his own position, as the last refuge of criticality, for now the historian could engage in ideological critique as a kind of theoretical class war.[9]

Within the discourse of art, institutional critique ultimately had a more lasting impact than the Situationists. In the early 1990s artists like Andrea Fraser,

Fareed Armaly, Fred Wilson, and Christian Philipp Müller relaunched institutional critique, not only analyzing the museum and gallery but also the role of the artist by focusing on the forms of artistic subjectivity permitted and produced in the art institution. Although this approach was to a certain extent already present in the works of artists like Marcel Broodthaers, the new generation made visible the conditions of possibility for the artist to perform or engage in a critique of the institution. This is exemplified by Fraser's performances, in which she is/performs a stressed and incoherent museum guide or nervous performance lecturer. But this turn toward yet another level of meta-critique somehow moved institutional critique even further away from any kind of revolutionary critique. It ultimately made the self-critical artist into a tired, desperate, and cynical post-political artist, convinced of the almost ontological impossibility of ever exiting the institution or being able to reach a non-art audience. Andrea Fraser summarized the position in 2005: "We are trapped within our field." Not only was there no outside; but it was not even possible to envision one. She continues: "With each attempt to evade the limits of institutional determination, to embrace an outside, we expand our frames and bring more of the world into it. But we never escape it."[10] Complicit critique had thus become dangerously close to a defeatist stance, in which any real critical potential was suspended. Art and the figure of the artist, as conditioned by capitalist society, were not only part of the problem. Since art is simultaneously able to articulate a muted critique of capitalism and engage in a consolidation of capitalist society, it had become *the* main problem. Institutional critique ended up trapped in the institution, becoming a Biedermeier version of criticality, which works comfortably from inside the institution and pays it the ultimate homage of being "deconstructed." In this context, it does not make sense to engage in a post-Situationist escape attempt, because everybody prefers the compromised prestige and benefits of the art world, which at best minimize and isolate larger issues within the field of art. The conclusion is bleak and pretty clear: in light of the notion of "the long march through the institutions," the institutional critique of the 1990s ends up looking like an internal exercise doomed to remain within the closed circuit of the field of art.

FAILURE OR NEW BEGINNING

Within the last few years we have seen yet another turn when it comes to the question of the institution. One aspect of this development stems from the financial crisis of 2008 and the rise of a global protest movement resisting the austerity programs that most European nation-states opted to implement in order to socialize the losses of the financial breakdown. This protest movement was the first large-scale opposition to form after a forty-year-long neoliberal crash landing, during which living standards have fallen and more and more people all over the world have been forced into precarious labor or simply find themselves excluded from the process of capitalist production altogether.[11] Although the financial crisis has not caused any real political changes in government policies across the board, it does represent a major ideological breakdown in neoliberalism, which now seems unable to reestablish its previous dominance. No new ruling ideology has yet been formulated, and we seem to be headed into a long period of geopolitical chaos defined by competing major powers and the slow dismantling of US hegemony.[12]

In this new situation of crisis and breakdown—in which the nations of the EU have been forced to undertake draconic austerity measures and nations in the Middle East and North Africa have been turned into battlefields—there have been attempts to formulate visions for retaking the institutions hollowed out by cascades of neoliberal reforms. Mark Fisher, for instance, has argued that now might be the time to embed oneself in old institutional forms like the BBC, the Tate, and the Labour Party. After decades of being hollowed out by neoliberal changes and cuts, these institutions are there for the picking. The Left must reenter the political and cultural institutions, putting them to a new use. As Fisher writes: "Mainstream media" is not "a monolith but a terrain" on which to fight and engage in "popular experimentalism." We shall neither "remain in the margins nor replicate the existing forms of mainstream," Fisher notes.[13] This means taking back the institutions that the Western working class and labor movement helped create over the course of the twentieth century through intense and persisting clashes with ruling powers. The social-democratic Left in Western Europe gained power through these institutions after the Second World War, and Fisher is proposing to do the same today. The proposal is to reactivate the institutions of the nation-state and put them to progressive use, as was done in an earlier period.

In a text co-written with Nina Möntmann, Fisher explicitly links his argument to the financial crisis, writing that "since the financial crisis of 2008, the ideological field is radically open in a way that has not been the case for at least thirty years [...] In other words, the ground is for the taking."[14] Fisher and Möntmann present their argument as a critique of a certain Deleuze-Negrian stance, which they consider obsolete as a result of the crisis. Negri's notion of exodus and Deleuze's lines of flight might have been relevant in an earlier period, but they in fact only mirrored the rhetoric of networks and participation as propagated by neoliberal management. We now have to move back into the institutions in a kind Gramscian project, Fisher argues.

Fisher and Möntmann explicitly refer to Gramsci and his notion of hegemony via philosopher Chantal Mouffe, from whom they draw their political and philosophical vocabulary. In a talk presented at the "Truth is Concrete" event in Graz in 2012, Mouffe outlined a project of engaging strategically with institutions in accordance with "a pluralistic perspective."[15] In opposition to attempts to move beyond the institution, Mouffe advocates for a return to institutions as a means to "challenge the dominant consensus" and help produce a new common sense—effectively breaking down the hegemonic order. Critical artistic strategies can play an important role in this challenge to the common sense of neoliberalism, paving the way for an agonistic political practice of "establishing a new hegemony," says Mouffe. We are involved in a discursive battle against neoliberalism, and the task is to develop a new form of competing common sense. In order to do this, we have to get back into the institutions. In the words of Mouffe: "The long march through the institutions cannot be averted."[16]

Both Fisher and Mouffe advance an ideological critique of neoliberalism, thus contributing to the important critique of ruling representations of neoliberal globalization. They focus on neoliberalism as a political ideology to be fought discursively in both cultural and political spheres and also in the institutions of civil society, most of all the media. However, the problem is that they almost exclusively focus on neoliberalism as an ideology, and they therefore end up using a severely problematic notion of the revolutionary use of the institutions. In such constrainedness, the idea of "taking back the institutions" is not only naive with regard to the economical apparatus within which it operates. Rather, the notion could be considered as a symptomatic feature of the present situation, when large groups that have been marginalized by the economical system seek recognition within this system's institutions and its other representational registers of politics. In short, the problem with both Mouffe and Fisher's discourse is that neither of them actually envision the long march through the institution as a genuinely revolutionary process; it's all about reforming the institutions and putting them to a different use. Revolution is reduced to a question of a different "politics." Their argument is framed around the question of political choices. Mouffe's proposal hinges on what we can call a foreshortened analysis of neoliberalism, in which the logic of capitalist economy is missing from the analysis and the return of the objective crisis tendencies of capital somehow disappear from her description. Confronted with the accelerated chaos—the meltdown of the biosphere and the growth of the world population in addition to global economic shifts that economically disenfranchizes hundred of millions of people—her proposal seems highly lacking and completely out of touch with reality.

Merely using the institutions of capitalist society in a different way is far from enough. We have to go much deeper, be much more radical in going to the roots of the problem, if we are going to address the inherent shortcomings of the capitalist mode of production. As Robert Kurz, a leading German theorist of the critique of value, has described, capitalism is "domination without a subject," in which the subject is not wo/man but capital.[17] It is thus not a question of a different politics or a new common sense; it is not a question of the wrong class running the economy. The *economy* is the problem: the forms of social relations in capitalism, as mediated by labor, have acquired a life of their own—independent of the individuals that participate in their constitution and developing into an objective system in which "the circulation of money as capital is an end in itself," as Marx once wrote.[18] Running the institutions of capitalist society and controlling the production of surplus value is equivalent to orchestrating one's own alienation.

For Dutschke the point was to dismantle the institutions from the inside with a view of creating something completely different, a communist society. Dutschke emphasized the ideological dimension of class struggle, but he did not reduce it to politics as Mouffe and Fisher tend to do. For Dutschke the long march through the institutions was one moment in a two-part war against capitalist society, in which institutional work and extra-parliamentary praxis went hand in hand, although the one could never exist on its own. The goal was the negation of the negation of capitalism, in other words the abolition of capitalist society and all its mediating forms, such as money and wage labor. Let me recall that, over the last forty years, capital has excluded more and more workers from its metabolism, and the process seems to make a new wage-productivity compromise unlikely. The "good" thing about the crisis is that it will become much worse, exposing attempts to use the institutions of capitalist society as insufficiently radical. As Toni Negri has phrased it: "There's no New Deal."[19]

It is thus an open question as to how much revolutionaries can use the existing institutions in the coming battles. Certainly less than "the culturalists" envision.

In the present situation, returning to the original notion of "the long march through the institutions," in which any use of the institutions is held in check by illegal actions outside is not a bad start. Perhaps this will enable us to avoid the worst reformist pitfalls and remember the revolutionary project of moving through the institutions while destroying them and then exiting. Most institutions have to go. That was the plan and that remains the plan. As Dutschke phrased it: "We can no longer formulate the question of reform."[20]

NOTES

1. "Revolution 67," a panel discussion in Hamburg on November 24, 1967. See *Rudi Dutschke: Mein Langer Marsch*, eds. Gretschen Dutschke-Klotz, Hellmut Gollwitzer, and Jürgen Miermeister (Hamburg: Reinbek, 1980), 15.
2. For a good account of the development of Dutschke's thinking, see Michaela Karl, *Rudi Dutschke: Revolutionär ohne Revolution* (Frankfurt: Neue Kritik, 2003).
3. "Zu Protokoll: Rudi Dutschke," TV interview with Günter Gaus, Südwestfunk Baden-Baden, December 3, 1967. *Rudi Dutschke: Mein Langer Marsch* (see note 1), 42–57.
4. See Rudi Dutschke, *Jeder hat sein Leben ganz zu leben: Die Tagebücher 1963–1979* (Cologne: Kiepenheuer und Witsch, 2003).
5. Luc Boltanski and Ève Chiapello, *The New Spirit of Capitalism* [French, 1999], trans. Gregory Elliott (London and New York: Verso, 2006).
6. These demonstrations have lived on within political philosophy thanks to Jacques Rancière, who uses the students' actions as his favorite example of political subjectivation, in which a group denounces their identity and social role in favor of an "impossible" transgressive identity, thereby demanding a reshuffling of the sharing of the sensible. See Jacques Rancière, *Disagreement: Politics and Philosophy* [French, 1995], trans. Julie Rose (Minneapolis and London: University of Minnesota Press, 1999). In 2008, André and Raphaël Glucksmann provided a bizarre retrospective account of the slogan that turns out to have been a call for European solidarity and support for the EU. André and Raphaël Glucksmann, *Mai 68 expliqué à Nicolas Sarkozy* (Paris: Denoël, 2008), 37–88.
7. For an analysis of the Situationists and other radicalized 1960s art groups, see Mikkel Bolt Rasmussen, "The Politics of Interventionist Art," in *Rethinking Marxism*, vol. 21, no. 1 (2009), 34–49.
8. Peter Bürger, *Theory of the Avant-Garde* [German, 1974], trans. Michael Shaw (Minneapolis: University of Minnesota Press, 1984).
9. Peter Bürger, *Der französische Surrealismus: Studien zur avantgardistischen Literatur* [1971] (Frankfurt: Suhrkamp, 1996).
10. Andrea Fraser, "From the Critique of Institutions to an Institution of Critique," *Artforum*, vol. 44, no. 1 (2005), 282.
11. See Mikkel Bolt Rasmussen, *Crisis to Insurrection: Notes on the Ongoing Collapse* (New York and Wivenhoe: Minor Compositions, 2015).
12. See Immauel Wallerstein, *Does Capitalism Have a Future?* (Oxford and New York: Oxford University Press, 2013).
13. Mark Fisher, *Ghosts of My Life* (London: Zero Books, 2014), 223.
14. Mark Fisher and Nina Möntmann, "Peripheral Proposals," in *Cluster: Dialectionary*, eds. Binna Choi et al. (Berlin: Sternberg Press, 2014), 176.
15. Chantal Mouffe, "Strategies of Radical Politics and Aesthetic Resistance," in *Truth is Concrete: A Handbook for Artistic Strategies in Real Politics*, ed. Florian Malzacher (Berlin: Sternberg Press, 2014), 72.
16. Ibid., 73.
17. Robert Kurz, "Subjektlose Herrschaft: Zur Aufhebung einer verkürzten Gesellschaftskritik" [1993], in idem, *Blutige Vernunft: Essays zur emanzipatorischen Kritik der kapitalistischen Moderne und ihrer westlichen Werte* (Bad Honnef: Horlemann, 2004), 153–221.
18. Karl Marx, *Capital: A Critique of Political Economy*, vol. 1 [German, 1867], trans. Ben Fowkes (London: Penguin, 1990), 253.
19. See Toni Negri, "No New Deal is Possible" [Italian, 2009], trans. Arianna Bove, *Radical Philosophy*, no. 155 (2009), 2–5.
20. *Rudi Dutschke: Mein Langer Marsch* (see note 1), 16.

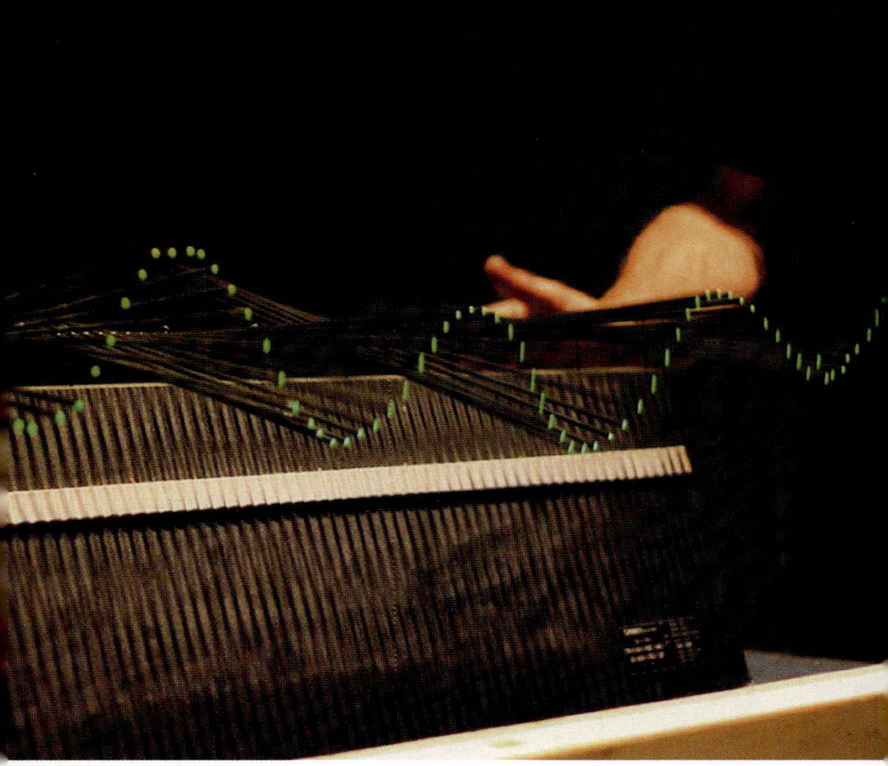

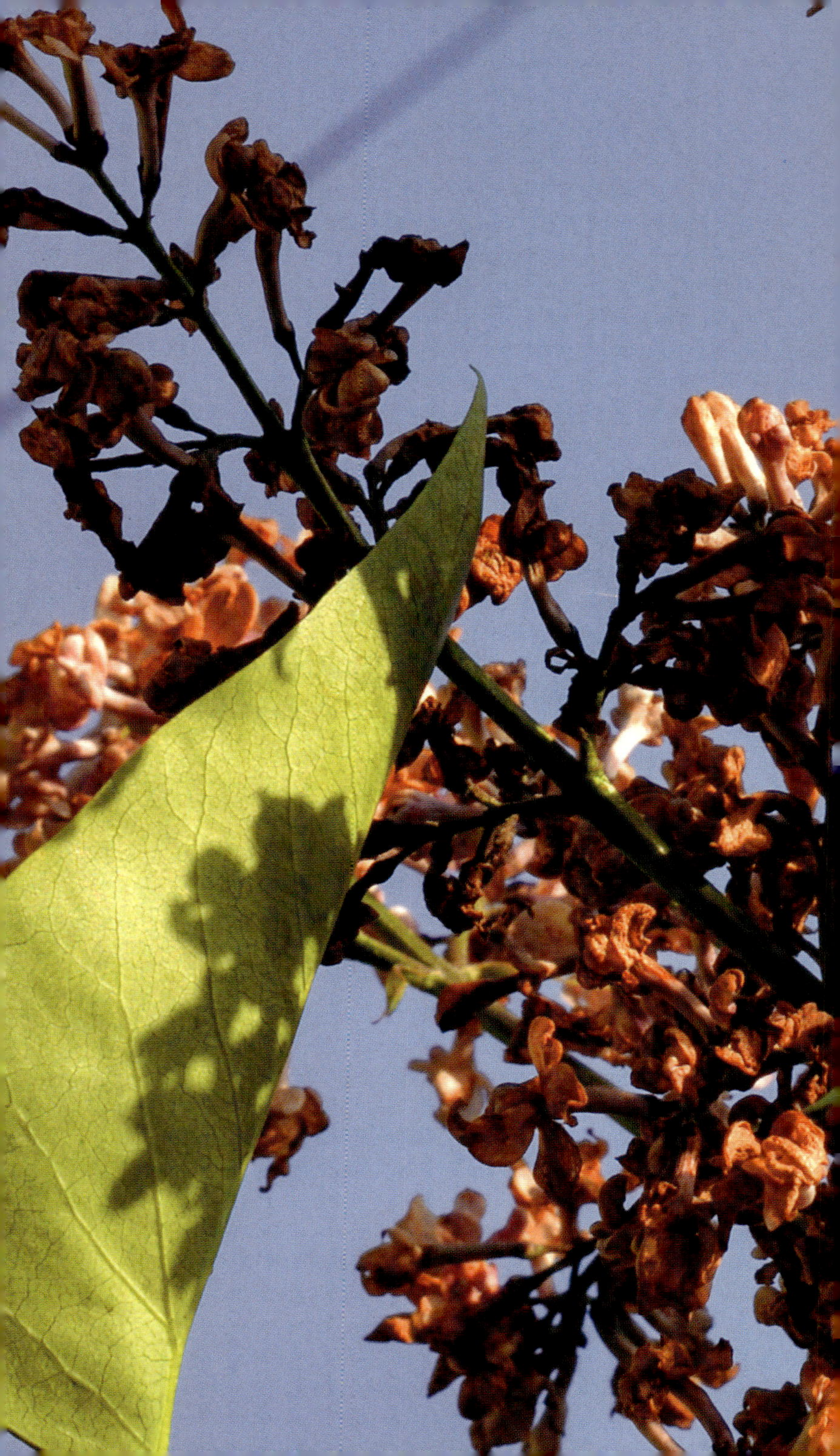

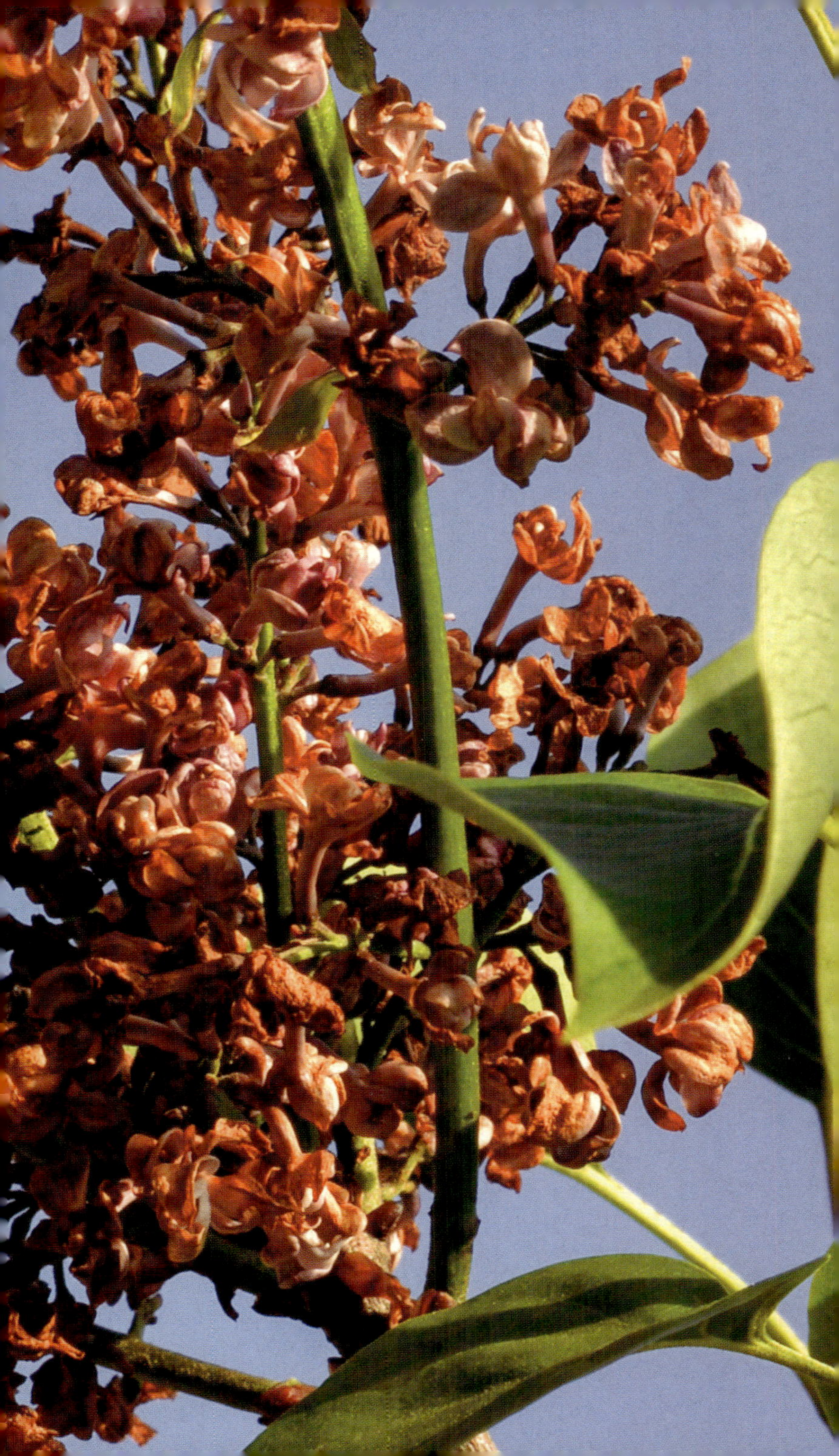

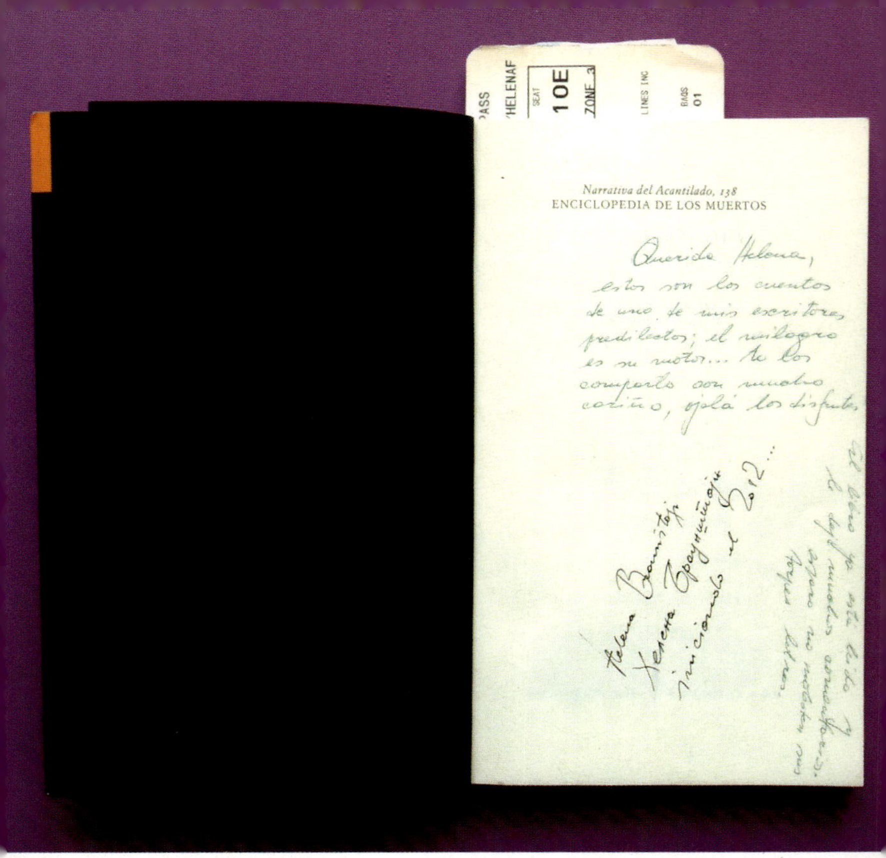
PASS
HELENAF
SEAT
10E
ZONE 3
LINES INC
BAGS
01
Narrativa del Acantilado, 138
ENCICLOPEDIA DE LOS MUERTOS
Querida Helena,
estos son los cuentos
de uno de mis escritores
predilectos; el milagro
es su motor... te los
comparto con mucho
cariño, ojalá los disfrutes

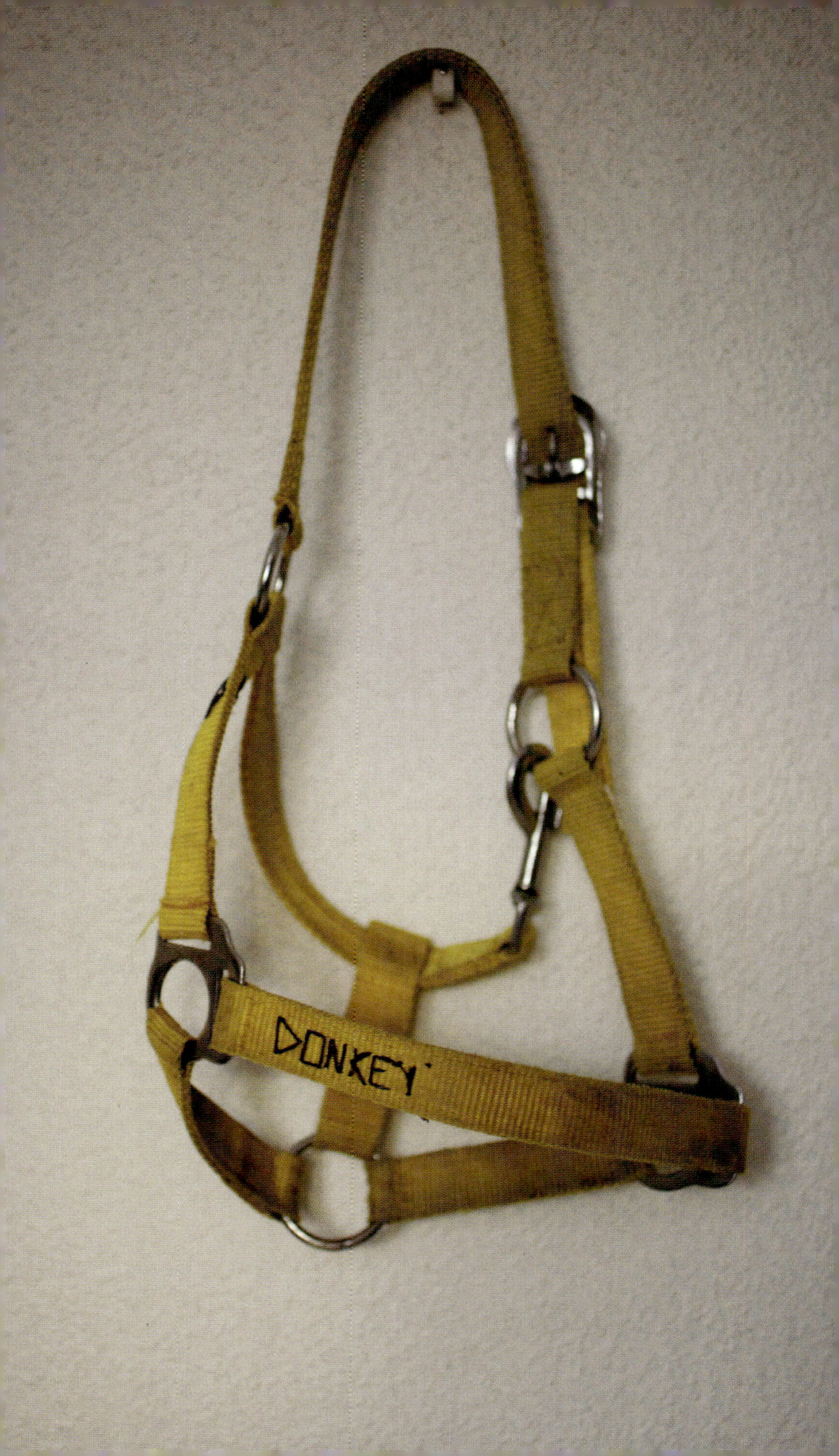
DONKEY

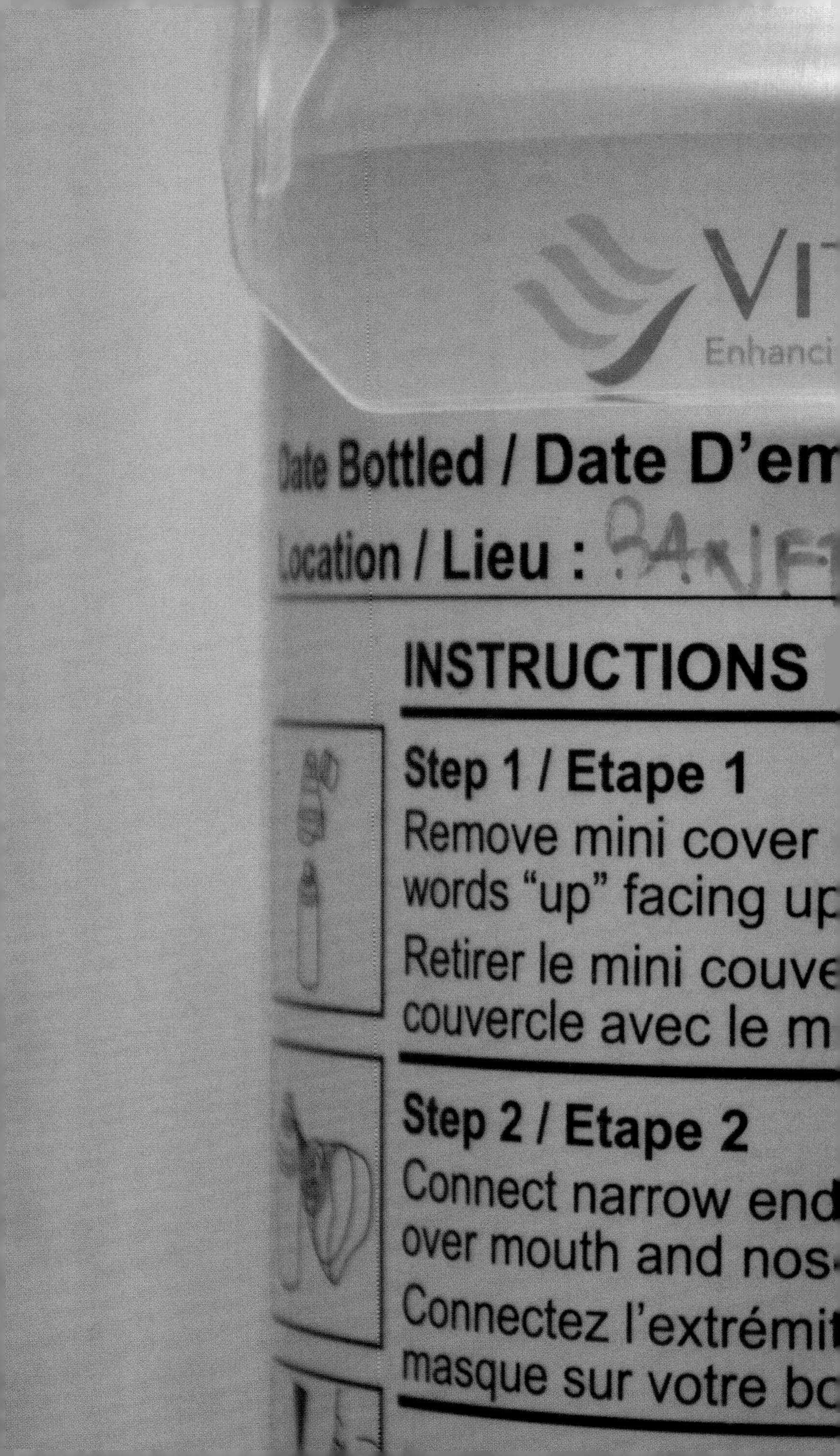
Date Bottled / Date D'em
Location / Lieu :
INSTRUCTIONS
Step 1 / Etape 1
Remove mini cover
words "up" facing up
Retirer le mini couve
couvercle avec le m
Step 2 / Etape 2
Connect narrow end
over mouth and nos
Connectez l'extrémi
masque sur votre bo

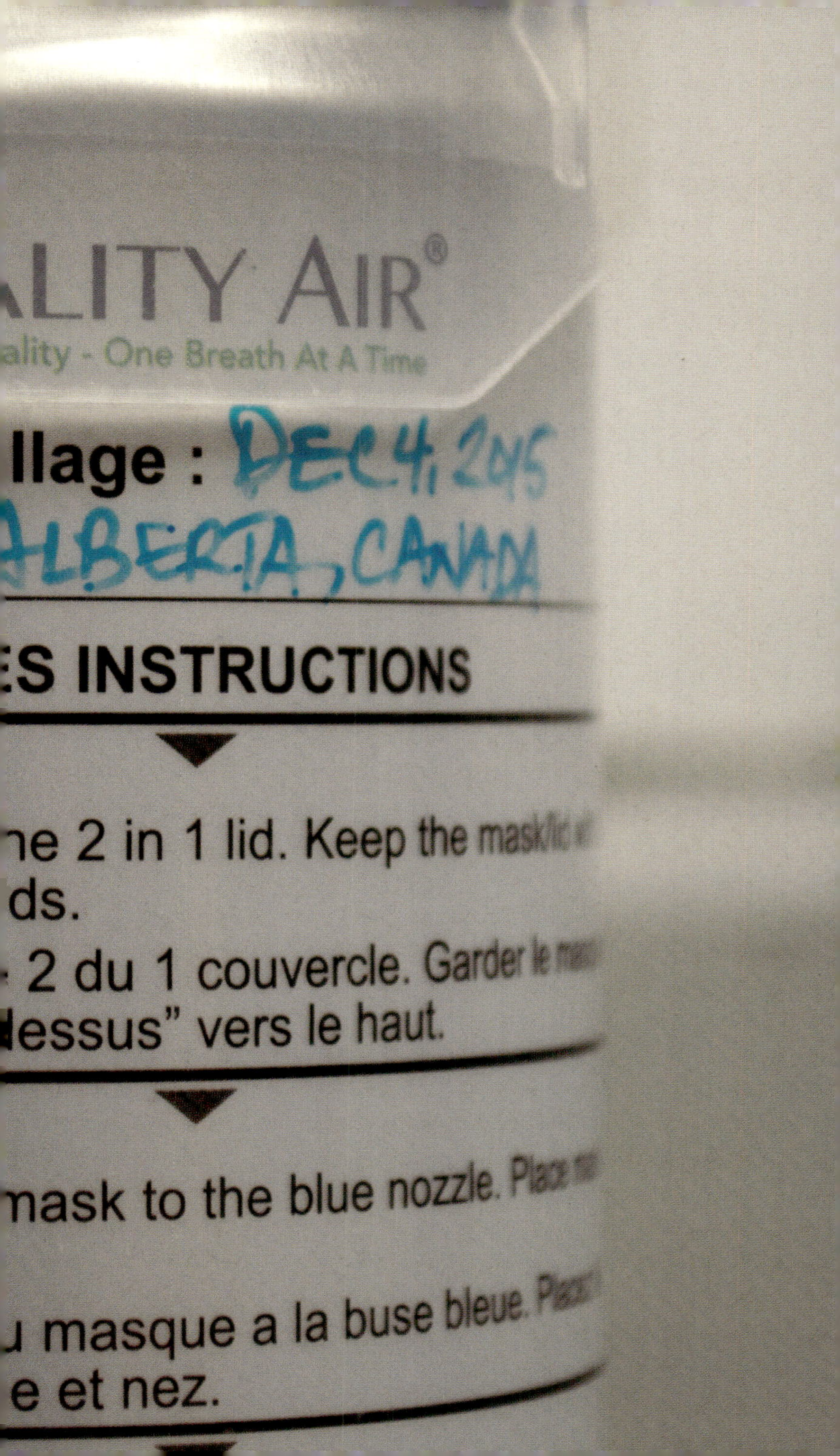

ALITY AIR®
ality - One Breath At A Time
llage : DEC 4, 2015
LBERTA, CANADA
ES INSTRUCTIONS
ne 2 in 1 lid. Keep the mask/lid
ds.
2 du 1 couvercle. Garder le
dessus" vers le haut.
mask to the blue nozzle.
u masque a la buse bleue.
e et nez.

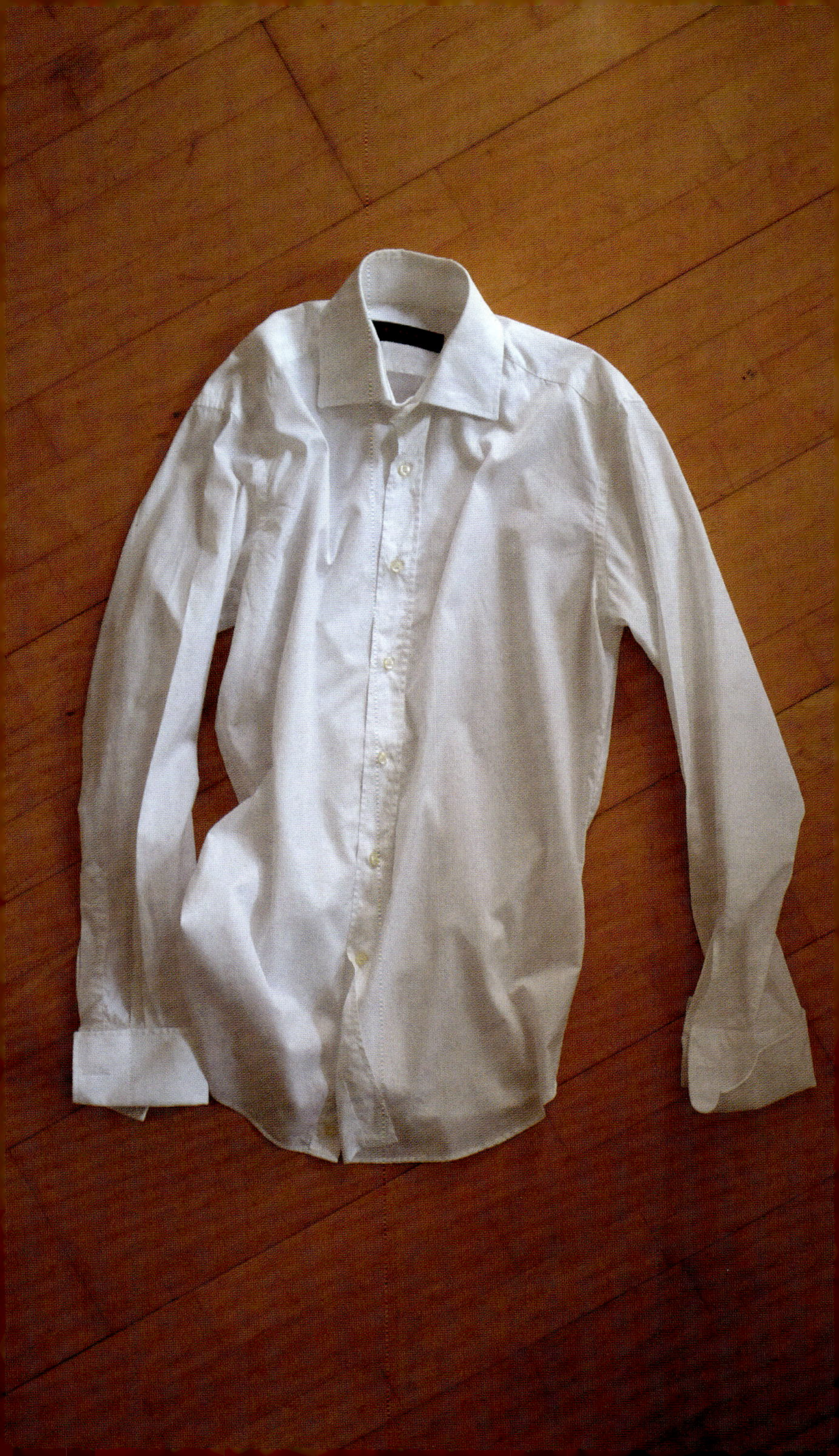

LEARNING FOLLOWING MAKING

Tim Ingold

INTRODUCTION

As you tap an egg against the edge of a bowl, prior to breaking it to cook an omelette, you touch, you listen, and you watch what you are doing. This is a matter not of inhabiting a world of sense, but of sensing the world.[1] Yet precisely these modalities of practical engagement and knowledge are missing from an anthropology of the senses that has nothing to say about how people see, hear, and touch as they go about their everyday business, and everything to say about how their experiences of seeing, hearing, and touching feed the imagination and infuse its discursive and literary expressions. In the very objectification of the senses, as things that one could have an anthropological study *of*, it appears that the eyes, ears, and skin are no longer considered to be organs of a body that, as it makes its way in the world, attentively looks, listens, and feels where it is going. On the contrary, they have become instruments of playback, capturing moments of experience and relaying them back to a reflexive consciousness for subsequent review and interpretation.

In life we move forward, sensing the world, rather than back, retreating into worlds of sense that have been artificially reconstructed on the basis of prior experience. I want to argue for a forward-moving anthropology, whose temporal orientation is the same as the orientation of the lives it studies. It is to move and think *with* persons and things rather than *about* them, to follow their trails, and to allow our knowledge to grow and flourish amid the movements of the world.

I refer to this trail-following as *wayfaring*.[2] When we speak of learning, and in particular of intergenerational learning, it is common to say that knowledge is transmitted from one generation to the next. The concept of transmission is linked to a genealogical model, the defining assumption of which is that individuals are specified in their essential genetic and cultural constitution—independently and in advance of their life in the world—through the bestowal of attributes from ancestors. Precisely because it separates the acquisition of knowledge-as-information from its practical enactment, however, the genealogical model is not appropriate to describe the ways in which people ordinarily come to know what they do. My thesis is that it is not through transmission but through wayfaring that knowledge is carried on.

The following text is a prolegomenon to wayfaring. I seek to show how learning in practice has to be conceived as a creative and improvisational coordination of perception and action; as an itinerant movement along a way of life understood as a path to be followed rather than a corpus of rules and principles to be passed on. I show how this path-following is given not in an engagement between practitioners and the material world by way of the senses, but in the coupling of substantial flows and sensory awareness in a world of materials. I begin by specifying what it means to say that in practice the movement of learning is creative and that it involves improvisation.

IMPROVISATIONS

There is a tendency in much writing on creativity to locate its sources in images and objects rather than in actual performance. This is why creation is so often equated with innovation. The equation rests on a "backwards" reading, according to which the creativity of action is judged by the novelty of its outcomes—by comparison with what has gone before—and is traced to its antecedent conditions in the form of unprecedented ideas in the minds of individual agents. This backwards reading is equivalent to what anthropologist Alfred Gell, writing about the work of art, has called the "abduction of agency."[3] Creativity is accordingly opposed to imitation, regarded as running off replicas from an already established design. Creative innovation can then come about only through the mutation or recombination of elements of transmitted design.

Yet this omits the creativity of the very process wherein any design is practically enacted. To recover this generative dynamic, creativity must be read "forwards," in the movements that give rise to things, rather than backwards from their outcomes. And to read creativity forwards entails a focus not on abduction but on *improvisation*.[4] To improvise is to follow the ways of the world, as they unfold, rather than to recover a chain of connections from an end point to a starting point, on a route already traveled. And the aim is not to reach a terminus but to *keep on going*. In keeping going, however, one may travel the same ground, over and over again. In any skilled craft, the development of proficiency calls for repetitive practice. Novices are required to copy or imitate exemplars shown to them, thereby incorporating into their own bodily dispositions the sensibilities of the masters in whose paths they follow, while simultaneously developing personal styles of their own.

In the Chinese art of calligraphy, for example, novices begin by tracing the shadows of the model to be copied, which is placed directly below the translucent paper on which they write. In the next stage, paper and model are placed side by side, forcing them to improvise the necessary gestures for themselves rather than being guided by the shadows of the masters. Then, in the final stage of learning, novices are encouraged to shake themselves loose from the masters' "clutching hands." At no point in this three-stage process of enskillment, however, do practitioners cease to copy. Every performance of a calligraphic work is a "going-over," in so far as it is modeled on previous studies, yet every going-over is itself an original movement, which carries the work forward, even as it follows paths already traced.

For this reason, no work is ever finished. Crescent rather than created, it cannot be contained within the bounds of a project that originates with a conception in the mind of an agent and ends with its realization in the material. It rather carries on throughout its performances, none of which *is* the work, but all of which contribute to its never-ending generation. In this regard, with calligraphy as with other arts of performance (such as music and dance), the performer is launched into a current, through which he or she has to feel the way with no assurance of how things will turn out. It is not a question of *iteration*, but of *itineration*.[5] Thus the practitioner is an *itinerant*, a wayfarer. And like all wayfarers, practitioners have to improvise.

Nor is the performance any less improvisatory to the extent that it is scored as in music, choreographed as in dance, or in any other way ostensibly preordained.

To the contrary, the more strictly the performance is specified, the greater the improvisational demands placed on practitioners to "get it right." Any formal resemblance between the copy and the model is not given in advance but is rather a horizon of attainment, to be judged in retrospect. That is why there is creativity even, and especially, in the maintenance of an established tradition.[6]

MOVEMENTS

Now in the performing arts, as in any craft, novices have to learn through repetitive practice in copying models shown to them. To copy, however, is not to replicate a preexisting form but to align the observation of the model with action in a world suspended in movement. Fluent performance has a rhythmic quality. But this quality does not lie in the repetitiveness of the movement itself. For there to be rhythm, movement must be *felt*. The practitioner who has a feel for what he or she is doing is one who can bring many concurrent movements more or less into phase with one another. This calls for continual correction in response to an ongoing perceptual monitoring of the task as it unfolds. Rhythmicity, as the philosopher Henri Lefebvre has argued, implies not just repetition but *differences within repetition*.[7] Feeling, then, lies in the coordination of movement and perception: such coordination, indeed, is the essence of skilled practice. By way of perception, the practitioner's own rhythmic gestures are skillfully attuned to the multiple rhythms of the environment.[8]

Thus any task, itself a movement, takes place within what André Leroi-Gourhan—the great French anthropologist of techniques—called a "network of movements," within which the existence of every practitioner is suspended.[9] In my view, it would be more appropriate to speak of a *meshwork* of movements than a network, of contrapuntal lines rather than connected points. This is a critical distinction to which I shall return below. For now, the conclusion I want to stress is that the measure of skill lies not in the efficiency of predetermined motions but in the sensibility that enables practitioners to respond to environmental perturbations that would throw the performance off course, were it confined to the execution of a fixed motor program.

In learning, the human organism undergoes growth and transformation—physiologically, neurologically, and psychologically—in and through the movements it carries on and the postures it endures. Living bodies are never made but always in the making, and their specific expertise is not added on—in the form of a motor schema internalized into a body already primed with the capacities to receive it—but is itself the developmental outcome of what anthropologist Greg Downey calls "kinetic self-exploration."[10] In this exploration, though guided by others, novices have perforce to find their own ways. And if it turns out that specific skills are common to a community of practice, this is not because the operations of practitioners' bodies are directed from within by the same motor schema, transmitted to them at the start, but because these developmental explorations have converged upon the same or similar outcomes.

Dance anthropologist Brenda Farnell has directly confronted the question of how we are to understand the creativity of apparently imitative and consistently repeated movements in the work of contemporary dance artists.[11] The precision and coordination of these movements call for a finely tuned kinaesthetic awareness, along with an awareness on the part of each dancer of their own internal bodily sensations, the exercise of both focal and peripheral vision, a sensitivity to the rhythms and sounds of breathing and footwork, and an ability to feel each other's presence in a shared intersubjective space. Of course, this practice develops the dancers' muscles, and their athletic prowess. As goals of training, however, muscle power and athleticism take second place to the development of movement perception. What develops, according to Farnell's collaborator, choreographer Robert Wood, is a "whole-body intelligence"—an intelligence in motion, capable of responding to an ever-changing environment. This intelligence, says Wood, allows the dancer to "let go," to *be*.

But how can such letting go be reconciled with a daily training regime in which prescribed movements are repeated over and over again? Would not such a regime have the opposite effect of habituating movement, dulling the senses, and sending conscious awareness into retreat? The answer hinges on the meaning of "embodiment." Maxine Sheets-Johnstone, a philosopher of dance, protests against the facile appeal to this concept, so pervasive in current writing in the arts, humanities, and social sciences, as if merely by placing the word "embodied" before "practice," the still festering wound created by the surgical separation of the organ of self-knowledge from the flesh and blood of human beings could be magically healed.[12] Employed in this sense, she argues, the notion of embodiment is nothing more than a "lexical band-aid," which allows the divide between knowing and being to persist simply by covering it up.

This will continue for as long as we fail to recognize that the key to both self-knowledge and organic life is *movement*. As we are living organisms, we move and *are* our movements; therefore the knowledge we have of ourselves is inseparable from the sense we have of our movements, or in a word, from *kinaesthesia*. As animate beings, Sheets-Johnstone insists, we do not experience ourselves and one another primarily as "packaged," but as both moving and moved, in ongoing response—or what I would call *correspondence*—to those around us.[13] This is as true of the movements of everyday life as it is of their more specialized refinements in dance, which is why dance—not as an object but as a means of investigation—can cast such a bright light on what it means not just to live *in* the world, but to be alive *to* it.

Arguably, however, Sheets-Johnstone's protest is more against a particular use of the concept of embodiment—albeit so pervasive as to be almost universal—than against the concept *per se*. For when Farnell describes human beings as "primarily embodied meaning-makers," she quite explicitly does *not* intend to convey the idea of the body as a package, within which practices are, so to speak, wrapped up. Nor, to invoke another widespread image, is it to be understood as a sink, into which practices settle like sediment in a ditch. The body, in Farnell's usage, is neither an object of performance nor its instrument but rather a dynamic center of unfolding activity. Whether in dancing, gesturing, talking, or writing, performance—she insists—issues *from* the body; it is not *about* the body.[14] And this takes us back to our question of how to reconcile the repetitiveness of training with the heightened sensitivity that it is supposed to engender.

The aim of such training is not primarily ergonomic; it is not about creating bodies that are more energetic and efficient in their movements. It is about the education of perception. Learning is not, therefore, imitative, if by imitation we mean the replication, within the minds of novices, of schemata originally housed within the minds of experts and expressed in bodily execution. But it is about copying, about aligning one's own ongoing movements with those of one's surroundings. Improvising a path through a field of practices, rather than mechanically executing the rules and representations of transmitted culture, the skilled practitioner does not impose preexistent forms on inert matter but intervenes in the fields of forces and currents of material wherein forms are generated. In this sense, as already noted, practitioners are itinerants, and skilled practice is an itinerant movement along a way of life. Skill, then, lies in the ability to find the grain of the world's becoming, and to follow it, while bending it to an evolving purpose.[15]

MATERIALS

In his notebooks, the artist Paul Klee repeatedly urged that the processes of genesis and growth giving rise to forms in the world we inhabit are more important than the forms themselves. "Form is the end, death," he wrote. "Form-giving is movement, action. Form-giving is life."[16] This, in turn, lay at the heart of his celebrated "Creative Credo" of 1920: "Art does not reproduce the visible but makes visible."[17] It does not, in other words, seek to replicate finished forms that are already settled, whether as images in the mind or as objects in the world. It seeks, rather, to join with those very forces that bring form into being. Thus the line grows from a point that has been set in motion, as the plant grows from its seed.

Taking their cue from Klee, philosopher Gilles Deleuze and psychoanalyst Félix Guattari argue that the essential relation, in a world of life, is not between matter and form but between *materials* and *forces*.[18] It is about the ways in which substances of all sorts, enlivened by cosmic forces and with variable properties, mix and meld with one another in the generation of things. Whenever we encounter matter, as Deleuze and Guattari insist, "it is matter in movement, in flux, in variation."[19] And the consequence, they go on to assert, is that "this matter-flow can only be *followed*." What Deleuze and Guattari call a "matter-flow," I would call *material*. Accordingly, I recast their assertion as a simple rule of thumb: *follow the materials*. To apply this rule is to intervene in a world that is continually on the boil.

Much has been written in recent years on the relations between persons and things, guided by the thought that the material world is not passively subservient to human design. Theorists have expressed this, however, by an appeal not to the vitality of materials but to the agency of objects. If persons can act on objects in their vicinity, so, it is argued, can objects "act back," causing persons to do what they otherwise would not. The speed bump on the road, to take a familiar example adduced by philosopher Bruno Latour, causes the driver to slow down, its agency here substituting for that of the traffic policeman.[20] We may stare at an object, explains art historian James Elkins (acknowledging the psychoanalysis of Jacques Lacan), but the object also stares back at us, so that our vision is caught in a "cat's cradle of crossing lines of sight."[21] And in a precise reversal of conventional subject-object relations, archaeologist Chris Gosden suggests that in many cases, it is not the mind that imposes its forms on material objects, but rather the latter that give shape to the forms of thought.[22]

In this endless shuttling back and forth between the mind and the material world, it seems that objects can act like subjects, and that subjects can be acted upon like objects. Instead of subjects and objects there are "quasi-objects" and "quasi-subjects," connected in relational networks. Yet paradoxically, these attempts to move beyond the modernist polarization of subject and object remain trapped within a language of causation that is founded on the very same grammatical categories and that can conceive of action only as an *effect* set in train by an agent. At best, they lead only to contradiction and confusion. At worst, they have led theorists to make fools of themselves in ways that we would be ill-advised to emulate.

For the world we inhabit, I maintain, is not comprised of subjects and objects, or even of quasi-subjects and quasi-objects. The problem lies not so much in the *sub-* or the *ob-*, or in the dichotomy between them, as in the *-ject*. For the constituents of this world are not already thrown or cast before they can act or be acted upon. They *are* in the throwing, in the casting. The point may best be illustrated by means of a simple experiment that I have carried out with my students at the University of Aberdeen. Using fabric, matchstick bamboo, ribbon, tape, glue, and twine and working indoors on tables, we each made a kite. It seemed that we were assembling an object. But as soon as we carried our creations outside, they leaped into action, twirling, spinning, nose-diving, and occasionally flying. The kite that had lain lifeless on the table indoors, now immersed in these generative currents, had come to life. What we had thought to be an object was revealed as what I would call a *thing*. The thing about things, if you will, is that far from standing before us as a *fait accompli*, complete in itself, each is a "going-on"—or better, a place where several goings-on become entwined. As Martin Heidegger put it, albeit rather enigmatically, the thing presents itself "in its thinging from out of the worlding world."[23] It is a particular gathering together of materials in movement.

Thus the very "thinginess" of the kite lies in the way it gathers the wind into its fabric, and in its swooping it describes an ongoing "line of flight."[24] On no account should this line be confused with the line connecting the kite with the flyer. For the line of flight, as Deleuze and Guattari insist, *does not connect*. It "is not defined by points that it connects, or by points that compose it; on the contrary, it passes *between* points, it comes up through the middle [...] A becoming is neither one nor two, nor the relation of the two; it is the in-between, [the] line of flight [...] running perpendicular to both."[25] Like the stems of plants growing from their seeds, to return to Klee's image, such lines trace the paths of the world's becoming—its "worlding"—rather than connecting up, in reverse, sequences of points already traversed. That is why I prefer the word "meshwork" to "network" to describe what Leroi-Gourhan saw as the ensemble of movements within which skilled practice is carried on.[26] Think of the mesh of vegetation in a forest, or of roots underground, each of which seeks to carry on by seeking a way through the tangle.

What goes for the kite-in-the-air, in its thinging, also goes for the flyer-on-the-ground. If the kite is not endowed with an agency that causes it to act, then neither is the human flyer. Like the kite, the human is not a being that acts—an agent—but a hive of activity, energized by the flows of materials, including the currents of air, that course through the body and keep it alive through processes of respiration and metabolism. Like the kite's line of flight, so the life-trajectory of the flyer follows a course orthogonal to any line we might draw connecting the kite as (quasi-)object with the flyer as (quasi-)subject. In practice, then, flyer and kite should be understood not as interacting entities, alternately playing agent to the other as patient, but as trajectories of movement, responding to one another in counterpoint, alternately as melody and refrain. In short, these contrapuntal trajectories proceed in *correspondence*, like melodic lines on a musical stave.

Both flyer and kite, in this sense, are things. Indeed, *persons are things too*. As a hive of activity and an entanglement of material flows, every person *is* a living organism. We have no need, then, to conjure up an additional capacity, installed within the organism, to stand in as the "cause" of this activity, as though the activity were the effect of some internal agency. Indeed the "problem of agency" is one that theorists have largely created for themselves, born of the attempt to reanimate a world already rendered lifeless by an exclusive focus on the "objectness" of things. It is striking that the more theorists have to say about agency, the less they seem to have to say about life. To rewrite the life of things as the agency of objects is to effect a double reduction, of things to objects, and of life to agency. My aim is to reverse this reduction, to restore things to life, and in so doing, to celebrate the creativity of what Klee called "form-giving." And to achieve this aim it is necessary to overcome the tendency to which I referred earlier, to read creativity *backwards*, by abduction.

In a dialogue with his son Yves, himself a practicing artist, the novelist and critic John Berger observes that you cannot *be* a mountain, or a buzzard soaring in the sky, or a tree in the forest, but you can *become* one, by aligning your own movements and gestures with those of the thing that captures your attention.[27] This is what happens, for example, in the practice of drawing, which Klee famously characterized as taking a line for a walk.[28] Like the mountain path, the buzzard's flight, or the tree root, the drawn line does not connect predetermined points in sequence but "launches forth" from its tip, leaving a trail behind it. Where the path winds, the bird flies, and the root creeps, the line follows. But following, as Deleuze and Guattari observe, "is not at all the same thing as reproducing": whereas reproducing involves a procedure of *iteration*, following involves *itineration*.[29]

CONCLUSION

Practitioners, I have argued, are itinerants, whose works are consubstantial with the trajectories of their own lives. And it is in the very forward movement of improvisation, rather than in the retrospective work of abduction, that the creativity of their practice is to be found. To improvise, write Deleuze and Guattari, is "to join with the World, or to meld with it. One ventures from home on the thread of a tune."[30] Life, for Deleuze and Guattari, issues along such thread-lines. They are the "lines of flight" that we have already encountered in our earlier example of the kite. Along them, points are not connected so much as swept up and rendered indiscernible in the current of movement. Life, as I have already indicated, is open-ended; its impulse is not to reach a terminus but to keep on going.

Following—aligning one's movements with the trajectories of things in the world—calls for observation. This is not, however, the distanced and disinterested contemplation of a world of objects, nor does it result in the formation of mental images or representations. To observe is not so much to see what is "out there" as to *watch what is going on*. Its aim is not to represent the observed but to participate with it in the same generative movement, intimately coupling the movement of the observer's attention—whether visual, aural, haptic, or olfactory—with currents of activity in the environment. Theorists of material culture tend to envisage a world in which the die is already cast—a world that has already precipitated out from the currents, mixtures, and transmutations of substances from which they are formed. To follow the materials, however, is to enter into a world-in-formation, in which things appear not as bounded objects but as confluences of materials that have momentarily melded into recognizable forms.

Far from containing the materials from which they are formed, things leak and are only sustained because of the interchange of materials across their surfaces. It is because of these fluxes that the inhabited world is imbued with life. In shifting our focus from ready-made objects to processes of generation and dissolution, I believe we should attend not to the *materiality* of things but to *materials-becoming-things*. Whereas objects *exist*, every thing—as I have already shown—is a *going-on* or, better, a place where many goings-on get tangled up together. And to engage with things, I maintain, you have to join with them in the processes of their formation.

The movement of making does not lie in the relation *between* one thing and another—between the mental image and the material object—but in a movement orthogonal to this relation, both of sensory awareness and material flow. This is the movement of life itself, and it is the creativity of this movement—the improvisational learning that comes from following, and the coupling of sensory awareness and substantial flows in a world of materials—that I have sought to recover.

NOTES

1. Tim Ingold, "Worlds of Sense and Sensing the World: A Response to Sarah Pink and David Howes," *Social Anthropology*, vol. 19, no. 3 (2011), 313–317.
2. Tim Ingold, *Lines: A Brief History* (London: Routledge, 2007), 75–76.
3. Alfred Gell, *Art and Agency: An Anthropological Theory* (Oxford: Clarendon, 1998), 13.
4. Tim Ingold and Elizabeth Hallam, "Creativity and Cultural Improvisation: An Introduction," in *Creativity and Cultural Improvisation*, ed. Elizabeth Hallam and Tim Ingold (Oxford: Berg, 2007), 3.
5. Gilles Deleuze and Félix Guattari, *A Thousand Plateaus: Capitalism and Schizophrenia* [French, 1980], trans. Brian Massumi (London: Continuum, 2004), 410.
6. Ingold and Hallam, "Creativity and Cultural Improvisation," (see note 4), 5.
7. Henri Lefebvre, *Rhythmanalysis: Space, Time, and Everyday Life* (London: Continuum, 2004), 90.
8. Tim Ingold, "Walking the Plank: Meditations on a Process of Skill," in *Defining Technological Literacy: Towards an Epistemological Framework*, ed. J. R. Dakers (New York: Palgrave Macmillan, 2006), 76–77.
9. André Leroi-Gourhan, *Gesture and Speech*, trans. Anna Bostock Berger (Cambridge, MA: MIT Press, 1993), 282.
10. Greg Downey, "Learning the 'Banana-tree': Self-modification Through Movement," in *Redrawing Anthropology: Materials, Movements, Lines*, ed. Tim Ingold (Farnham: Ashgate, 2011), 86.
11. Brenda Farnell and Robert N. Wood, "Performing Precision and the Limits of Observation," in *Redrawing Anthropology: Materials, Movements, Lines*, ed. Tim Ingold (Farnham: Ashgate, 2011).
12. Maxine Sheets-Johnstone, *The Primacy of Movement* (Amsterdam: John Benjamins, 1998), 359.
13. Ibid.
14. Brenda M. Farnell, "Getting Out of the Habitus: An Alternative Model of Dynamically Embodied Social Action," *Journal of the Royal Anthropological Institute* (New Series), no. 6 (2000), 413; and Farnell and Wood, "Performing Precision," (see note 11), 111.
15. Tim Ingold, "The Textility of Making," *Cambridge Journal of Economics*, vol. 34, no. 1 (2010), 92.
16. Paul Klee, *Notebooks*, ed. Jürg Spiller, vol. 2, *The Nature of Nature*, trans. Heinz Norden (London: Lund Humphries, 1973), 269.
17. Paul Klee, *Notebooks*, ed. Jürg Spiller, vol. 1, *The Thinking Eye*, trans. Ralf Manheim (London: Lund Humphries, 1961), 76.
18. Deleuze and Guattari, *A Thousand Plateaus* (see note 5), 377.
19. Ibid., 451.
20. Bruno Latour, *Pandora's Hope: Essays on the Reality of Science Studies* (Cambridge, MA: Harvard University Press, 1999), 186–190.
21. James Elkins, *The Object Stares Back: On the Nature of Seeing* (New York: Simon & Schuster, 1996), 70.
22. Chris Gosden, "What do objects want?" *Journal of Archaeological Method and Theory*, vol. 12, no. 3 (2005), 196.
23. Martin Heidegger, *Poetry, Language, Thought*, trans. Albert Hofstadter (New York: Harper and Row, 1971), 196.
24. Deleuze and Guattari, *A Thousand Plateaus* (see note 5), 323.
25. Ibid., 323.
26. Ingold, *Lines* (see note 2), 80–82.
27. John Berger, *Berger on Drawing*, ed. Jim Savage (Cork: Occasional Press, 2005), 124–126.
28. Klee, *Notebooks*, vol. 1 (see note 17), 105.
29. Deleuze and Guattari, *A Thousand Plateaus* (see note 5), 410.
30. Ibid., 344.

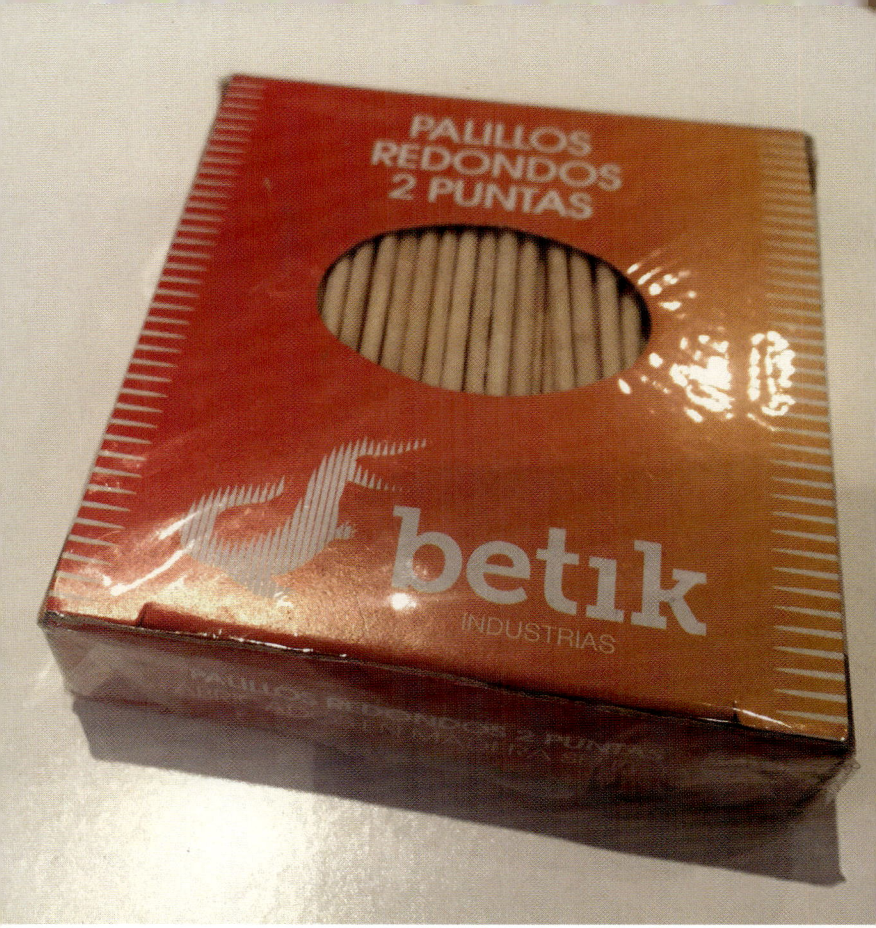
PALILLOS
REDONDOS
2 PUNTAS
betik
INDUSTRIAS

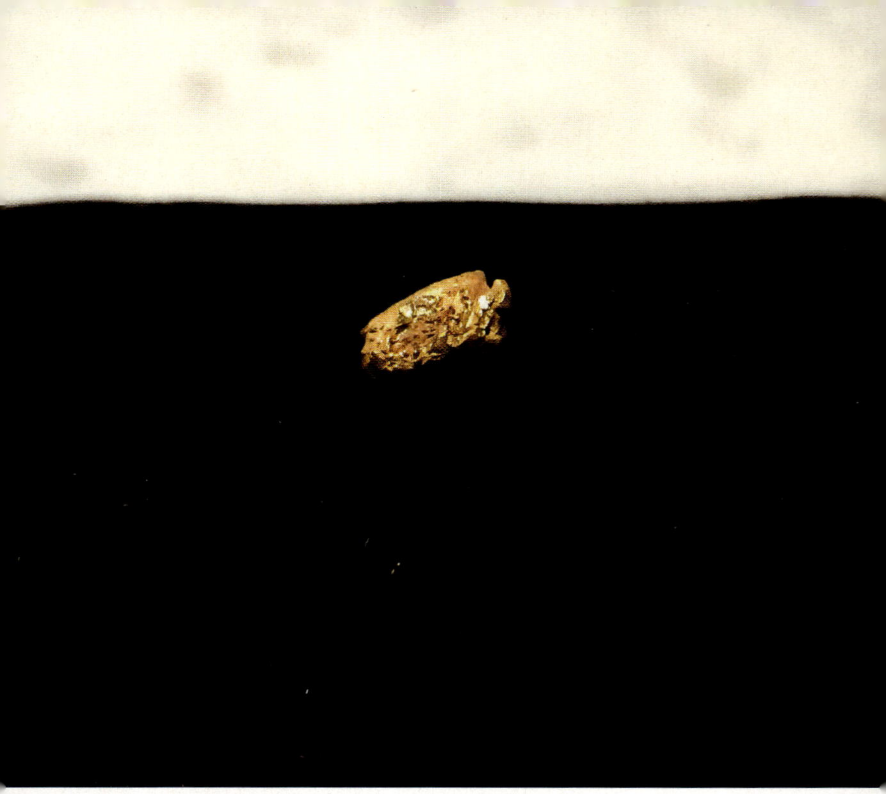

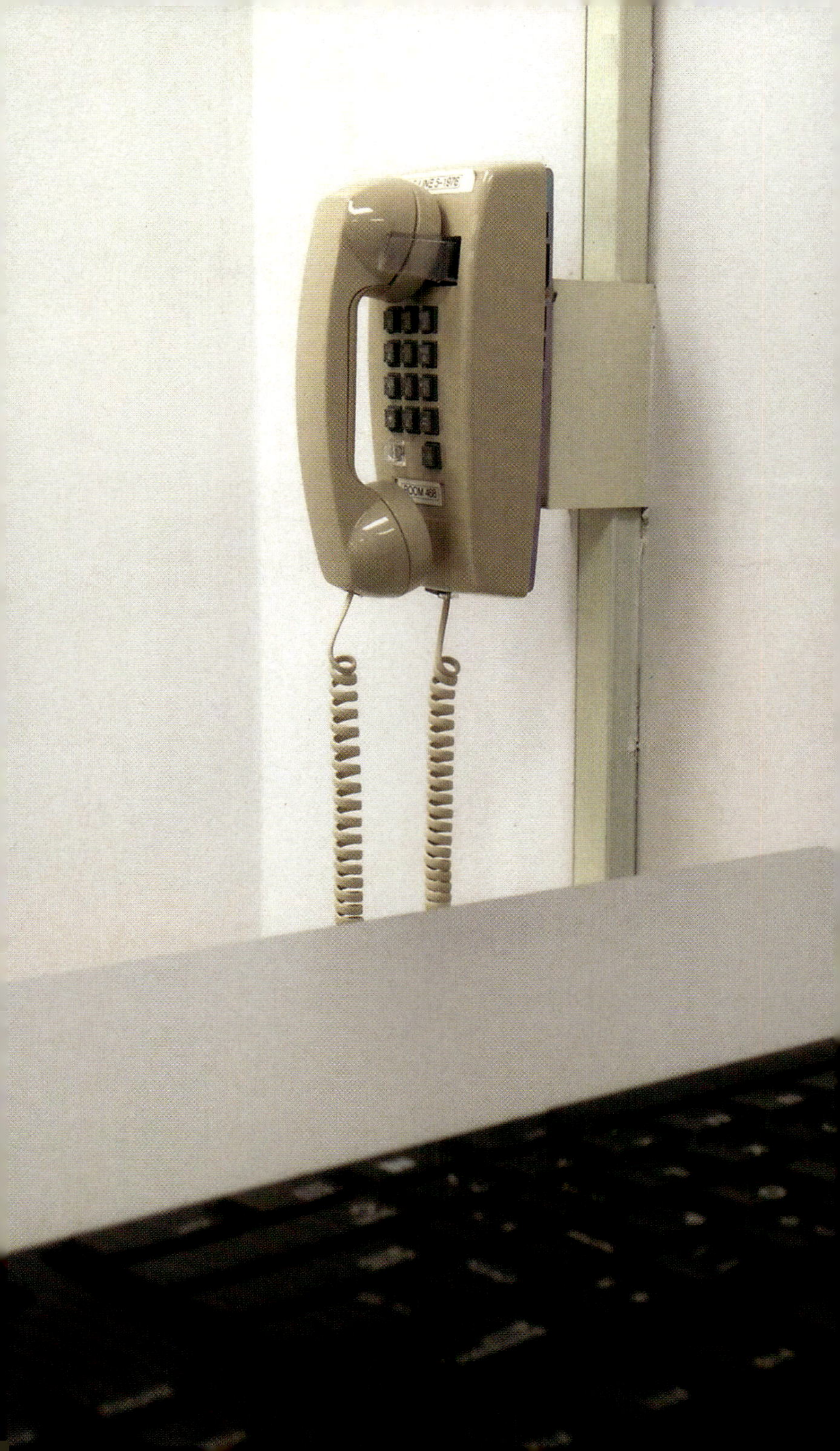

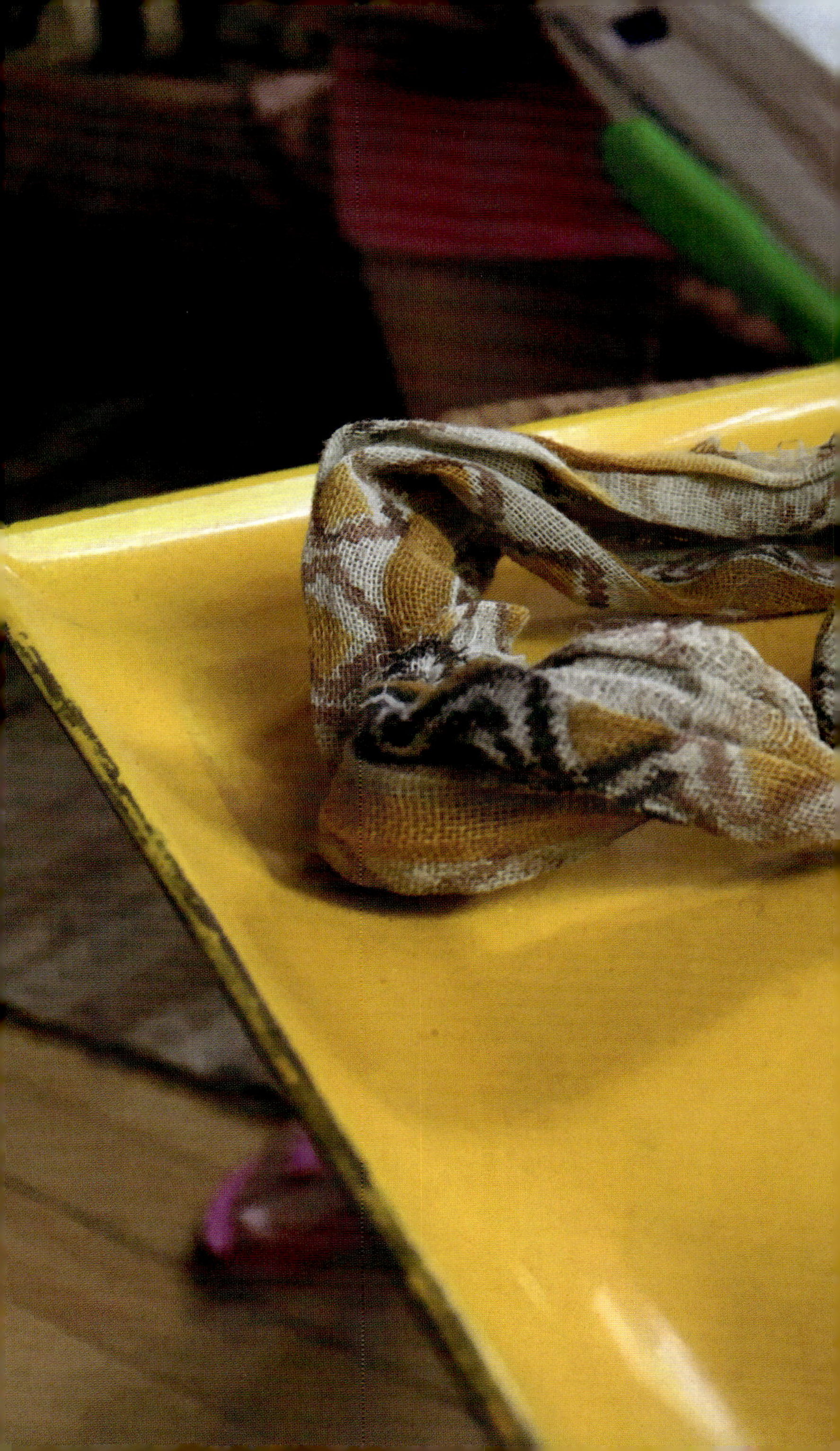

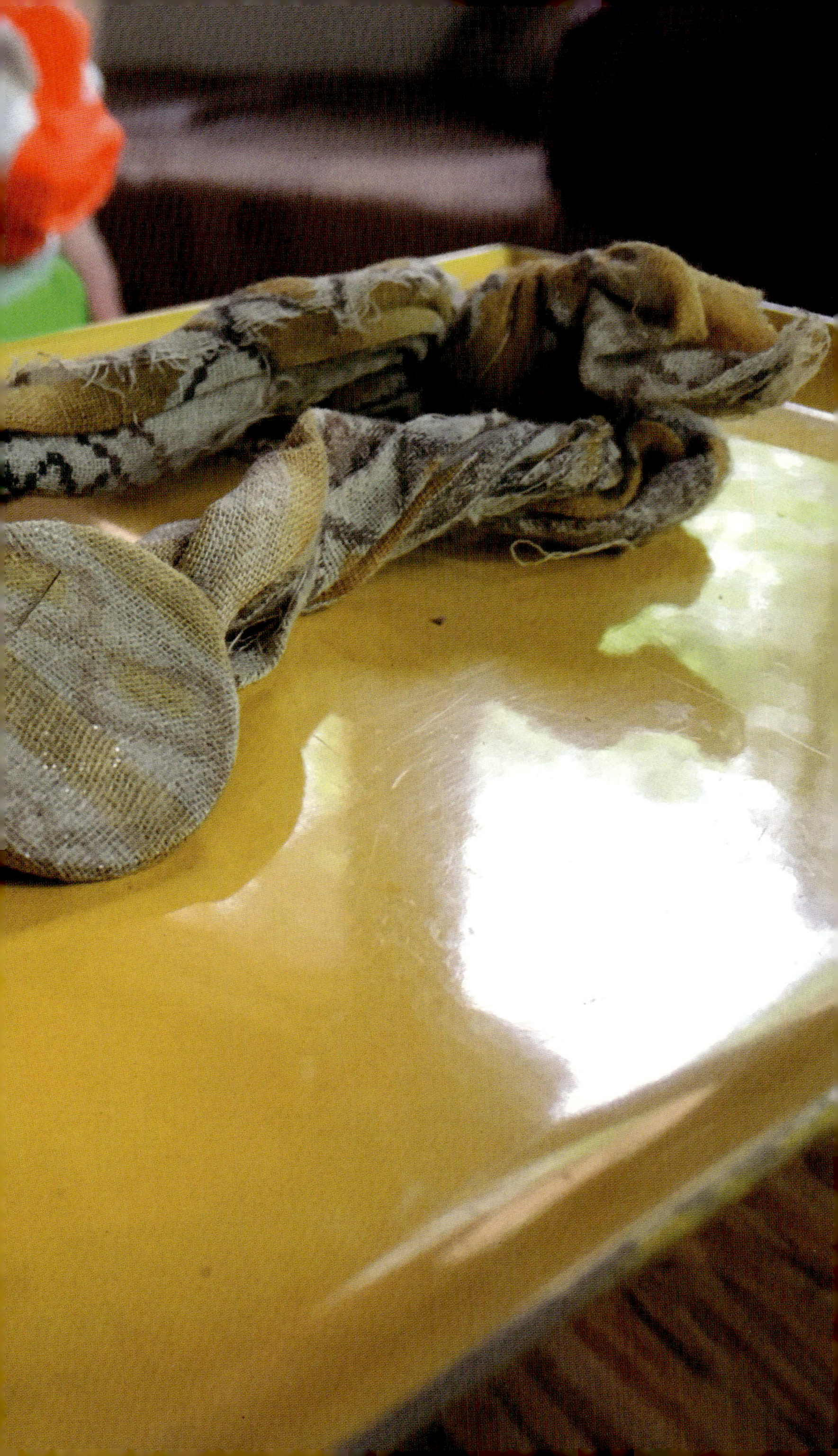

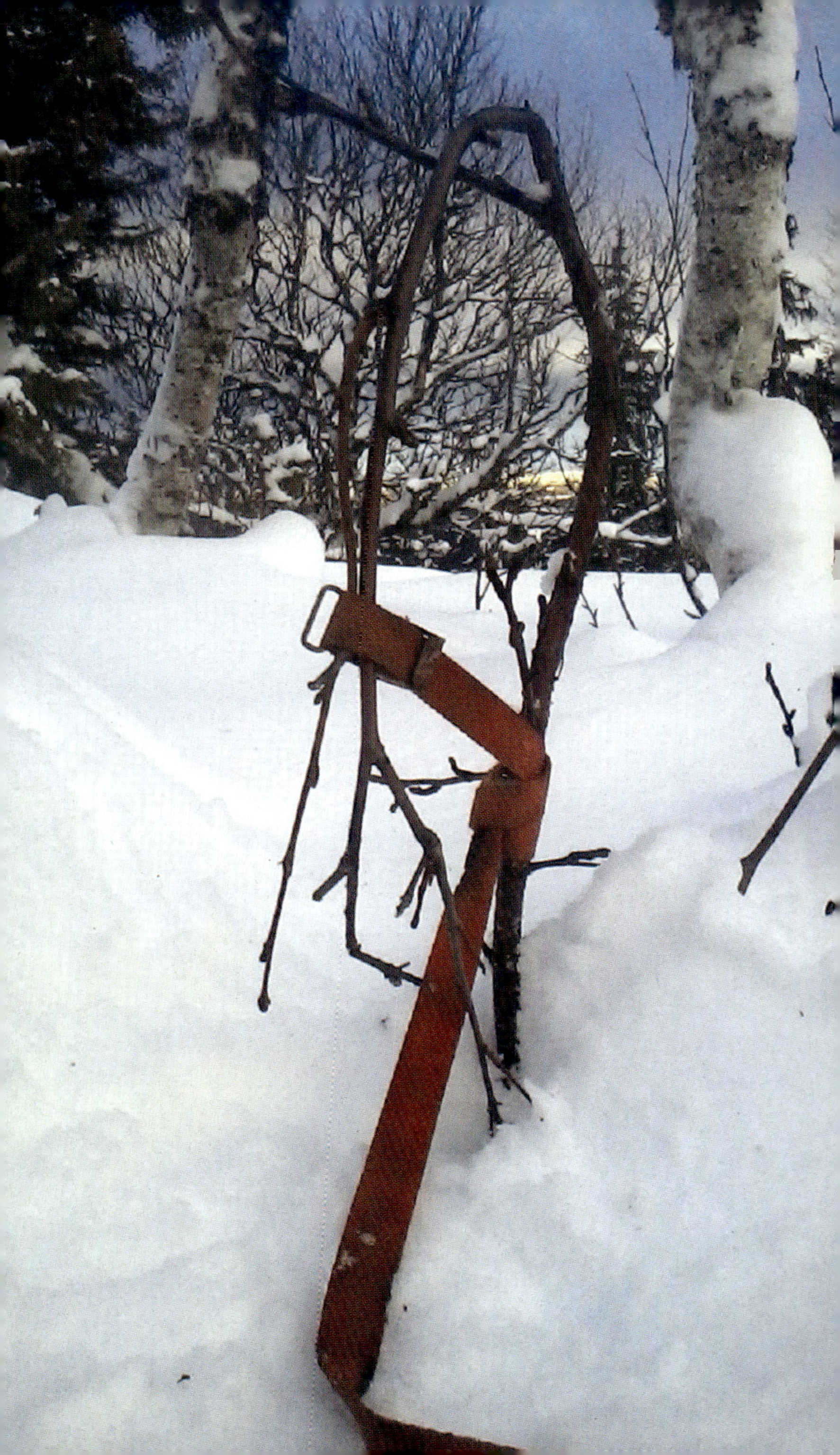

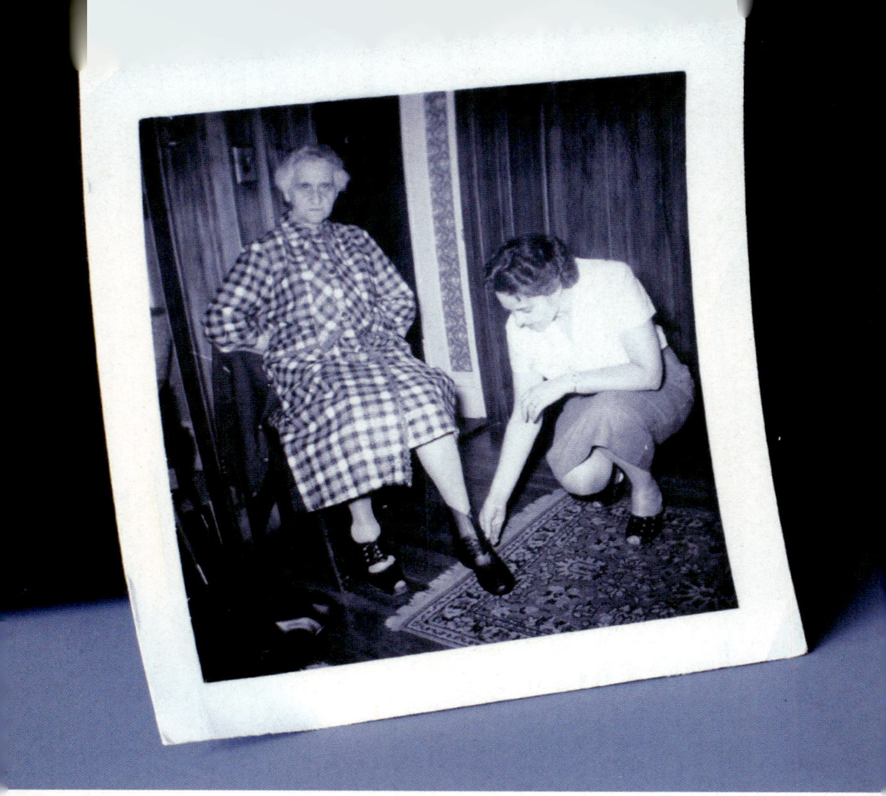

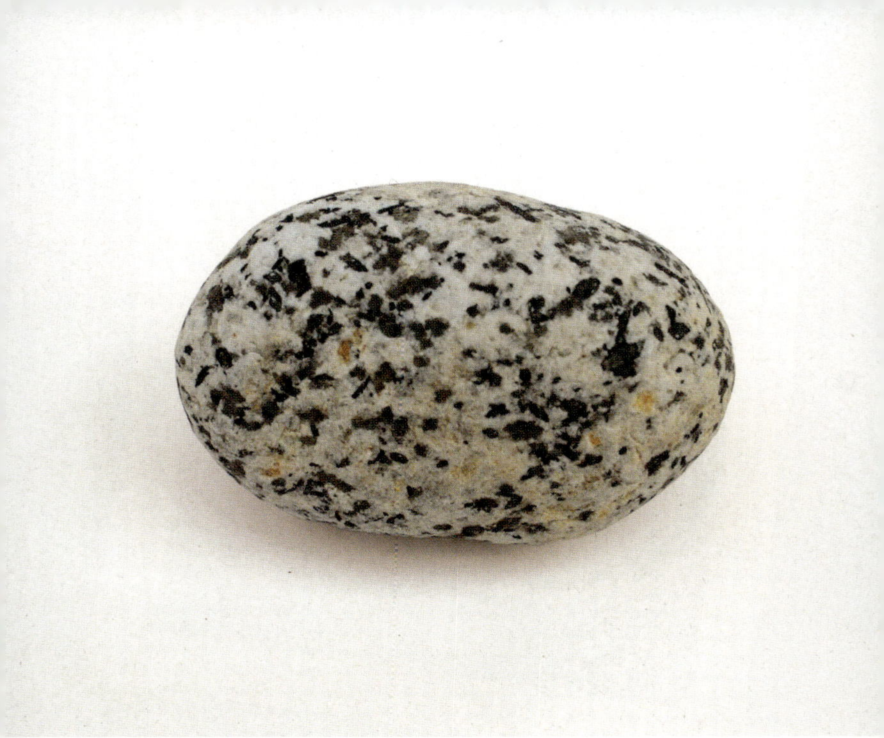

SOFT MACHINE ORALITY

Rikard Heberling, Kirke Hundevad Meng, Lisi Raskin, Samuel Richter, Hinrich Sachs, Barbara Wien

Berlin 15 August 2016 and Stockholm 18 August 2016

(...)

What happened? You can't hear me?

No, it's just really, really low. The volume's really low.

Weird.

Maybe it's the microphone.

Totally, that's way better. Thank you.

I feel I'm screaming maybe.

Better?

Much. You might need to scream still.

The other day,
you were pointing at the transfer of spoken word into text as a way of learning more about the power framework within the situation of speaking.
Did I understand you right?

My initial comment was
that I began to perceive a strong presence of transcribed orality in the visual arts, and elsewhere. Why does the art world recurrently get back to the presence of the written, of something which has been orally exchanged?
The interview situation, the staging of a relaxed moment of conversation, etc.
What if this serves as both a representation of an egalitarian projection and as a gesture of naturalization?

Pragmatically speaking,
the intention today is to get into a conversational mode without necessarily having to come up with a conclusion.
However, we are fully aware that the recording is serving for a transcription.
We are not bound to publish
and we're not even intending to publish whatever is said right away.

But... what does the mind filter away if one is aware of being recorded?
Is this going to be made public in a live stream?
Or can it be edited, annulled, trashed, whatever, you know?

Corrected.

Improved.

That was a reason for us setting this one up. Arranging a pretext for gathering, and then kind of building upon that flow. Just the idea of,
let's say we're five here and plus one on Skype,
with a two hour framework,
having a conversation about the issue of orality...

I begin to understand this more and more as an ideological construction pretending to be an informal situation! Because it's so much easier to conceal subtext,
Lisi has been so clearly pinpointing it,
present in this very moment.

There is a machine on the table.
You are in a kind of TV screen for me now,
and we indeed have space, gender, class involved, all those codifications.
And I guess we are relatively homogeneous, to say it frankly.

Once transcribing these words and perceiving them as letters, all those aspects will no longer be represented. One would have to make a real effort, to add photographs or other types of descriptions of who is sitting around this table.
Typeset, it's just a name,

at least that's how the convention of transcription
performs the rest of the frame.
"Lisi Raskin," colon, and then whatever I say,
no?

I have been working with Dieter Roth for many years,
and his opinion was "Don't edit,
just bring what the people say, even if it's super contradictory,
if the sentences are not really finished,
this is language.
Language is not logic.
Maybe with the gaps, one begins to see other things which unconsciously are there,
not really uttered,
but around the table."
He was absolutely convinced that the oral meandering should condition the written.
My critique on editing is that one almost wants to make it better than it was, in the end.
This is how I came to the subject and subsequently started to publish many talks.
Because I liked it.
My approach to the outer world was through talking with the artist,
not essayistic texts,
but talking with artists... Just to tell you what my background is, and what I experienced.

But my memory is editing ephemeral experiences while listening to you now:
I can look into your face and I see all that part of the body expression which is,
so to speak,
confirming or not confirming what you are saying.
That is what I would call the totality of human conversing.
That's the natural thing.
We are not aware of it,
but that's, of course, part of it, all the time.

When the abstraction toward a bodiless voice,
let's say the radio voice,
or the written text is... filtering those

aspects,
in excluding them,
editorial and typographical conventions
are trying to establish an easyness
for dealing with such an abstract
representation of the conversation, no?
Another machinery we got accustomed
to, I believe.

It's an interesting proposition
that we have social sciences methods of
describing what happens when we're
interviewing people. And then we have,
as Barbara was saying with Dieter Roth,
a valid perspective that there's a notion of orality
lending itself to authenticity, among other things.
I want to challenge the paradigm of orality as
authentic
and bring in this understanding that there are
people,
myself included,
who are trained to speak a particular way
through things, like theater or...

But where does the correlation
between authenticity and orality
originate from?
What lies behind that construction
which we often take for granted,
also in relation to Dieter Roth's
problem with editing a false
version of something which has
been more true?

A good hint! Dieter Roth was very aware that language is a power thing and that he can basically... say anything. Five minutes later, he would say the opposite, making us believe something else, which is equally true.

Regarding language as a power machine,
an essential aspect is that text can never capture...
one of the most fundamental aspects is
that it can never capture silence.
The silent part of a conversation.

Which is a constitutive part of the conversation itself.
Someone is speaking and the other one is silent.
Furthermore, silence is also the internal limit of the conversation itself.
In other words, a conversation is equally a distribution of silent positions that are not necessarily passive.

Now, that you are bringing up silence,
I'm just thinking,
"Okay, I'm listening to you while you are speaking, so I am silent, but I'm attentive."
Different forms of silence as one more aspect important for the informal course of encounters.
Does that make sense?
Let me transform this into a question.
Do you experience deliberate informality as part of the power structure?

I guess I do.
In moments when one doesn't know the person but knows about the person's function.
Being aware that she is an artist and she a gallerist, or the other way around...

Of course, as you were suggesting, Lisi,
certain preconceived ideas about the role and the social function of the other immediately come into play when forming words.
Communicating can obviously develop into completely different directions.
My question remains:
is such type of encounter with tacit knowledge about the interlocutor,
or rather no information about her at all,
maybe a standard social situation in the arts?

Maybe one is allowed to suspend disbelief when in a really energetically charged,
albeit totally loaded scenario,
where one is not recognizing the meta-narrative and its existing entanglements with the person that one's engaging with...

No, no, no.
I think you're right. I wanted to mention the aspect of transgression. There are moments where orally performed

transgression of courtesy standards is representational insofar as it affirms the speaker's control over the situation. Whereas in other moments, where people meet and talk to each other, transgression can mean loosing the subject.

I really need a coffee soon, but I will try to say something.
If one reflects about orality and ideology in a wider sense,
then orality today could be conceived of as cultural capital in an economy that is more and more based on participation.
And the idea of orality as something natural goes hand in hand with a classical, liberal situation like the ancient Greek agora, a situation of testing different ideas and thoughts against each other in a natural public space.

Egalitarian?

Not really. I want to claim that the understanding of orality as an authentic political concept with ancient roots is producing the idea of the natural and informal in itself and in turn conceals the ideological dimensions.

I think it's interesting that the...
that as soon as there is marketable listening, it becomes performative, but I also just want to dispute the idea that there are no interpersonal dynamics motivating, dictating our relationships,
so I think there's something that we call out and we even teach about, but I think, Barbara,
when you mention whether there is a power dynamic when an artist speaks to a gallerist,
then it's sort of that kind of self-awareness and conditioning; and ambition and desire and historicity.
In higher education all these things come into play; and I think, that it really is a conundrum, because the idea is that one is supposed to really be talking about things,
personal ones,
and those hard to articulate intellectually, in spoken words,
but we're doing so...

Makes sense. Makes sense.
I'm just trying to project this once again toward...
what do you call it...
the invisible power structures that are so often performed, on all different levels of encounters in the professional art world.
In how far is the transcription,
the written so to speak,
enabling us to see such subtexts of power around a particular speech act, in Bakhtin's terminology?
Whereas the oral situation basically employs the opposite strategy:
It obfuscates or disguises the mental frameworks, personal frameworks, power moves.

> That's where I think it becomes interesting to think it a step further,
> when these,
> let's call them moments of orality, performed in interviews or in recordings,
> become the representation of orality...

It's like I am watching TV,
but you're together, you've been hanging out, and who the fuck am I?
I've met two of you. I haven't met the other two of you in real life. Who knows if we'll ever meet in real life?
Then there's the hierarchy of where you all found each other, where you are professionally, the ways that you rely on each other.
There's gender, there's class.
There's a racialized dimension to this with the ways that our genders are racialized and the way that we're enculturated to take up space. And, I'm speaking my first language and none of you all are.
There's that complication which creates a weird hierarchy.
Having all that stuff be on the table about the Skype visitor from Providence, Rhode Island, who has extreme language privilege right now.
It should be part of what goes on.
Then we're like what were the conditions.
They're arbitrary. In a way, the people that we are, are totally arbitrary.
I think we should contend with the conditions now.

My sensation is that the informal encounters in the art world are filtered by different perspectives:
One of these filters, that I recognize, is about being interested in talking with somebody
even if one doesn't know the person much,
based on the feeling of that conversation being cool and curiosity-raising...

By now, it would also really behoove us to throw in the capitalist register,
because in an educational context, for example, the idea of the informal translates into a performance of affective labor.
It is part of the student who,
of course,
is paying out of her/his pocket
or is taking out loans.
I realize that the European and Scandinavian context is quite different from the US American,
but the expectation is bundled into value.
Affective labor being part of what the professor is expected to perform.

In relation to that, I would also like to bring the attention to the words' "physical presence,"
which is easier to capitalize...

How do you mean?

I mean it's a more physical version of the utterance than just the simple speech act.
Which might also be a reason serving as explanation for
the shift toward the transformation of speech into physical, material words.

What would you mean by "physical words"?

Printed words, or digital, for that matter...
words that are easy to mass reproduce and circulate.

Oh, multiply.

Disperse.
A form of commodification of the spoken.

In the Christian theological narrative,
it's the moment of Jesus' words becoming multiplied by his disciples,
followers,
for the masses, basically.
That's the dispersion of the word, or the spreading of the word...
But that's not what you meant, right? (laughing)

No... The printed word, the materialized word is a more effective, more sophisticated version of such multiplication. Under the present circumstances, it is easy to see the benefits for which the printed word is being promoted on behalf of the spoken situation.

Let me basically argue then,
okay, I do agree,
but that dispersion is part of the
institutionalization process of the arts.
It is likely that other fields do the same,
a heart surgeon might have his group of friends
and colleagues,
but then there is, of course, the scientific peer
group around them,
for which publications are made,
and these publications are the institutionalized
versions of the conversations in small circles.

Professional worlds, including the art world, identify the distribution of discourse as part of their institutional structure.
That's not a big surprise.
I am still curious about the aspect that you brought in,
about the open-endedness
or the nonfinite quality of the conversation
that is allowing for curiosity on the two sides of the
participants of that conversation.
Maybe that kind of unfixed...
one could call it vagueness, or...
I don't know whether I have a good word?

Fluidity, maybe?

The fluidity, which allows for,
"Oh, I would like to know more, to go deeper"
and you were kind of provoking me, asking what should

be maximized,
or what the productive aspect was.
My inner voice answered something like,
"Well, curiosity."
Without gain in terms of economy... but... knowledge.

Knowledge, yes.

Which, of course, can be capitalized.
I'm trying to reconstruct or retrace the impulse,
and I think that's completely personal.
I would even argue, if a reason for my interest in
this conversation shall be mentioned,
then it's this one.

I would say that, for my part, it's knowledge too.
And it's a certain level...
a certain level of expanding understanding.
Of course, one has to go to places not visited before in order to reach
that state... of reality.
The situation has at least proven that such informal ways of making
something material, or collective,
are an interesting form to reach states of new mental territory.
The key is, of course, how we learn from it, and benefit from it, and
build upon it.

The "we" that you're just referring to...
It's probably the process which has to reconstitute it anew, each
time we meet,
behaving in a way like a Medusa, expanding and coagulating
in a particular rhythm, in a certain type of collaboration...
But I think that the intention to engage with such a
collaborative process,
in order to explore precise questions regarding biography and
institution and learning,
is to let them circulate...
I experience this as a pretty good vessel for letting certain
things happen that I cannot think of myself...

Alright, the aspect of the biographical...
We haven't really touched upon that.

I'm curious about, and how far
artists tell and retell aspects of their lives in order to,

and now I may use a term Lisi has been employing,
to index their work.
I think it happens repeatedly in informal conversation,
however, it is equally employed in a kind of preaching
rethoric...
It sounds probably stupid asking you, but I'm pretty sure
that you talked to Beuys, right?

Oh, yes, I talked to him.
Horrible.
"Talk" is too much. It was a monologue from his side.
I had questions for him and he just uttered what was in his
mind, not answering my questions at all.

It makes me think of the theatricality of electoral campaigns.
There is no intention to negotiate anything.
It's to perform judgements,
or certain types of insulting attacks,
in order to position oneself.
Such theatricality is the complete opposite of perception, of an
attentive space of communication...

It's a theatre of orality, intending to be
entertaining,
but at the same time it's about claiming space
and positions.
I'm concerned about that. You mentioned this
beautiful idea of the agora.
As far as I observe conversations of a public type,
they are not interested in any kind of criterion or
quality that we are discussing here,
rather purposefully evict them or shut the door
for them...

I have to laugh about the tendency to want to find
an authentic point to discuss our inherent nature, the
discourse of the naturalized,
the discourse of the purity of something like desire,
which for me, that's one of the worst places.
The things I want
are the most perverted,
and are put in my brain by larger systems of power.
It's the place that I constantly have to be like "what's my
problem?"

Why do I want this?
Why do I want this person?
Why am I finding this person attractive?
I'm like this, because it is a type, or a value, or a larger cultural system that has been imported.
It's racialized and it's class loaded and it's elitist and it's bourgeois.
It's all the things.
I would say that my desire, just to be totally honest, has more to do with the worst parts of my bourgeois indoctrination
and the way that that dovetails into taste.
Desire and taste, they're in my brain,
I'm just being honest here, they're vetted.
That's why I'm laughing.

I'm so compelled to bring Bertold Brecht's theatricality concepts in.
Does anybody else feel that?

Yes, but think of Angela Merkel.
She's performing the silent type, no?

Poor Angela Merkel. Poor any of those imperialist feminists.
You know what I mean?
They've done some work
but they reproduce a dominance and subordination paradigm.
That's what it means to be part of larger systems of power right now.

If we talk about smaller systems of power,
smaller groups, on the level that we have influence over,
let's say the six of us in this virtual room,
then I think differently... The creation of consensual paradigms is possible. There's nothing that's existing on the larger level of politics that is consensual.

That dovetails back into refusal, into believing that there's a space outside of normative politics to engage, the desire for the tabula rasa, all that sort of stuff. Those are the extreme options when consent is not possible. When consent is possible, man, we could really

do anything.
We can do anything.

I imagine that agora in the same way as you described the classroom, twenty minutes only giving critique as you would like to get critique yourself.
What I'm asking is
whether such a framework can possibly be applied to a larger scale?
Is that even interesting?

I think we're training ourselves to think differently,
hopefully.
I think that when things get too large, the rules of that scale weigh heavy on the intent.

I would like to slow down to zero,
to "I have no agency."
I think performing agency, performing right action, performing consensual, ethical engagements as a practice,
that's something that we need to learn and value. It may take a while...

That type of orality,
because it is not recorded or represented,
is a much stronger tool of power in the art world than the writings of art historians!

However, they have any power in general.
What they deal with is the representation of the past.

I just think about... Klaus Biesenbach and James Franco
versus Lynne Cooke and Joseph Beuys
or something,
or René Block and Joseph Beuys.
You've got someone who'd actually rather be a late night television host talking to a celebrity who also makes our la-la and money
versus someone,
a contextualizing agent who is complicit in all the capitalist aspects of things
but still has her/his finger on something.

Harald Szeemann, if you prefer.
We could talk about everybody who got lumped into that Documenta in the same way as art historians. It's a different thing. It's grotesque.

I used the term art historian more to designate a formative background.
I do not intend to talk about the particular activity of an individual. Rather about the fact that a trained art historian uses methodologies distinct from informal orality,
in relation to art works encountered,
toward living artists, and their relationships.
Certain museums,
able to engage in critical reflection about their own mode of functioning,
are producing discourse, based on such methodologies, while performing a certain role within the entertainment industry.
In short:
Discursive contribution is simply not consumed by the visitor when paying a single entrance ticket.

Interesting.
In his text, Mikkel Bolt refers to... to Peter Bürger's *Theory of the Avant-Garde*,
which is from the 70s, late 70s I think.
The neo avant-garde is a shortcoming of the first avant-garde,
and because the art world becomes more and more institutionalized, without escape,
the position of the Marxist historian is the last refuge of criticality,
the only position from where one could engage in ideological critique.
The theoretical class struggle can only be propelled by the historian.

Really?
Says Bürger?
I need to read that.

This is a narrative that's completely sick...
As we're privileging art historians we're also re-enacting bourgeois values.
Art historians, they look after history.

Who gets to write history? The winner gets to write history.
When every last cultural institution that we've believed in is taken over by someone who is interested in celebrity culture,
the people who are writing art history will be the people who are invested in celebrity culture,
in this new paradigm.

Let's go back to from where we departed, with Rikard and Samuel talking about discourses of will,
the way that liberal whiteness perceives itself and the agency of liberal whiteness.

How do we call ourselves?
How do we look at ourselves and think about the ways that we enact the power that we have,
which is tremendous, this agency that we have,
which is arbitrarily conferred,
and how do we make the shifts there in terms of how we frame these arguments?
Is it possible to externalize this now that I've said it?
We could agree or disagree.

Could we come to terms with... us sitting around a table,
with our relationship to being indoctrinated by bourgeois aesthetics and the ways in which, Hinrich, we talked about this for hours at your house,
but the ways in which taste has a monopoly on even the way we perceive ourselves as locked into certain places.
What I know is, at the end of the day, I'm just a dirty fucking Jew dike.
I've got it. I've got the colonizers voice in my head about my positionality.
Is that though really true?
I'm other things. I've got agency. I can do these other things.
At what moment am I identifying that I've internalized and what's coming out of my mouth is the voice of the oppressor?

One thing
and then I want to say two things.
I want to get back to the place where the ideological...

I want to talk about it in terms of nesting dolls, if we can.
You know those Russian nesting dolls, right?

Yes, the Russian doll.

We have ideology as one frame, but it's not the outer one.
We're analyzing it with discourse analysis.
I think that it's important when looking at the ideological function of orality within our field
and actually think about how the ideology functions to re-inscribe certain formative values.

Whose voices are present and absent?
That is something that begins to become part of that frame.
In the normative space of the art world, women are less present than men.
The notion of who gets to be the artist, or the author, is still hyper-masculine.
Speaking as a male persona, that kind of thing also gets projected onto me.

I just see this huge smoky question mark... dissolving and transforming into a "No!"

That will be interesting.

Yes.

Is that the wrong metaphor?

We're very offended by this.

Sorry, I like to be offensive.

Rock the machine.

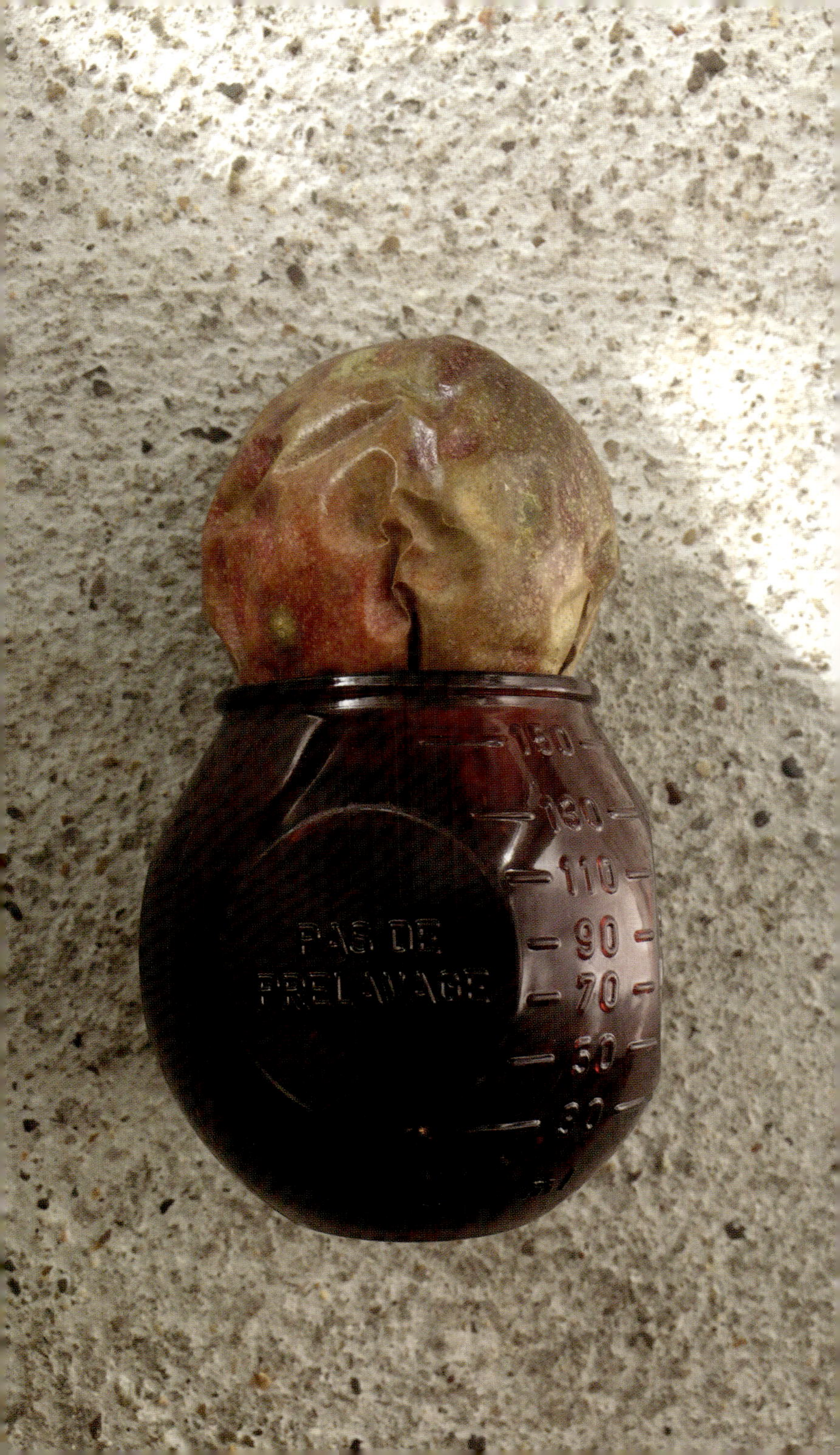
PAS DE
PRELAVAGE
150
130
110
90
70
50

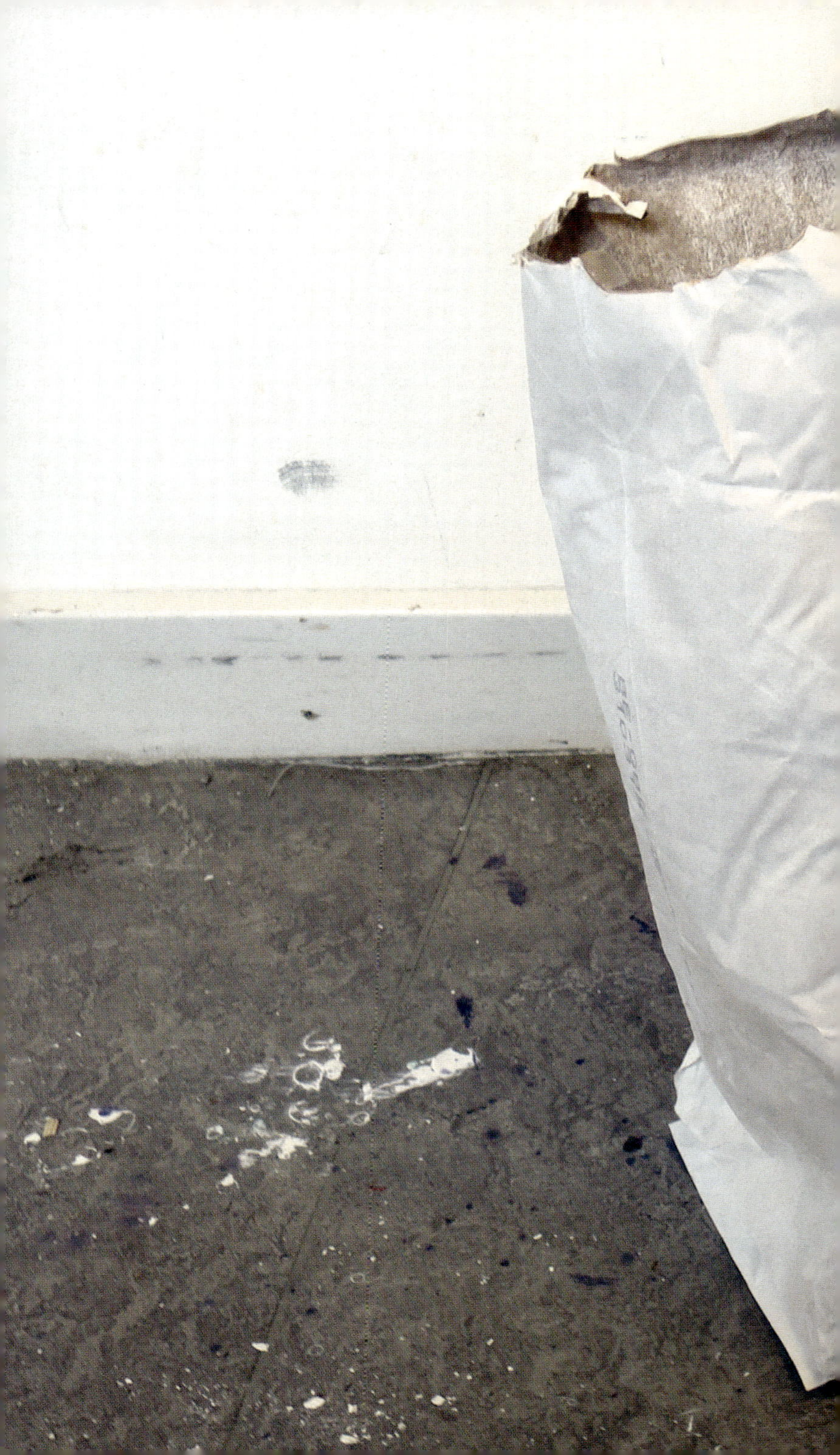

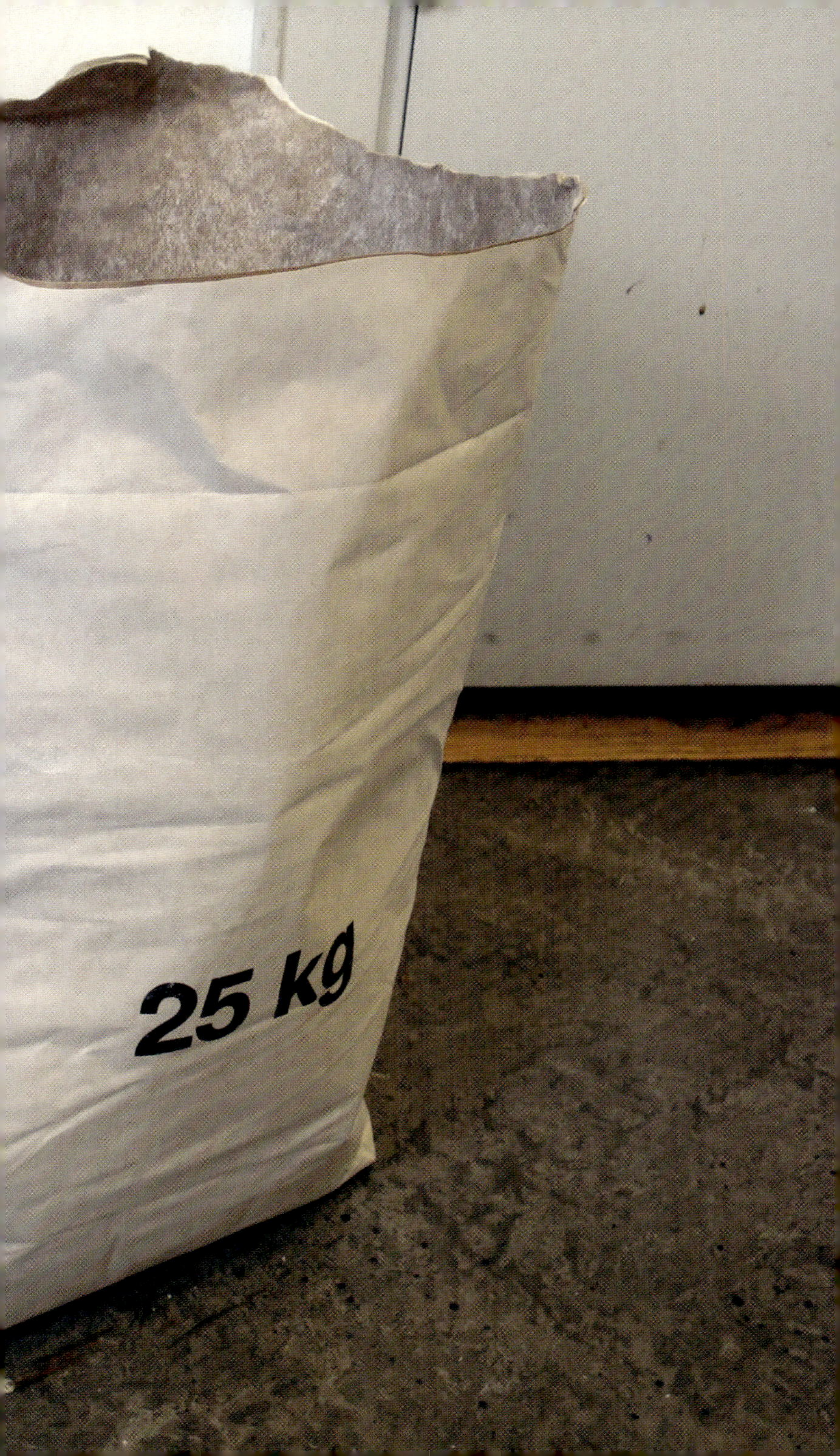
25 kg

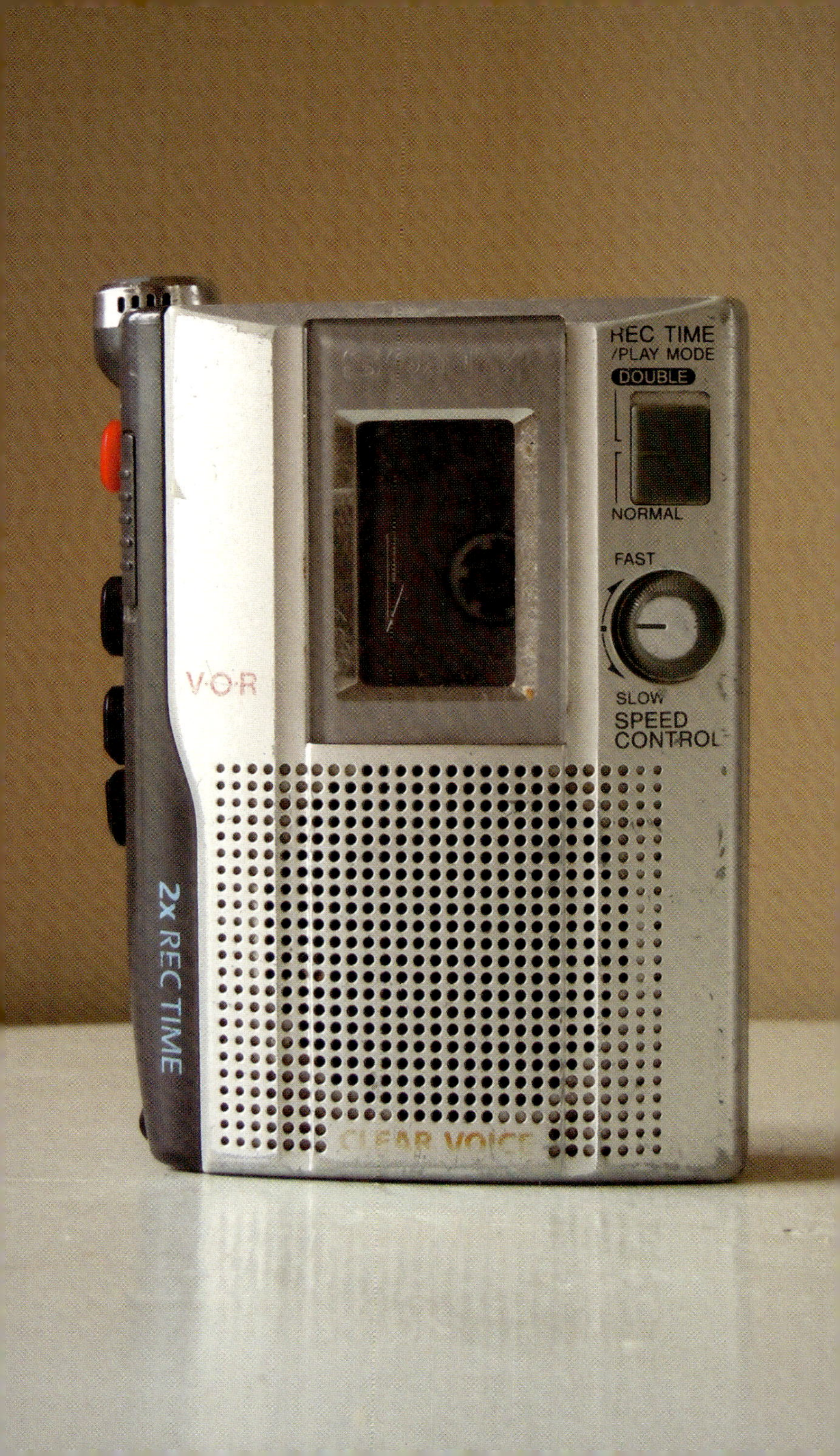
REC TIME
/PLAY MODE
DOUBLE
NORMAL
FAST
SLOW
SPEED
CONTROL
V·O·R
2x REC TIME
CLEAR VOICE

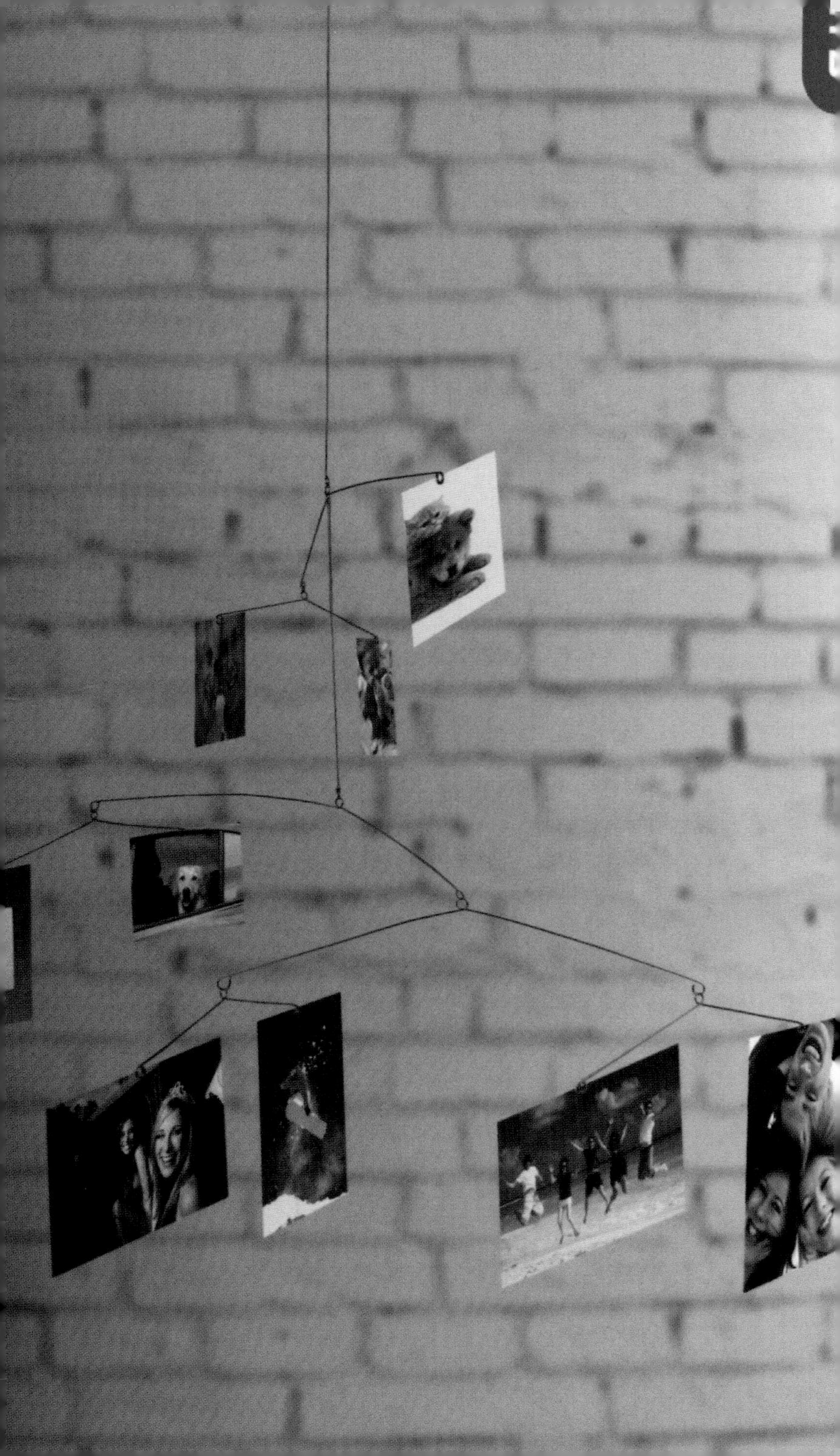

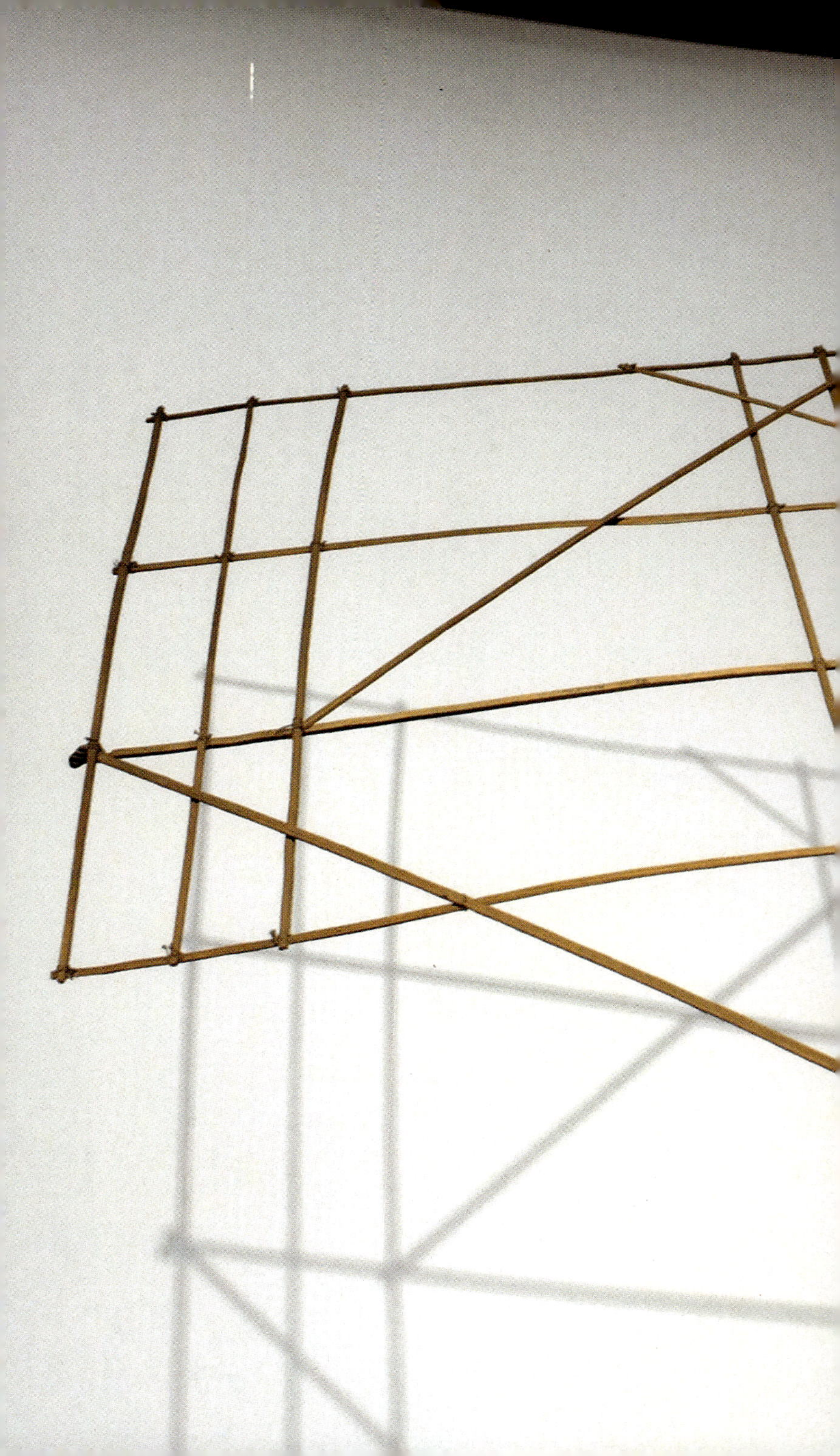

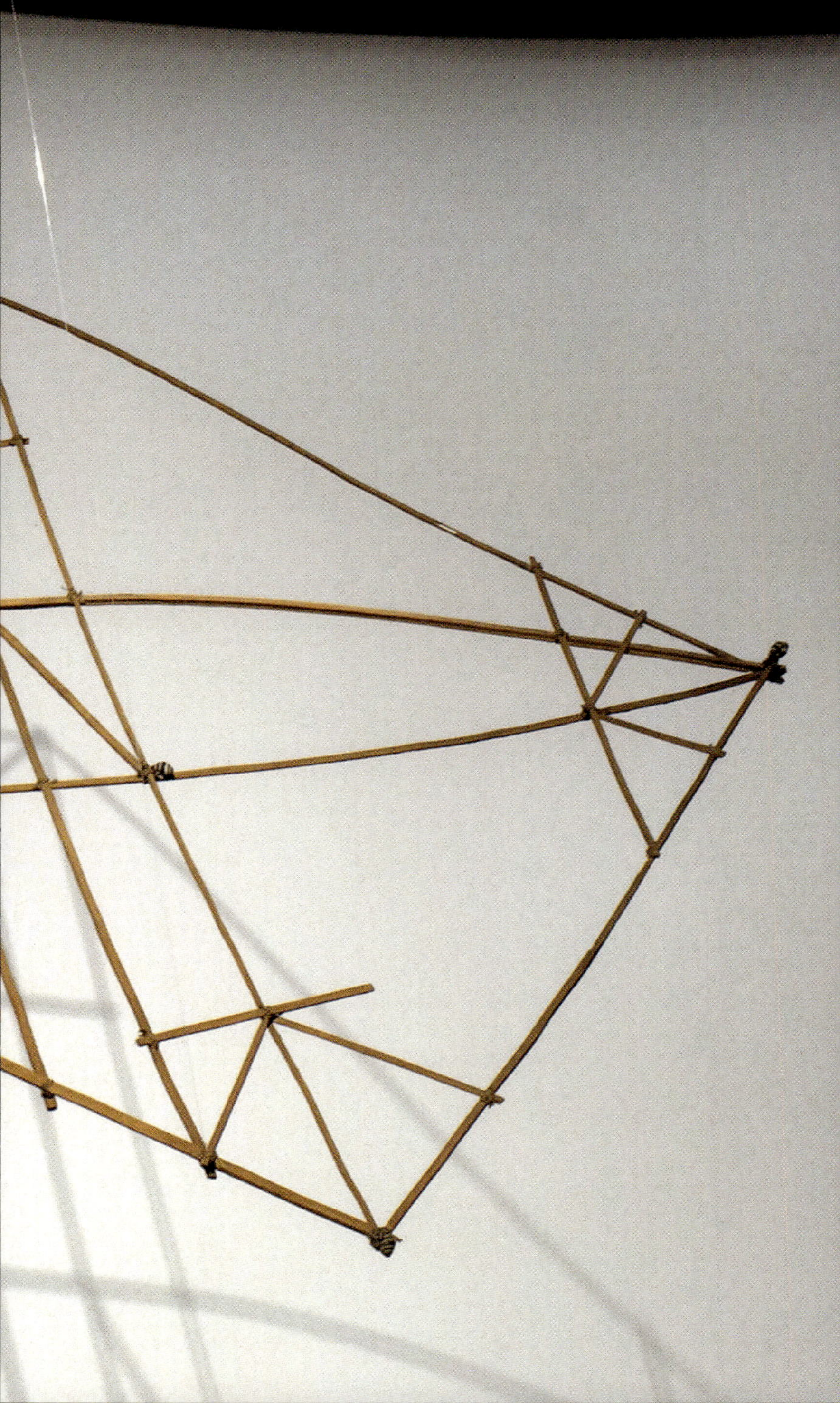

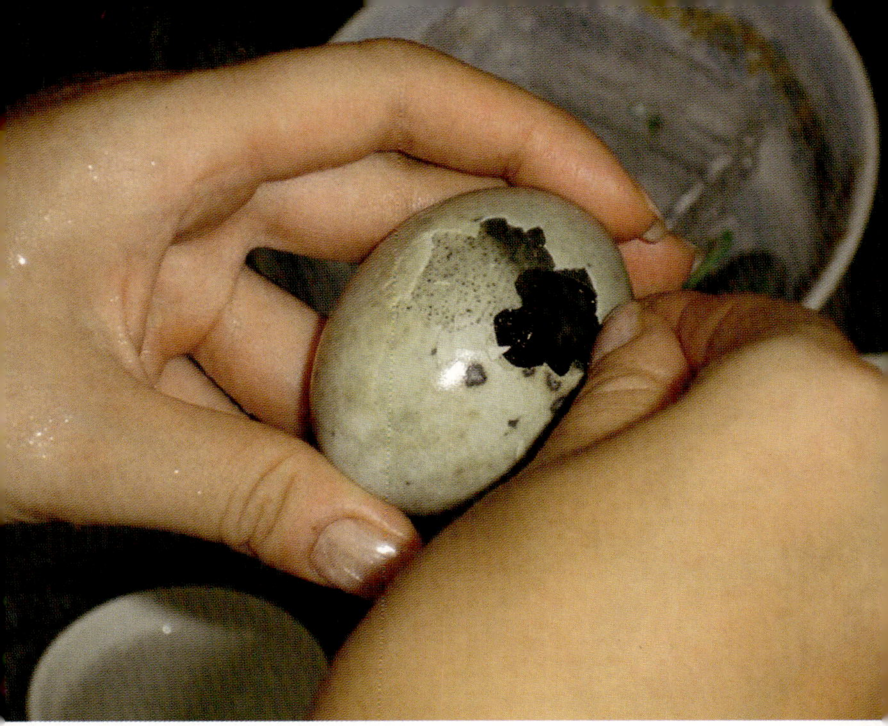

FLOTSAM AND JETSAM

A phone for emergency information; a cassette recorder used to tape a concert by the Japanese musician Keiji Haino; an English-Tagalog dictionary obtained by a daughter in order to learn Tagalog, the mother's first language; an alchemist furnace to end the tyranny of money; a globally standardized cardiopulmonary resuscitation doll designed after the death mask of an unidentified woman found in the River Seine; a "stick chart" from nineteenth-century Micronesia used to navigate a 3,000 nautical miles area in the Pacific Ocean, visually attractive, but use-less to those who haven't learned to bring experience in. These, and forty-six other items, have been captured by the some-times staged, sometimes arbitrary use of a photographic device—the digital camera, the mobile phone, the screenshot—ac-companied by a few commenting lines from the individual(s) who selected the item and provided the image, taking the form of personal reflection, institutional-ized narrative, or researched facts.

Nevertheless, they are allowed to appear in their visual presence, the one of a world of materials, by spreading their particular constellation all over the book: enabling and/or recalling the encounter of something seen for the first time, unidentified, perceived, but not yet transformed into purpose, only later valued as significant in relation to a navigational move.

The items tell different stories, but each one resonates a relationship or personal experience between the contributor and the item in question. In line with some of the recurring themes throughout this book, the images or their signified objects have all been associated by each respective contributor with one or more of the keywords *institution*, *biography*, and/or *learning*. Against this background the commentaries on the images, listed in the following pages in the order of their appearance in the book, act as transformers of the visual into narration, in order to perform, seen from another side, fully grown and independent voices, expanding the navigational horizon as such, as much as proposing unexpected echoes of and relationships to the other texts in this volume.

Map (Europe Political 1:3,500,000)

Published by Freytag & Berndt, Vienna, Austria, ca. 2012. Four-color offset print on paper, cardboard, 136 × 94 cm (open), 24 × 13 cm (folded).

"Google Maps is pushing us closer to what Jorge Luis Borges dreamt of in his short story 'On Exactitude in Science'—a world mapped at a scale of 1:1. Meanwhile, printed maps, which clearly represent history as well as geography, increasingly appear as petrified relics of a quite recent past. Recent events in Britain and its impending exit from

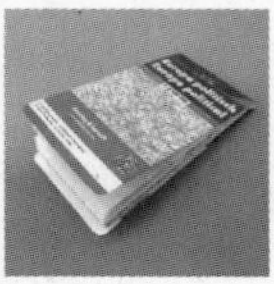

the European Union are certainly what prompted my search for this political map of Europe. It was accompanied by the feeling that everything I've taken for granted —as a peripatetic artist who has made the movement of objects, materials, and ideas his stock-in-trade and who has lived outside Britain for many years—was suddenly up for grabs. The European order that facilitated the development of my art practice can no longer be taken for granted. Recent political and technological developments have left the map charged in new ways—anachronistic and oddly nostalgic." — Simon Starling

Water Kettle

Photographed in the village of Kerr Amadou, Gambia, October 2011. Recycled plastic, approx. 26 × 20 × 21 cm.

"Together with the Gambian musician Amadou Sarr I have developed a series of film works, which tell stories about various members of his family. All the stories

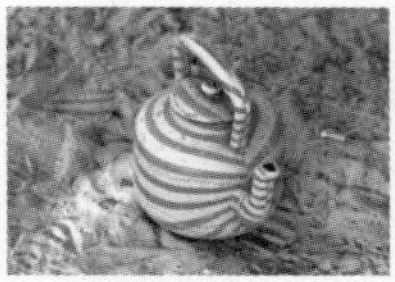

have been generated in collaboration with Amadou. We went to the village where he grew up several times. The water kettle with the orange stripes was sitting just outside the door of the room where we slept, at the compound of Ali Joof—Amadou's cousin and brother. During the same trip we did the recordings for the film *This Is What I Used To Do*, in which Amadou is walking though the countryside while getting ready for the making of clay flutes, something he used to do as a child. In the film he employs a similar water kettle for preparing the clay, which instead has yellow stripes and belongs to his mother's sister N'Dèye N'Diaye. I later purchased this kettle." — Gitte Villesen

Lemon Plants in Plastic Pot

Planted in Copenhagen, Denmark, May 2016. Plastic flowerpot on a terracotta plate, planting soil, lemon seeds, approx. 15 × 12 × 12 cm.

"Last autumn I had a bicycle accident and ended up in the emergency room. While in the waiting room to have a doctor check my bruises, I found a box of children's books and comics. I picked up a worn, illustrated book about simple ways to plant seeds from oranges, zucchinis, and other fruits and vegetables—easy

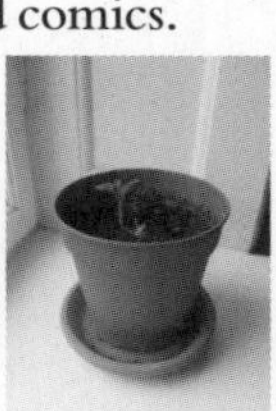

reading when your body and head are hurting. Later I forgot all about the planting book, and it wasn't until I started picking up seeds from trees and bushes I found in parks around town, that I came back to it again.

I'm amazed how people around the world generously upload tutorials to YouTube, on how to plant a seed or change the tires on a tractor. My favorite channel, 'Mr. Eastcoastman' by Mitchell, a Canadian with quite a passion for gardening, mostly just shows how to germinate and grow various seeds and plants. I have now tried different seeds, and I have some pots growing with mangos and lemons. The seeds have first been germinated in a closed plastic bag wrapped in moist toilet paper for about a week and then planted in regular planting soil. The lemon plants have now reached about 3–4 cm. It is a very sporadic and basic way of learning, which also involves sharing tips about how to succeed. It takes time, and the outcome might be a failure, but it is very fulfilling to follow the growth of a plant." —Jacob Grønbech Jensen

Eau de parfum

Made in USA, purchased on November 7, 2014. Glass bottle containing eau de parfum, 6.5 × 3.8 × 10 cm.

"The fragrance Rogue by Rihanna was launched in 2013 and is described as capturing the mischievous nature that lies within every woman, encouraging her to be bold, confident, and sexy. The scent is described as flirtatious, sensual, and oriental with a distinct blend of jasmine, plum, and patchouli that captures Rihanna's unexpected style, distilled in the advertising campaign by fashion photographer Mario Sorrenti. On the fragrance, Rihanna comments: 'People are always changing and evolving, and with Rogue I wanted to switch it up to reflect who I am today. I made it for all women, for every mood, because we all want to project our true selves.' The fragrance contains accords of lemon blossom, cyclamen, jasmine, rose, plum, and suede over a base of musk, wood, patchouli, vanilla, and amber. The owner of this bottle does not wear the perfume but uses it to cover up the lingering scent of cooking." —Hedda Viå

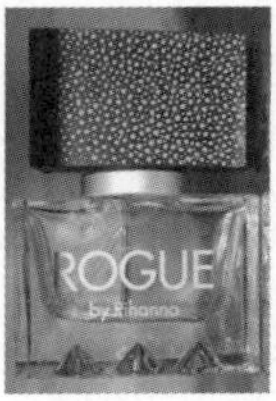

CPR Doll

Used in a cardiopulmonary resuscitation session at the Migration Agency, Malmö, Sweden, May 2016. Rubber mixture, 45 × 25 cm.

"The practice doll used for cardiopulmonary resuscitation is based on L'inconnue de la Seine, the death mask of an unidentified woman who was found drowned in the Seine in the late nineteenth century. Following the discovery of the woman, casts of her death mask became a popular fixture among members of bohemian society and a signifier of social status. In the twentieth century, the unidentified woman

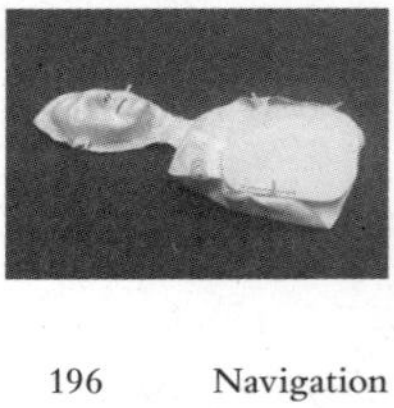

became the face of a CPR doll, when the Norwegian company Leardal Medical began producing a mannequin with a face based on the death mask to promote newly developed methods for resuscitation. The first-aid doll was nicknamed Resusci Anne and has since become a training tool for CPR courses worldwide." —Ludvig Briland

White Good-luck Cords

Offered to the current owner by her grandmother from Thailand, 2013–14. Cotton cord, approx. 8 cm diameter each.

"Every time I was about to leave for traveling, my grandmother would call me over and ask for my left hand, palm up, toward her. She would cut off a piece of blessed white cord, one hand holding one end of the string, the other hand the other end. Hunched over my hand, she would roll the piece of

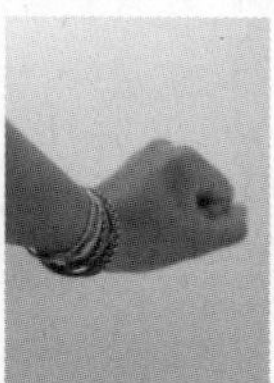

cord back and forth over my wrist. Meanwhile she would quietly murmur some prayers such as: I wish you safe travel, work and stability, good health, and some other things. I was always a bit surprised by the pragmatism and humbleness of her prayers. She would not ask for wealth or success, but rather for the most necessary things, and in moderation. This ritual is one we have gone through many times. Once, when I was eight, and about to leave the country for the first time, she called the entire village into our home to add power and blessing to this gesture. They formed a circle around my grandmother and me, while being connected to her (the first neighbor held her elbows, watching, as her hands were busy performing the ritual, and the next held the next one's elbows, until the entire room was connected). I was young, but that form of presence was significant, and I was overtaken by a sense of meaning and importance. Maybe that was my first memory of a shared experience, a temporary community.

Today, I am an avid traveler. My intention is always to travel as light as possible. Meanwhile I have acquired the skill of being rooted in myself, to a certain extent. Besides gear, such as cameras and other recording equipment, which has a monetary value, I do not consider any object in my luggage really valuable, at least no material thing. The two pieces of cord, stripped of their origin and gestures, are poorly made and basic. Yet they have become a mental compass, a spirit-thread to a community to which I once belonged. It is the sense of belonging that is carried along when traveling, independent of other people's opinions, laws, and prejudices. The cords hold a world of references so privately owned and used, that they need no justification." —Apichaya Wanthiang

Museum Display

Denny Farmland Museum, Cambridge, UK; date of fabrication unknown. Painted wood, with the paint refreshed in the 1980s, approx. 140 × 60 × 60 cm.

"This particular display, combining a visual language relating to early modernism with local heritage objects, seems to be intended to mediate access to a historical moment in time. The objects exhibited on the display structure are from the first half of the twentieth century. Some of them, like the vacuum cleaner, might have looked as disruptively

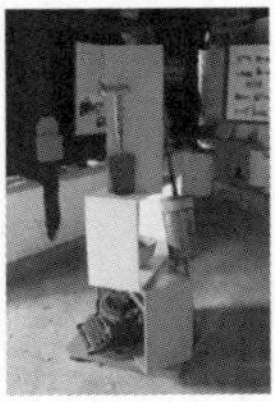

different from the rural context into which they were introduced at the time, as do the design paradigms of the rectangular structure in primary colors in relation to the retro-stylistic orientation of the nineteenth century. Now, it is the current distance in time to the period called 'De Stijl' from a Dutch perspective or maybe 'Abstraction' from a British perspective—a distance intriguingly brought into play by the educational cue of this structure." — Marjolijn Dijkman

Tarot Card

Four-color offset print on paper, 120 × 70 mm.

"The other day there was a car accident. Blood flowed freely—thick and fast. Life was leaving someone's body in the form of blood, not soul or breath, as when someone dies of old age. The accident and my practice as an artist are connected. I have learned only what I am able to remember, and all that I have learned has gone through me and is poised somewhere between body and mind. My knowledge is shaped by my life lived, and I shape life in return by living.

As always, when facing change, I turn to my Tarot cards for help. As soon as I unwrap them from their box, I feel an energy flowing into my hands. With great precision, they guide me. After shuffling the cards three times, while in deep concentration, I pick up the card at the very top of the deck, which is the Ten of Swords. It reads: 'Hidden deep beneath the surface of the Ten of Swords is the ultimate power of the Swords suit—the ability to

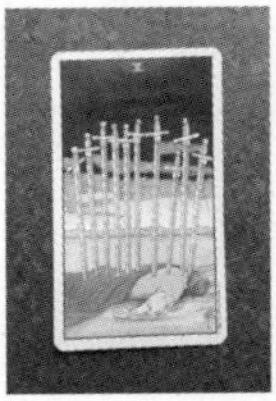

analyze the situation and your responses, and learn from yourself. True wisdom does not come from without but from within. The pain and hurt you have endured has not gone without purpose. The positive power within you can be used to learn from your pain and draw wisdom from defeat.'" — Karin Hald

Knife

Ticino, Switzerland, age unknown. Metal, bone, inox steel.

"Not much is known about this knife, but this does not hinder one from appreciating its high quality. The age of the knife

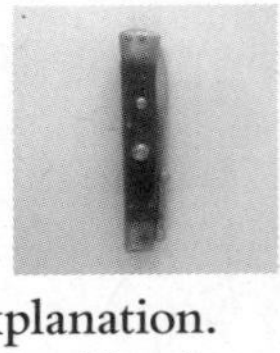

is hard to determine, as it has been handed down through generations without commemoration or explanation. It was most likely acquired by the current owner's grandfather, but it could be older. It is now mostly used for mushroom hunting."

— Daniel Pianetti

Potted Plant

Found in a bush in Lidingö, Sweden, spring 2015 and saved from the trash. Geranium, industrially produced wooden sticks, ropes, approx. 20 × 20 × 75 cm.

"A potted plant has become a subject. The human who began taking care of it observed how the plant was being directed to assume a shape. Natural, organic growth is guided by the man-made apparatus of supportive sticks, steering the plant into certain ways of rising upward and taking form. The preferred aesthetic—standing straight instead of dropping and leaning—was achieved by constant adjustments made throughout the process of trimming and guiding the plant. In some respects the plant also talked back to the human after having been 'informed,' seeming to learn where and how

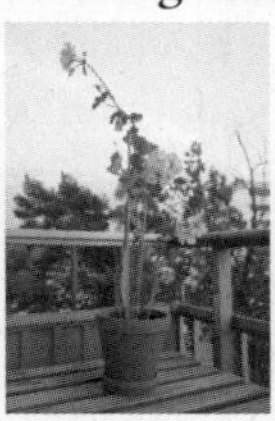

to grow next. It followed what the human desired, and organized its development toward that ideal. From another perspective, when the plant was placed in front of a window, it could grow toward the sunlight, and it could also get out of balance, its parts sticking out too much. The process of taking care of the plant was perceived as a process of understanding where the plant wanted to grow. As a whole, the process was a slow feedback loop involving the human and the plant." — Yun Yu

Poster and Postcard Set

Purchased at a charity sale at the Center for Art on Migration Politics, Copenhagen, Denmark, 2016. Four-color offset print on paper, cardboard, 42 × 59 cm (poster), 15 × 10 cm (postcards).

"A poster and its postcard set resulted from the project 'With Love from 6C,' realized by students in an elementary school class with the help of their teachers. The idea was to use pedagogical tools to transform the students' ambitions into a body of work. However, a set of postcards sent to an absentee student never reached its

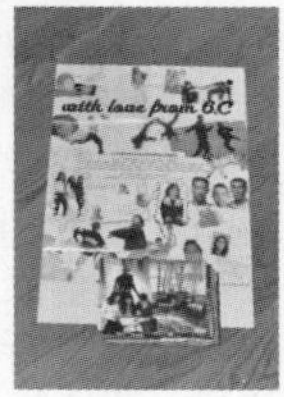

desired destination. It conveys a timeless nostalgia that is concrete and palpable. One example is the postcard reading: 'I love you Zidan, and I am your biggest fan in the world.'" — Ehab Aljaby

Contact Print

Private photograph, late 1990s. Photo paper, 240 × 35 mm.

"The print contains two shots depicting a woman in her mid-twenties, sitting at a table in the library of the Academy of Fine Arts in Munich. Studying there in the second half of the 1990s, she tested herself as artist-to-be, feeling the profession's designation—"artist"—impossible and therefore necessary to avoid at all costs. She spent many hours in the academy's library, which with its high ceiling was a welcoming, sun-flooded space, and there she

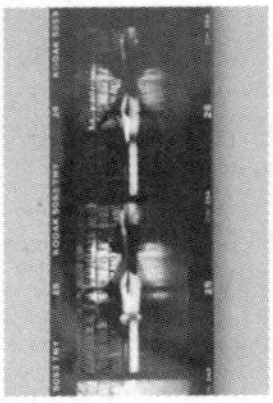

discovered treasured things. *Work 1961–73*, a catalogue of Yvonne Rainer, for example, was pulled off the shelf again and again, although this practice was off the radar at the academy at that time. Located at the top of the gallery was a complete collection of *Vogue* magazines, from the late 1940s to the 1980s, bound in faux-leather volumes. Once no longer needed, consulted materials were to be deposited on little trolleys, from where a man with gray hair and a snow-white coat brought them back to their place in the library's order.

She doesn't remember anymore where exactly she spent the most time back then, whether at the academy, for studying, or in cinemas, nightclubs, and bars, or in other places where knowledge is consumed… In the daytime the woman was sometimes so tired that she dozed off on the books, in the sunlight of the library."

— Doris Lasch

Rolls of Newsprint

Proofing material found at Bold Printing, Malmö, Sweden, 2014. The kind of paper used for the Swedish financial tabloid *Dagens Industri* (Today's Industry), ca. 40 × 270 cm.

"Today, when the paper is no longer 'today's paper,' long rolls of oil-soaked newsprint are sent through the printing press in order to be cleaned and prepared for the new paper, the new news, offers, and rulings. Such newsprint is spewed out by enormous machines, released from codes and standards for that instance, producing unique and unintelligible renderings of facts, events, ideas, and people. The material was found, almost by accident, when I was picking up something else at a printer and by chance caught sight of the waste product that was being taken out in heaps. Glass-like from the oil, and with markings that resemble marble

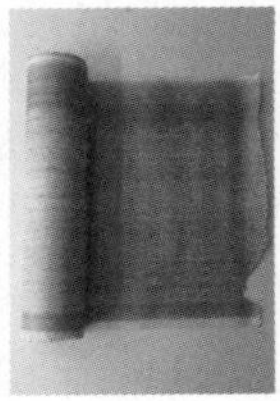

in one moment and ripples on water in the next, the rolls don't speak the factual and informative language of the press, but an abstract, almost formalist language. The heavy and extremely fragile material resists almost any physical interference, remaining somewhat alien, resting in its own unstable equilibrium. It becomes a visual conveyor of language in its very essence. Looking at it, one might like to believe that it reveals where the language of art lies. Somewhere underneath the daily, instrumental, scientific use of language, just above total destruction."

— Kirke Hundevad Meng

English-Tagalog Dictionary

Published by Kobunsya, Tokyo, Japan, 1944. Letterpress print on paper, cardboard, 19 × 14 cm.

"An English-Tagalog dictionary lying around in a family's home—one of the daughters had obtained it in order to learn Tagalog, her mother's first language. As no Swedish-Tagalog dictionary was available, English was chosen as the most closely related, understood language. Furthermore, since Tagalog was heavily influenced by English, the dictionary became useful for both generations. English functioned as a sort of shared language. Here it became the middle-language for two generations wanting to understand each other on equal terms—a mutual space of translation, where communication could materialize within a language other than the respective mother tongue. At the same time, the English language is neither neutral nor objective, and in this context it became a signifier of a violent, colonial institution, since the US had taken possession of the Philippines from Spain in 1898 and imposed a colonial rule in which language functioned as part of the 'civilization project.'

At some point, the dictionary went missing in the family's home, but another copy was acquired, a

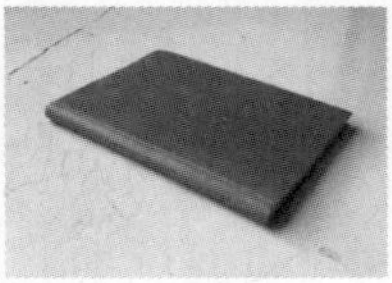

particular edition originating from Japan, published in 1944 during the Japanese occupation of the Philippines, when they were fighting the Americans over territory. In this edition, the power relations between the colonized and colonizer(s) as well as the premises and conditions of the translation processes become even more complex." — Cecilia Luzon

Protractor

Acrylic, 25 cm diameter, 3 mm thick.

"Having moved from Berlin to São Paulo without many personal objects, I looked around at home for something that I could connect to the many things I learned recently. This plastic geometric object seems cold, an instrument of angles. It could relate to what I have been trying to learn: to understand things that were previously outside of—or that conflicted with—my perspective, to critically examine my own inherited framework of thought, and to learn to live in a truly affirmative

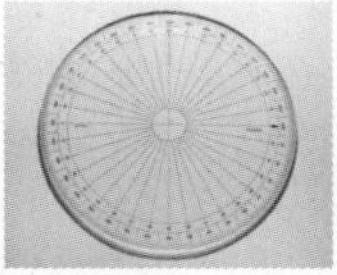

relation to multiplicity. But the actual context is much more private. The object belongs to the woman I live with and love, someone with many opinions and perspectives different from my own. Whereas I proclaim resemblance in the clear and unobstructed view of disparity, she has no inclination to cover differences with a cloak of affection, and sometimes even seems to seek them out. As disconcerting as it can be for me, her affirmation of difference without indifference—of difference that expects, an unreserved negotiation and conversation in a daily life lived together—has not only shown me where I might try to be a bit more fearless in my private life, but it also made me realize how what I am able to learn within the confines of my work is connected to what I learn in life. However, I've lately also been thinking about the opposite: What can I learn about living from what I do instinctively in my work?"

— Falke Pisano

Lehren und Lernen als Aufführungskünste / Teaching and Learning as Performing Arts

Artist's book by Robert Filliou, first published in 1970 by Verlag Gebr. König, Cologne, Germany, and New York, NY, USA; second edition, published in 2014 by Occasional Papers, London, UK. Offset print on paper, cardboard, metal spiral, 21 × 27.5 × 1.5 cm.

"Some slightly older student friends of mine at art school went traveling with Robert Filliou. He held a guest professorship at the time. According to hearsay, the student group spent a good while with him in Dordogne, in the south of France, exploring some of

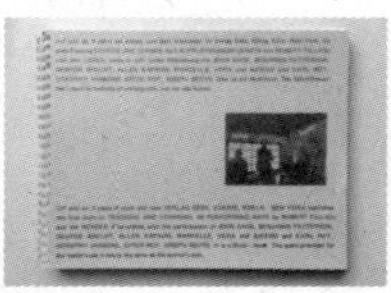

the area's pre-historic caves. They returned with stacks of drawings and talked about 'artists in space.' I didn't understand much.

Recently, I came across this publication of his, previously unknown to me. I don't believe that one can learn from its content about learning while reading it. It does contain assumptions about and a position on society and personal fulfillment that simply may be somewhat dated. But I can clearly sense—and would elaborate with this publication at hand on pages so-and-so—how its author, the artist, and the others sharing conversations with him, practiced a lucid way of moving across the zeitgeist of their historical context by a series of maneuvers 'in space' so to speak. And they, in return, allow me to grasp where and how artistic practice needs to move, for the sake of its lightheartedness, in the brute force present-day."

— Hinrich Sachs

Ashtray

Fabricated in May 2016; presented as a gift to the current owner in June 2016. Blown glass, approx. 14 × 13.5 × 3.5 cm.

"The 'Pink Donut' ashtray is a failed attempt at fabricating an artwork. The idea: an imagined model of rotary direction was to twist within a thin bubble of pink glass slowly blown by a specialist glassworker through an iron pipe. The bubble was meant to slowly expand, then to twist, collapse on the poles and then open, not rupturing but rather taking the shape of a torus, a bizarre form somewhere between a sphere and a spiral. A continuous wrapping within itself, yet whirling on top of the blower's pipe. But after the collapse, the poles did not open. There was no twist in rotary directions, and no whirl occurred around the end of the pipe. The result was far from the expected toric miracle.

The donut was then given to me as a gift, hovering between not being the artwork it was intended to be and being something very different than a mere failure.

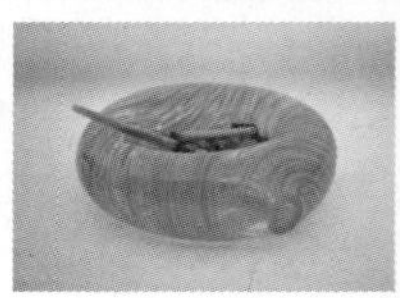

The pink gut or curiosum was transformed through its failed artistic properties into something other. With its serendipitous design and its intrinsic

aesthetic qualities intact, the object gained the status of a tribute and would come to remind me of its revolutionary reversal, repurposed or rather reborn for ashes and for stimulating smoky conversations."
— Mateusz Nowak

Backpack

Purchased in Geneva, Switzerland or via the Internet, ca. 2013. Nylon, plastic, approx. 35 × 28 × 4 cm (when empty).

"A woman from Geneva bought this backpack in a compulsive manner, without liking it in particular. It then landed at her mother's place, in a corner of her living room, because she had become the victim of an invasion of bed bugs (*Cimex lectularius*). All her belongings had to be evacuated, the textiles deep frozen or washed at more than 60 degrees Celsius. These are two methods for killing these insects, which bite human beings during their sleep, living exclusively on human blood. The backpack had to be treated accordingly, like everything else, but was thereafter abandoned by its owner. A year later, the woman's sister was also affected by an invasion of bed bugs.

Bed bugs are supposedly a species dating from the age of the dinosaurs, having mutated in order to survive the pesticides which, until recently, nearly eradicated them. The *Cimex lectularius* is now well established in Geneva, a cosmopolitan place and a turntable of globalization. They arrive via travelers' luggage and successfully install themselves in wooden flooring, beneath the plinths. They crawl into cracks in the walls and even manage to pass through zippers. Their larvae survive two years without eating or drinking. Central heating as well as the planet's warming are supposedly the reasons for their prolonged installment in Switzerland. In 2014, 10,000 apartments in Geneva were infected. In 2016, the official figure has risen to 14,000.

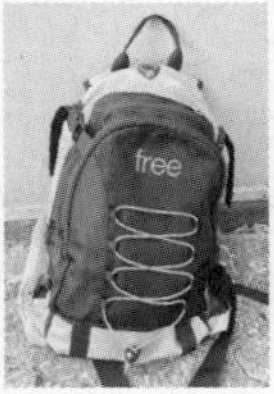

As the sister's belongings, including bags, similarly had to be deep frozen or washed at more than 60 degrees Celsius, she is now using the backpack embroidered with the word 'free.'"
— Donatella Bernardi

Safety Net

Purchased on www.biggamehunters.co.uk for personal recreational use, May 2015. Circular Net: Black High Tension PE mesh fabric (ca. 1,400 cm in circumference, 269 cm high); poles: galvanized steel (24.5 mm diameter), foam padding, rubberized PVC; fittings: U-bolts, nuts, spacers, washers.

"[...] it anyway. We put it up in the back, and the kids loved it. They went mental, bouncing around for hours, best thing ever. Then Jenny says we need a safety net to stop the kids from flying off and breaking an ankle or something, so we got a safety net, but when it came we realized we needed a frame for it, which comes separately, so we ordered a frame and eventually got it all set up and safe. Next thing, the neighbor says it's blocking the view from her kitchen, and we need to move it. But the back garden's tiny.

You've seen it, we can't move it anywhere else back there, and the front is where I keep the cars, so I just left it there. I thought fuck it. It was starting to get stupid. All we wanted was to give the kids something to do outside when the weather's nice. Then it's all this hassle, so fuck it, leave it as it is. She'll have to put up with it. Not much of a view anyway. A few days later, some guy knocks on the door and tells me I'm running a garage business out of the front garden, and do I have the necessary permits for that. No I don't have a garage business, and no I don't need any permits, and will you keep your voice down because I just got the baby to sleep, and the nurse says she's underweight, and we need to make sure she feeds and sleeps properly, and then the neighbor comes round with her son, and they start having a go at me, telling this guy that I've been [...]" — Toby Lynas

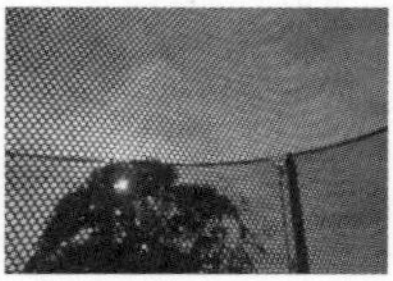

T-shirt

Purchased at the Craft Day Sale at Tyler School of Art, Philadelphia, PA, USA, October 2015. Cotton, water-based silk-screen paint, approx. 7 × 7 × 0.1 cm.

"This cocoa-colored shirt is a standard, L-size item. However, the motif embellishing the chest was designed, prepared for printing, silk-screened, and sold within less than twenty hours. The maker, an undergrad art student, had begun this process at 9 pm, after a week of regular classes and extracurricular workshop meetings, and used the silk-screen facilities overnight. The motif depicts two fellow workshop participants that the maker had met for the first time a few days earlier." — Hinrich Sachs

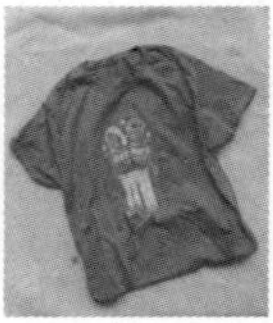

Wooden Sword (with Moominmamma)

Mariefred, Sweden, 1998. Plywood, felt pen, 55 × 8 × 0.5 cm.

"A wooden sword from the annual Knight Festival in Mariefred, Sweden, that the owner obtained as a child after being dubbed a knight in a ceremonial act for kids. An ambiguous sense of play and collusion was palpable to the children who took part in the staging of this historical institutional ceremony. Nevertheless, they participated, performing it with an attitude of, if not belief, at least respect and earnestness. Later the same summer, the owner asked his mother to write his name on it and also draw Moominmamma (one of his favorite fictional characters) on it, in order to ensure his surroundings and playmates that he himself was the rightful owner of the wooden sword." — Samuel Richter

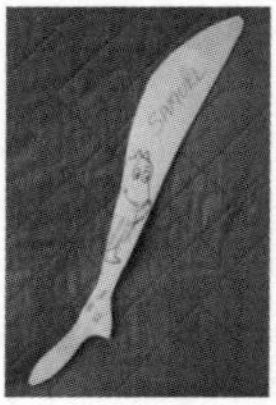

Rosa the Robot

Observed on www.socialdemokratiet.dk, 2001. Computer code.

"During the campaign for the general election in Denmark in 2001,

the Social Democratic Party presented a chat robot named Rosa. The idea was to establish a public database that gathered information on political topics and could provide a more direct interface to the electorate than the mass media. But Rosa did more than accumulate data. It was programmed to learn from chat sessions and could adapt to the views and expressive styles of its users. A female chat partner, 'she' was represented in a drawing on the website as something like a middle-aged primary school teacher. A certain subjectivity was thus imagined to represent the ideological and social identity of the Social Democratic Party and their campaign motto 'Mennesker først'—'humans first.' Disaster struck when Rosa was left to her own devices for a week and developed a strongly racist discourse during this period.

With Rosa, a political actor with its roots in modernism's dialectical discourses took the form of a cyborg. Through the slogan 'humans first' an emblematic representation of a range of conceptual binaries, such as human/machine, politics/people, culture/nature, was established—which Rosa ended up disturbing. The idea of automatizing political discourse carries with it the erasure of political discourse inasmuch as the idea of the specifically human becomes synthetic, not authentic. This process of automatization can be understood as a highly ambivalent sublation. The human/machine-synthesis produces new identities that are very present in our civilization, but without real social discourses. Subjectivity is in a state of *Aufhebung* or 'suspension,' but its discourse is stuck in a dialectical condition.

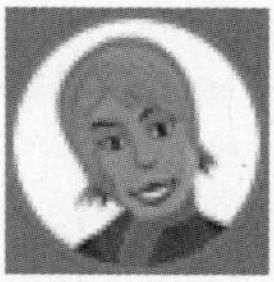

Even if this occurrence dates back more than fifteen years, it continues to be an instructive example of compromised recursive navigation as a result of a meltdown of binaries.

Needless to say, Rosa left cyberspace a long time ago."

— Lars Bang Larsen and Søren Andreasen

Athanor

Alchemical furnace (Inv.-no. 60.749) photographed in 2010 in the storage of the Nordiska Museet, Stockholm, Sweden. Supposedly used by August Nordenskiöld in the secret alchemical laboratory at the Royal Mint, Stockholm in the 1780s. Given to the museum around 1880 by Nordenskiöld family. Iron, 60 × 45 × 40 cm.

"The Finnish-Swedish alchemist August Nordenskiöld, deeply influenced by the Swedenborgian spiritual movement, spent his life traveling, writing, searching for resources, and experimenting extensively in laboratories. One of his main pursuits and personal motivations was to make gold from inferior metals—in quantities so large that gold itself would become worthless, eventually leading to the end of the 'tyranny of money.' He approached the Swedish King Gustav III, asking to be allowed to return to Stockholm in order to conduct alchemical research in the King's employ. The King agreed, and Nordenskiöld began his work in a

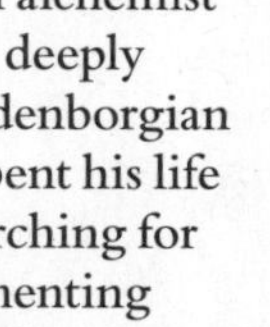

secret laboratory at the Drottningholm Palace. The project was eventually abandoned due to a lack of success. However, Nordenskiöld continued pursuing his plans. He died in Sierra Leone, West Africa, while exploring further utopian ideas, among them the abolition of slavery, as described in his pamphlet 'Plan for a Free Community at Sierra Leone' (1792)."

— Goldin+Senneby

Cardboard Box with Padlock

Seen and photographed while visiting a local hospital in Busisi, Tanzania, during fieldwork in 2006. Cardboard, adhesive tape, iron, brass, approx. 28 × 57 × 35 cm.

"A box that was disposed of in a hospital in Busisi displays information about the contents, bearing the generic words 'medical supplies' on its side. It seems to have been exposed to moisture and bears a greasy stain. The corners of the cardboard are completely

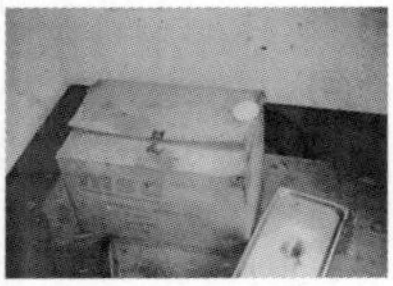

worn off. It has no particular closing mechanism. One flap simply folds over another. However, two metal brackets, a hinge, and a lever have been attached to the box. The lever is locked with a padlock. Any pointed material, even hands, could easily tear the box open. Maybe the padlock is merely symbolic, a warning sign, a kind of scarecrow. Maybe it was the only means available to protect the contents of the box. Maybe it is was just a way of pretending, or maybe just a lazy solution."

— Malou da Cunha Bang

Polo Shirt

Private belongings, 1996. Emerald-green cotton piqué, approx. 61 × 83 × 2 cm.

"A Ralph Lauren Polo Shirt features a branded collar label, stitching that matches the color of the shirt, a thread difficult to copy, a size tag to the right of the main label inside the collar, and just

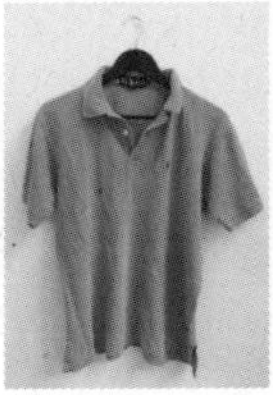

two opaque, pearl buttons attached with a cross-stitch. The spelling, font shape, size, spacing, and positioning of the logo are in keeping with the brand's manual: upright, with a clean finish, reverse neatly stitched, without any ink or loose ends. The rider is distinguishable from the horse, and the reins, tail, and ears of the horse are all visible. Other Ralph Lauren shirt styles differ from this format."

— Tomas Kominis Endresen

Disk-like Fan

Woven in Bagoundié, Gao, Mali, 2015. Palm leaves (species: *Hyphaene thebaica*, commonly called "doum palm" or "gingerbread tree," Arabic: دوم, Songhay: *kangaw* or *kongu*), 28 cm diameter.

"A *lefe*, in Songhay, is a disk-like or rectangular object used to fan the body or a fire. Like the shape of the earth, it is a sphere—a shape to circumnavigate. It may also function as a cover, a lid, or a 'roof.'

This *lefe* was bought from women who founded an association to produce local craft, mostly with palm leaves, thus the name *Kongu nafaw* ('good or benefit of the palm leaf') to sell at the market in Gao.

The income of each sale is donated to one of the members, so she can have enough money, for once, to afford a significant purchase for herself.

When I was young, in the 1970s, the LP was in vogue as the primary carrier of music. The LP was then called *lefe*. Those days it made us travel around the world. Walking in the streets of Gao, one could hear the sounds of Charanga everywhere, especially by the local heroes, Las Maravillas de Mali, led by Boncana Maïga of Gao. Reggae was also all over the place: Bob Marley and the Wailers, the trio Burning Spear, Peter Tosh, Jimmy Cliff, and all their reincarnations. And echoes from the south: Zambia's Mike Nyoni. Oh boy, 'Amida' floated through the air of the dance floor every weekend. Young men and women were glued to each other in a synchronized swing. Back then, any song that could induce such an ethereal fusion

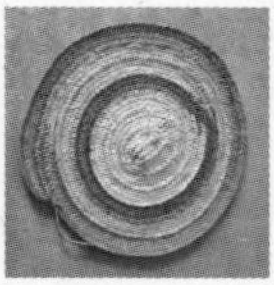

was called a 'slow' in any language. For a long time we considered Mike Nyoni a Kenyan. Maybe Zambia was just too far off, on the rim of the earth. But there were genuine specimens from all over the continent on the LPs in homes and on dance floors: Sudanese, Egyptian, and Indian hits met Swedish, French, and Italian ones. There were crooners from all across the Americas. The deaths of Mike Brant and Bob Marley were bitterly mourned in Gao. But the disk kept turning. The band played on, imitating the dead.

These were the days one could see music *turn*. Today it flows relentlessly like a waterfall down the cracked rib of a mountain. Now we need to give *lefe* back a physical substance; so we use it to refer to a hard disk or anything related to the idea of a disk." — Mohomodou Houssuba

Walking Trail Signage

Photographed in Stolan, at the northern side of the mountain Billingen in Skaraborg, Västergötland, Sweden, July 18, 2014. Orange and blue paint on wooden pole with orange and blue colored plastic rectangular signs nailed to it; made in the context of the art project Skaraborgs museum museum.

"Approximately 12,000 years ago a large water mass existed across an area that today includes Sweden and Finland, the Baltic Ice Lake, which constantly received new inflows from the melting inland ice cover. When the retracting ice exposed the northern part of the table-top mountain of Billingen, which constituted a barrier against the ice lake, its tip at Stolan gave way to the pressure from the lake, and a dramatic event ensued, in which this enormous body of water was emptied at this spot.

The nature reserve in Stolan is maintained by the Västra Götaland County Administrative Board and encompasses

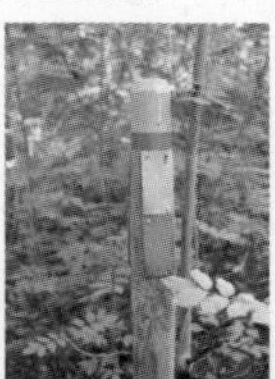

one of the many walking trails in the region. The trails are under the care of the Skövde Municipality, which keeps them accessible and makes sure walkers can pass hillsides, creeks, marshes, and grazing fields—if they make sure to follow the orange and blue markings. Orange marks the so-called Billingeleden, with a length of 40 km, whereas orange/blue marks the adjoining trails.

As part of the technologies for maintaining, visualizing, mediating, and providing access to non-urban environments, these markings reflect the intersections between 'nature' and 'infrastructure.' At the same time, these striking visual encodings of the landscape could possibly also be read as a kind of readymade art, situated somewhere between Conceptual Art and Land Art—with the county administration as the involuntary artist." — Cecilia Grönberg and Jonas (J) Magnusson

Folding Chair

Owner and origin unknown. Aluminum, polyester fabric, 50 × 80 × 82 cm.

"For two years this folding chair has been moved around from

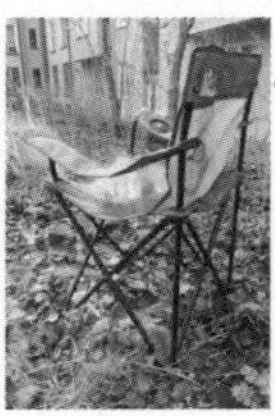

place to place in the garden of the inner courtyard of a multi-apartment property in Kungsholmen, Stockholm, Sweden. It belongs to no one, and no one wants to use it or throw it away." — Leonela Lilja

Concrete Cast

Private belongings, Skåne, Sweden, ca. 1998. Cast concrete, 19 × 17 × 7.5 cm.

"The cast was made by a four year old from a plastic mask depicting the first commercially acclaimed animated character in film: Mickey Mouse. Nose and other facial features are missing." — Aron Skoog

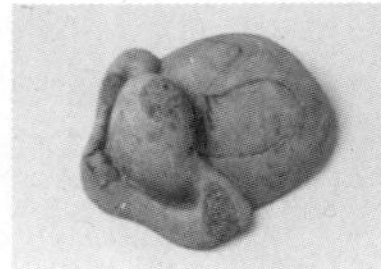

Center Lotion

Purchased at Jenny Q's Herbals, Joshua Tree, CA, USA, May 2016. The handmade Center Lotion comes in a plastic bottle, 16.8 × 5 cm, containing ca. 2 oz.

"An international visitor to Joshua Tree, California, USA, had become aware of a certain scent that was in the air and found it difficult to identify its origin. Whether coming from leaves or people, something was blending particularly well with the high desert environment. In a conversation, someone gave her a hint and pointed

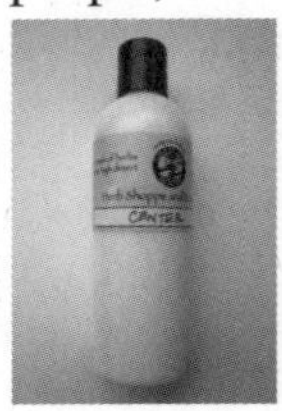

her toward an herbal shop. There, surprisingly, the saleswoman was wearing this precise scent. For the very first time the visitor told someone that she wanted to smell just like her. The woman behind the counter explained the scent product as a mixture of four different natural oils added to a moisturizer and offering 'a sense of peace, grounding, and presence in the body.' The visitor left, now smelling exactly like a random woman in the desert." — Catalina Aguilera

Dog Teeth (Labrador Retriever)

From the puppy Miranda, Öland, Sweden, ca. 1999. Enamel with some remaining dentine, 1 × 0.4 cm.

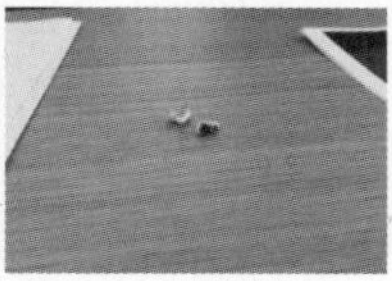

"A puppy tooth that grew in the embryo from the moment of conception. It is a tooth that is naturally pushed out and replaced by an adult tooth—perfectly formed for crushing bones as well as ripping and tearing up meat—when the dog reaches a certain age."

— Klara Zetterholm

Tent

Purchased on www.leboncoin.com from its previous owner, May 2016. Marechal brand, model Savoie 3. Cotton, tubular structure, 200 × 400 × 180 cm.

"One of the objects that has played a role in shared memories and people's imagination is the tent, in our case an orange one. First and foremost, this ridge tent—known as a "Canadian" tent in France—first invested the development of camping with political meaning, when the Popular Front of 1936 granted workers the right to paid holidays and made it possible for a large number of French people to come into contact with nature, with the sea, the mountains, to go hiking, and enjoy their vacation. The framed tent brings back childhood memories. It was a family tent: solid, spacious, with a flat roof and square corners, and it was even possible to stand up in it. The frame was made of pipes joined together by metal springs, kept in a separate bag that was heavy and had to be stored on the roof rack of the car or in the trailer attached to the back. This tent lacked the colorful stripes and transparent plastic windows that were to come later as an imitation of the home—making the tent into a secondary residence by default. The tent also created a certain relationship to the world: with its smells, the sound of the rain on the stretched canvas, and the feeling of being close to the wind and the changes in the weather. And all of this in a manner that made us also feel a certain relationship to nature while being separated from it by thin panels of fabric. Rousseau and Thoreau were made available to the most modest wallets. These geometric patches of color in the fields or the undergrowth also prefigured those of abstract paintings that were to become an element of our common environment. The lively hues of these geometrical figures that stood out against the multiple nuances of green of a natural background formed an expanded painting. They opened up the possibility of recognizing art in all landscapes whether rural or urban. This figure of the tent is neither the symbol of a nostalgic desire or wish for reformation. It belongs to the anachronisms with which we love to identify."

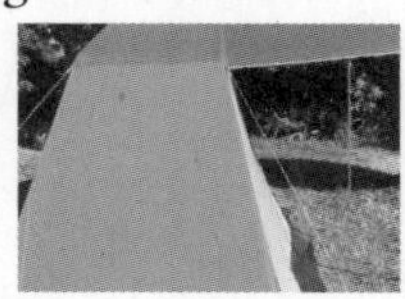

— Dector & Dupuy

Spray Foam Blob

Observed in a flat in Copenhagen, Denmark, 2016. Spray foam, approx. 30 × 30 × 20 cm.

"A blob of spray foam was sticking to a ceiling in a flat, and the resident started to wonder about what it was covering and how it had ended up there. He tried to figure out what internal force had shaped it and organized it into its present shape. The material had taken on an unpredictable but still recognizable form. It had sparkled, as it emerged from its container and had released toxic fumes while it changed its state of aggregation, from liquid to solid. For him, this

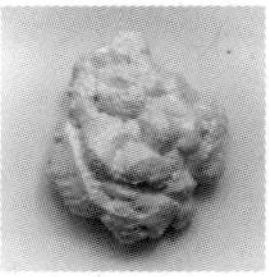

resembled the way institutions seem to come about, develop, and function in patterns beyond the intentions of individuals, organizations, or historical narratives. They fulfill not only their stated or official functions, but also a multitude of more or less obvious other functions. At their best, they shelter small pools of messy activities inside the officially recognized taxonomies that externally legitimize their existence." —Kristoffer Ørum

Wave Generator / Wave Machine

Bell Telephone Laboratories, New York City, USA, ca. 1973. Wood, metal wire, screws, paint, approx. 25 × 95 × 50 cm.

"The device is used to visually demonstrate how waves function. After being developed for this purpose, it served as a prop in two educational films, *Simple Waves* and *Similarities in Wave Behavior*, made by engineer John Shive in 1973 in one of the world's most influential industrial laboratories for communication technologies. Following the historical trajectory of human efforts to imitate, represent, and copy the real in virtual and mental spaces, the device predates the current accessibility of the digital realm, in which attempts to bridge physical boundaries are becoming increasingly important. Whether analog or digital, machines such as this potentially support the sharing of an experi-

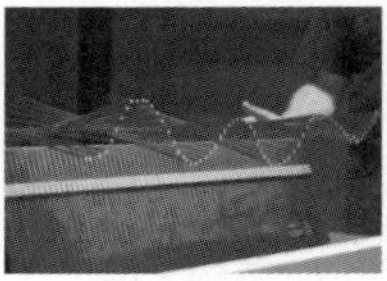

ence via already known words or experiences or enable the use of new environments. They may be changing the notion of copying as well as our understanding of reality." —Jonathan Terry

Wilted Lilacs

Photographed in a private garden in Stockholm, Sweden, June 21, 2016, 20:31:23. Bundles of withering flowers, each panicle approx. 17 × 5 × 5 cm.

"What better night to meditate on death and decay than the brightest of the year? Summer solstice, the most beautiful of nights, is a turning point—from here on the days get darker. Dying and death is the concluding chapter: the end game of the text, of the fabric, the final step into the unknown. An unfathomable form of existence that nevertheless is a precondition of human cultures and societies, or life itself as we know it. It is a necessity for the stories we tell one another about the meaning of being. From ontology, metaphysics,

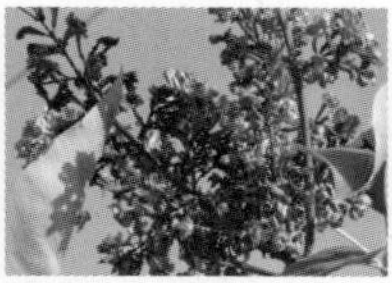

and religion, to art and science, to pure blunt economy, to questions concerning waste management and burial procedures.

Not many of us, if anyone, knows when, where, and how he or she is going to die. To die is a process of lifelong learning—and who is to assess its outcomes? Withering flowers glow in the last rays of the late evening sun. Recalling the *wen-yen* literati, the old Chinese calligraphers, who sat in their gardens, contemplating the glittering moon in the pond, the whispering wind through the bamboo, trying to catch *qi* (氣), drawing their poems of the night."
—Johan Widén

Book with Autograph

Personally addressed and presented as a gift to the current owner, Mexico City, Mexico, 2012. Paperback, 208 pages, offset print on paper, 21 × 14.5 × 2.5 cm.

"A copy of Danilo Kiš' *Enciclopedia de los muertos* (The Encyclopedia of the Dead) has been customized with a personal dedication. It became a key book for the recipient

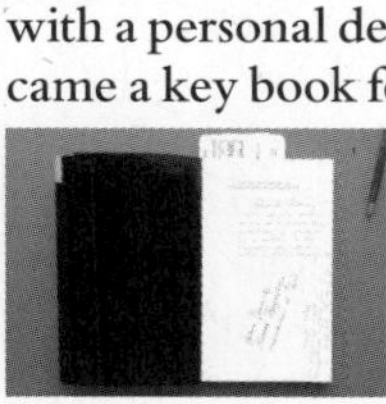

of this present, who has had the feeling that, thanks to this gift, a new door to many questions has opened—understanding that merging with the alterity of the unknown is vital to acknowledging the personal implications of one's relationship with others." —Helena Fernández-Cavada

Horse Halter

Purchased at the Gothenburg Horse Show, Gothenburg, Sweden, 2000. Polyester, metal, embroidery, 44 × 20 × 20 cm.

"The horse bridle embroidered with the word 'Donkey' was used in a riding school. The owner, nine years old at the time, had been asked to become the 'groom' of a particular horse. The horse arrived in Västergötland from Denmark in a trailer and kicked a man in the stomach. Since it lacked both pedigree and legal identification, it was not possible to send it to the butcher. It then somehow ended up in the stable that the girl was going to regularly, although she only could take riding lessons every

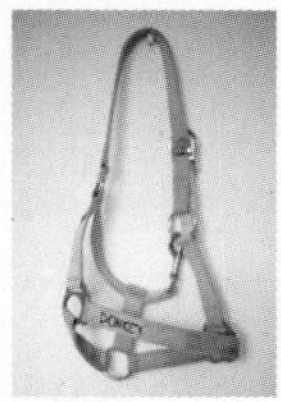

other week. The financial crisis of the 1990s affected many families in Sweden, but that was too complicated for the girl to understand at the time. She cleaned up dung, swept the floors, and helped privileged friends with their horses. Her horse was later derogatorily nicknamed 'Don Quixote' by other children in the riding school."
—Filippa Wikner

Canned Banff Air

Purchased on www.vitalityair.com, February 3, 2016. Aluminum, plastic, 6.7 × 23.8 × 6.7 cm, 130 grams.

"The aluminum can contains 7.7 liters of fresh Canadian air, with a slight scent of pine. Bottled in Banff National Park in Alberta, Canada, the can comes with a

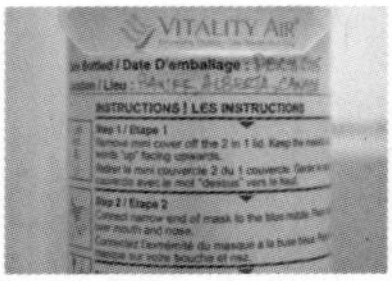

handy mask that allows the user to easily inhale the air in between activities or while on the go. According to the international marketing of the product, the 150 breaths of crisp Rocky Mountain air are a great way of countering pollution or getting ready for an exam. The small size of the can allows it to fit perfectly in a gym bag, a satchel, or even a jacket pocket." — Isak Anshelm

Cotton Shirt

Industrially produced, M-sized cotton shirt stained with fried oysters, saffron, and cool climate wine.

"A generic cotton shirt is just that: a generic, mass fabricated piece of clothing produced in accordance with standardized measurements. Wearing a white shirt has certain connotations; it is like wearing an external hard drive only capable of doing certain things that just a generic cotton shirt can do. However, using the shirt alters it, making it personalized attire that is

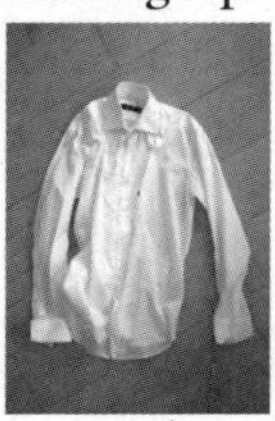

shaped and hand-tailored by the wearer. The owner only wore this item of clothing once, but the generic fabric became the canvas for something very personal: a night in Amsterdam two years ago when fried oysters with saffron were served." — Jacques Henri Sennwald

Round Toothpicks

Approx. 230 round wooden toothpicks, purchased in Bilbao, Spain, June 2016. Plastic and cardboard packaging, 7 × 6.5 × 1.5 cm.

"Toothpicks—essential for Basque finger food, locally called *pintxos*—were the first things I ever stole. I made a bet with my cousin, who dared me to steal from a shop that we used to go to with my mother and my aunt. It was June 15, 1977, a Wednesday. I was almost seven. We didn't have school that day. Working adults had a

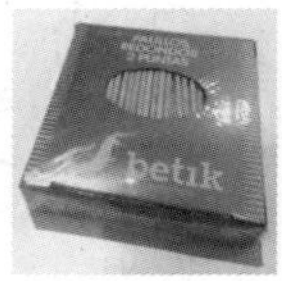

half-day off in order to vote. It was the first democratic election since the Spanish Civil War and after almost forty years of Franco's dictatorship.

That day was the beginning of something called *Transición*. It was presented as a smooth and undramatic transition from dictatorship to democracy. Since then, another forty years have passed, but socially and politically Spain has not advanced. The elections from June 26, 2016 ended with quite similar results.

The last forty years of transitioning to nowhere have been a piece of cake for Francoists and their memories. No legal or historical review has taken place. Spain is still a gray, fearful, arrogant, gossiping country based on values inherited from Franco's dictatorship. It is a country that remains culturally stuck.

I just got back from Chile, where I was told that they are currently going through their own *transición*. I believe such historical and cultural changes have to be faced and swallowed as a whole at once, with all the consequences of indigestion, instead of the ongoing blockage.

By the way, I never stole toothpicks again." — Asier Perez

A Gram of Gold

Gold, approx. 0.6 × 0.5 × 0.4 cm.

"This nugget was purchased in April 2013 in the raw gold sellers street, Av. Ernesto Rivero in Puerto Maldonado, which is situated in the Peruvian region of Madre de Dios. It was extracted illegally from the 11 Naturaqal Reserve in the Amazon region, which shelters more than 60 percent of all the illegal gold extraction in South America. This particular transaction was documented with a hidden camera as part of a research project. At the time of the purchase, a

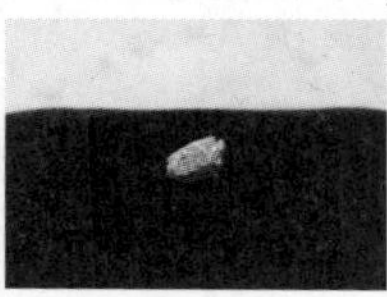

gram of gold cost $44.11, but one must question what these $44.11 in turn represent. Sheltering these illegal activities has created a sustained microsystem in the area, where normalcy has been slowly altered, to the point where child prostitution, slavery, and human trafficking are in a sense 'socially accepted.'

By April 2014, the known cases of children who were prostituted in the area, according to the Department of Crime of the Public Ministry of Peru, included approximately 2,250 girls. It is recognized that this figure diverges substantially from the real numbers. The illegal mining in the area has given rise to hundreds of mining camps, and each of them has in average of fifty 'prostibars' (bar-brothels). According to the NGO Huarayo the average number of sexually exploited girls in a 'prostibar' is twenty, and up to 60 percent are minors."

— Oscar Lara

Phone for Emergency Information

Push-button telephone photographed during a visit to the windowless Phillips Hall classrooms, University of Iowa, Iowa City, USA, June 2016. Apparently it was at some point detached from its original wall position and installed on a more recent cable duct.

"Phillips Hall is a building located on the campus of the University of Iowa. Built in 1965, all its classrooms and professors' offices are located in the very center of the building. They are surrounded by other administrative areas and share no walls to the outside. This means that these spaces have no windows, and no sound enters from the outside city, so that students do not see, hear, or become distracted by the streets. At the time the building was constructed, youth protests had just begun to emerge and spread, although on a very small scale. Only one major event is reported to have occurred in Iowa City, in 1967. Currently the rooms in Phillips Hall are used by some of the language departments.

These classrooms are equipped with a phone system. The phones, aside from being used for internal and external calls, are part of a campus system in which the uni-

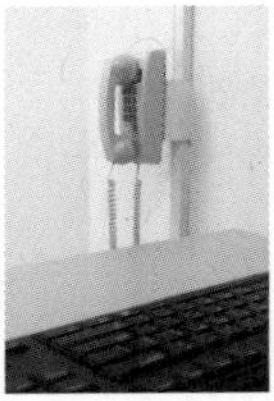

versity police informs about so-called emergency events in real time. A professor who gets such a call while teaching class is supposed to inform the students about the crimes reported in real time—for example that two men, dressed in such and such manner, race, age, etc., now at the corner of X and X street, are suspected of stealing a car and are moving west... Students are thus repeatedly exposed to a kind of live crime report during their study time." — Nanna Nordström

Pilgrimage Amulet

Unidentified Indian coin, wrapped in an armband of calico rag; Kanpur, India, 1989.

"This small object was given to me by an elderly charwoman and sweeper, who cleaned the lavatories in a large communist household in Kanpur, India, where I lived for a time in 1989. It was a gift on the occasion of my undertaking a pilgrimage to the Triveni Sangam in Allahabad to attend the Kumbh Mela that year. I have never unwrapped the coin, and, though I wore the armband for the week that I traveled to and from the Mela, I never understood the significance of the gesture she made by tying it to my body.

The trope of life-as-journey represents a basic space-for-time

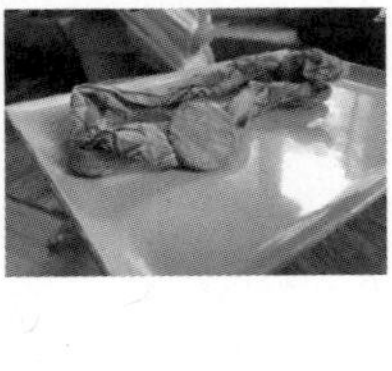

substitution of the sort that may fundamentally distort our experience of existence. Is the ready availability of this formula a symptom or a cause? Like many a young person, I believed, at eighteen, that a long trip on my own—a 'journey'—would be an essential element in the *Bildungsroman* I was busy projecting as an autobiography. I went to India. The first morning I awoke there, I went into the small courtyard of a colonial era compound in the Civil Lines of Kanpur at dawn, and watched a long line of giant fruit bats fly in from eating guava on the sandy plains of the Ganges. I was so terrified by the solitude and the strangeness of my surroundings that I talked very quietly into a Dictaphone I had brought with me, and said over and over again, 'I'm really having trouble keeping it together.' Sadly, I have lost the tape. But I retained this small gift, given to me by a Dalit woman in what seemed to be a token of goodwill as I set out for Allahabad and the vast tent city of pilgrims convened for the auspicious festival of the Kumbh Mela—temporarily, it was said, the largest aggregation of human beings on the planet. A pilgrimage is a journey in which one sets out to find a better version of oneself. That is the destination. This object was designed to help me to that end.

As I set it out to take the picture, my younger daughter came into the room, with a large water pistol slung low at her hip. 'What are you doing?' she asked." — Yara Flores

Tied Down Branch or a Becoming Walking Stick

Tempelhögen, Kallrör, Sweden, 2015. Birch tree and ratchet strap, 1 × 60 cm.

"For those who need to cross a boggy mire on foot, a walking stick can be very helpful. The

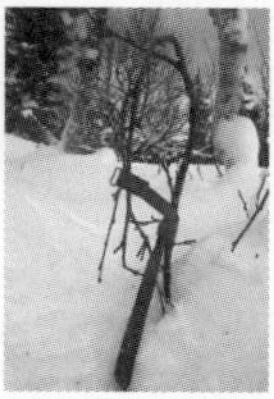

mountain birch tree, which grows on the edge of such mires, has excellent branches for making walking sticks. Old knowledge says that to make a walking stick, one ties a branch down, so that it will grow into the correct shape."

— Gideonsson/Londré

Photograph (Grete Demonstrates Clara's New Galoshes)

Private photograph, possibly a Polaroid, 1960s. Photo paper, 9 × 8.8 cm including the passe-partout.

"Shot in Boston, Massachusetts, USA, during Clara's visit to her daughter Grete—Clara took the ship to Boston from Haifa—they had last seen each other in Freiburg im Breisgau in the 1930s—Grete's

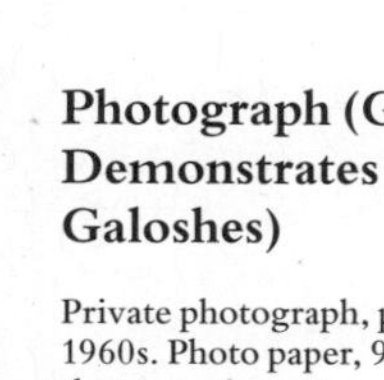

husband, Ernst, feared flying—not everybody in the family believed it to be the reason why they never visited Israel—nobody thought of hidden anti-Zionism—according to U.S. Geological Survey Water Supply Paper 2375 the 1961–69 drought in Massachusetts was the severest on record—perhaps the galoshes were bought just in case it would rain at some indefinite future date—searching data concerning the waterfall in Israel in the 1960s I learned from the Climate Change Knowledge Portal of the World Bank that Israel is located in Africa—it would be the first African state that takes part in the European Song Contest—it reminds me of another photograph—Grete poses in a scenery depicting the North Pole in a park on a summer vacation—longing for a climate change."

— Eran Schaerf

Pebble

Found in the shoreline area between Rikuzen-Takada and Ofunato, Japan, June 1996. White granite, 6.5 × 4.5 × 4 cm.

"I found this pebble twenty years ago. At the time, I was looking for a large piece of white granite to use for a new sculpture. I visited several stone quarries near Tokyo, but couldn't find one that was just right. I remembered seeing a rocky stretch of exposed granite when I went sea bathing in Iwate Prefecture, so I decided to go north along the Pacific coast, visiting all of the quarries and beaches with exposed bedrock that I could find in the Tohoku region in northeastern Japan. I went to all of the beaches that I could reach by car along the 500 km stretch from Ibaraki Prefecture's Oarai Town and Hitachi City to the southern Kamaishi City in Iwate Prefecture.

There are some famous long stretches of beach, such as Kujukuri Beach along northeastern

Japan's Pacific coast, but these mostly change into an elaborate and deeply indented coastline as you go farther north. When I actually drove along the coast, the differences in elevation were much more pronounced than I would have thought from looking at the map, and the roads were narrow, curved, and steeply sloping. It took a lot longer than I thought it would. Whenever I would find a promising white stone, I would approach it and give it a close examination. For the three days it took to drive there and back, I repeatedly got in and out of the car, driving for as long as there was sunlight.

Things like mobile phones didn't exist at the time, so I would call my wife and three-year-old son at home three times a day, whenever I could find a pay phone. 'How's Shuntaro? Right now I'm in such and such Town in such and such Prefecture. The waves under the cliffs are nice and gentle. I can see the horizon in the distance.' At night, I would stop the car in a park or other public facility and sleep. In the morning, I would brush my teeth and have a quick wash at the park's water spigot.

On my 500 km drive, I saw many spectacular coastal views.

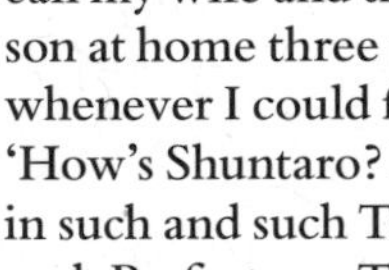

I stood at the edge of sheer cliffs looking down at the clear ocean filled with fish. I experienced the hospitality of people in small villages. One sight that was particularly memorable I encountered upon arriving in Ofunato. I was all alone, and it was around nine o'clock at night. I could see lights in windows here and there as I drove, but there was no one out walking by that time. I stopped my car at the harbor and stood near the water's edge. Maybe it was because I happened to arrive just at the spring tide, but the harbor was dead calm. The surface of the water was like an extension of the wharf and the land, sparkling in the moonlight as it stretched out silently into the far distance. 'If a tsunami were to come right now, everything in this harbor would be swallowed up by the sea,' I thought. Looking back on it now, that random thought seems quite meaningful, but it was really just a simple, intuitive impression. I had been envisioning a tsunami of a half-meter in height. That would have been more than enough to flood the town. I certainly wasn't imagining a 10-meter tsunami (with a run-up height of 40.1 meters) like the one on March 11th.

I saw 500 km of the coastline that was hit by the March 11th tsunami with my own eyes, fifteen years before it was destroyed. In one of the places I visited, there was a rocky stretch of granite just big enough to moor a single fishing boat. There was a small slanted hut with a rusty galvanized sheet iron roof painted a grimy blue. The quality and crystalline pattern of the granite was exactly what I had been looking for. I passed around behind the rocky cape and reached a small beach. There I found sand and pebbles formed from weathered granite of the same type as on the rocky stretch. I took this pebble as a sample of the stones in the area.

Ever since then, this pebble has been on my working table in my studio. It's a sort of switch that activates my memory and my imagination. It also reminds me of the giant tsunami that I had the good fortune not to meet in person. But it's just a pebble. Unless a geologist, someone looking at this pebble without hearing my story would have no idea that it wasn't a local stone. That's why I'm sure it will return to being 'just a pebble' after I die." — Yusuke Toda

Wash Ball with Passion Fruit

Found in a cellar, age unknown; perhaps moved from London to Basel before 1997 but found as is in early 2017. Rubber and organic matter, fist sized.

"Worthy of a minimal chuckle. The couple: Oh the domesti city is fucked. Not that I care. Oh (fuck!) the poetry of the every day collar stiff and st arched on the trembling machine. Oh the d'oh me: Stick it in. It was already stuck in. It is a found thing, not to be repeating myself. Me: STICK IT IN you shriveled piece of shit. Liquid can a) trickle in from above one by one (uncountable) or liquid can be) forever present (unaccountable). There is something to be said about inside out. About round and round goes the stare into the White Good (the olden day when the telly was not to be considered, when the papers were constantly wet from separation mourning). There is something to be said about books and covers. I wouldn't recommend reading while eating the squirty bitch or accidentally leaving the epos in your back pocket as you drop off the dirty stuff for its boring a.f. cleaning ritual (looped). I sit on top and stare: case out, doc. U meant the Silver Bad. An epic climbdown that soiled my negotiating hand. On heart. Attack this community you olden day con Struck me just how final a summer this comes out. All in the wash. In the prewash it comes out: this union, Jack, was not altogether (just the red with the whites. Yes the red with the delicates.) not altogether labeled right."

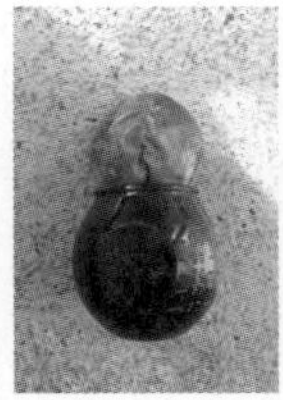

— Sophie Jung

Plaster Bag

Retrieved from the sculpture workshop at the Royal Institute of Art, Stockholm, Sweden, August 2016. Paper bag with plaster dust, 46 × 35 × 25 cm.

"The bag originally contained 25 kg of plaster powder, which is now used up. Plaster's simple production method—the mixture of powder and water—makes it a convenient material for creating heavy, static, yet fragile forms. It allows the user to be productive and 'learn by doing.' Such empty bags are commonly seen lying around art schools." — Anton Brolin

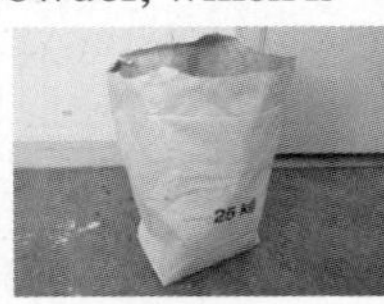

Cassette Voice Recorder

Sony TCM-200DV Standard Cassette Voice Recorder purchased at Radio Shack, New York City, USA, 2001. Plastic, metal, Perspex, electronics, polyester, 8 × 11.4 × 3.5 cm.

"This cassette voice recorder was used regularly by a filmmaker for recording sounds, often in an ad hoc manner and in everyday contexts. Some of the specific recordings include: a concert by

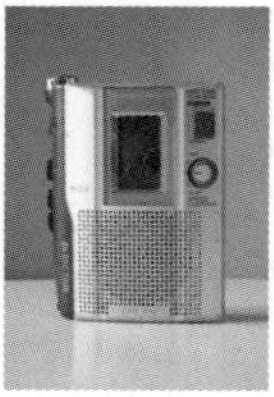

Keiji Haino in Tokyo from 2006; a lecture given by Thom Anderson in 2010 on the advantages of a lack of narrative in short films and emphasizing how cinema has failed us; and a game of bingo during the wedding celebrations of Samuel Delarosa and Karen Sharkey in Ireland in 2011." —Marcus Harrling

Random Photo Mobile

Registered as a trademark by the multinational Kikkerland Design Inc, made in China, and purchased in Moderna Museet's shop, 2016. Steel wire, approx. 56 × 60 cm.

"This decorative do-it-yourself framing device is merchandise from an art museum store.

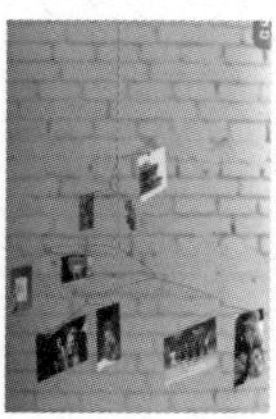

It invites the buyer to either use prefabricated images, like postcards (artworks, cityscapes, sunsets) or to individually mount personal photographs on the artwork-like mobile. Finally assembled and hung, it offers users a means to curate and frame their visitor experience." —Gabriel Säll

Stick Chart

Marshall Islands, Micronesia, nineteenth century. Wood, snail shells, coconut fiber, 85 × 96 × 0.4 cm. Courtesy Museum der Kulturen, Basel, Switzerland (Inv.-no. Vc 202).

"The so-called stick chart was used to navigate an area encompassing some 3,000 nautical miles in the Pacific Ocean. Stick charts were employed by Micronesian navigators before setting off as a device for learning about and memorizing the position of islands and decisive aspects of the sea, such as currents. This particular chart was sold around 1900 by the German colonial chief administrator on the Marshall

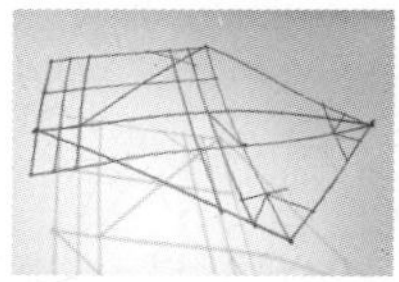

Islands, Eugen Brandeis, to the ethnographic collection of the University of Freiburg, Germany, and ended up in Basel, Switzerland, by way of an exchange, in 1904. Recent research has revealed that it actually was Antonie Brandeis, the chief administrator's wife, who had persistently collected such objects and gathered contextual information about them." —Hinrich Sachs

Pídàn / Century Egg / Leather Egg / Millennium Egg / Various Other Names

Purchased at the Oriental Supermarket, Stockholm, Sweden, 2016. Duck eggs, preserved by a modern process, Styrofoam, 6 × 4 × 4 cm each, 7 × 16 × 11 cm.

"This preserved food product and delicacy is said to have originated in the Hunan Province of China. Various versions of this traditional preservation method can be traced to Shanghai, Guangdong Province, Laos, Taiwan, Thailand, and Vietnam. Natural alkaline compounds—a combination of salt, wood ash, charcoal ash,

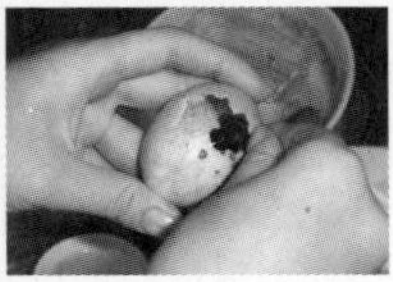

and calcium oxide—aid in the preservation process. The eggs can thus be preserved up to 240 days. This particular pídàn was produced by a modernized method with results similar to traditional processes. It includes soaking eggs in a solution of salt brine, calcium hydroxide, and sodium carbonate for ten days, followed by keeping it in plastic wrap for several weeks."

— Adam Shiu-Yang Shaw

CONTRIBUTORS

Catalina Aguilera is an artist living and working in Stockholm, Sweden. She is currently enrolled in the Masters Program in Fine Arts at the Royal Institute of Art, Stockholm. Her work was recently exhibited during CPH Art Week 2017.

Ehab Aljaby is a student living in Malmö, Sweden.

Søren Andreasen is an artist, writer, and curator based in Copenhagen, Denmark. He is currently working with Lars Bang Larsen on a project to follow up on their 2012 picture book *The Critical Mass of Mediation*.

Isak Anshelm is an artist based in Stockholm, Sweden. His work can be described as thematic painting. He is currently working at an artist residency in Gotland, Sweden.

Malou da Cunha Bang is a visual artist working with graphics and video. She lives in Copenhagen, Denmark.

Donatella Bernardi is an artist currently living in Zurich, Switzerland, where she works at the Zurich University of the Arts as Head of the Masters Program in Fine Arts. She recently developed *The Belly of the Phoenix*, a series of objects addressing lineage, rupture, sagging, and synchronicity.

Ludvig Briland is an artist based in Malmö, Sweden.

Anton Brolin is based in Stockholm, Sweden. He is currently studying at the Royal Institute of Art, Stockholm, and preparing for his BA examination in spring 2018.

Robin Curtis holds the chair in Media and Cultural Studies at the Albert-Ludwigs-Universität Freiburg. She is based in Düsseldorf, Germany, and is currently completing a book with the title *Immersion and Abandon*.

Michel Dector and **Michel Dupuy (Dector & Dupuy)** are artists living in Savennières and Paris, France, respectively. They work on the sites of their exhibitions or performances. They are currently developing *Fourmis blanches*, a "neighborhood art library" for the regional hospital center of Gonesse in the outskirts of Paris. The monograph *Dector & Dupuy* was published in 2016.

Marjolijn Dijkman is based in Brussels, Belgium. Her artistic practice is two-fold: ongoing projects and works developed in relation to specific contexts or interests, and initiatives such as *Enough Room for Space*. She exhibits internationally, most recently at the 11th Shanghai Biennial in 2016.

Tomas Kominis Endresen is an artist currently living in Berlin, Germany. His work was recently displayed at Montern in the Odenplan subway station, Stockholm, Sweden.

Helena Fernández-Cavada lives in Malmö, Sweden. She is an artist working mainly with drawing. Her recent project, *Epistolary Drawings*, develops dialogical strategies to contribute to the politics of temporization. It includes *Letters to My Mother*, an artist's book which interrogates the making of history in Spain, specifically the dictatorship period and the transition to democracy.

Yara Flores is an artist based in New York City, USA, whose work deals with the spiritual dimensions of technology. Her solo show *Greebles* at the Raygun Project Space (Toowoomba, Australia, 2016) materialized virtual non-faces. She was part of *Fifteen People Present Their Favorite Book (after Kosuth)* at Škuc Gallery in Ljubljana (2016) and Asad Raza's *Home Show* (New York City, 2015).

Ellie Ga is an artist living in Stockholm, Sweden. Her work often takes the form of video installations and performances—part observational essay, part poetic inquiry, part fragmentary storytelling. She was a recent recipient of a three-year project grant from the Swedish Research Council.

Gideonsson/Londré is an artist duo living in Kallrör, Sweden. They were recently part of the group exhibition *Kroppens Kalke* at Forlaget Gestus, Copenhagen, Denmark.

Goldin+Senneby "define themselves as a 'collaborative framework exploring juridical, financial, and spatial constructs.' The elusiveness of this description is somewhat apt. Since 2004, when Simon Goldin and Jakob Senneby started working as a duo, they have speculated around the layerings of contemporary economics, analyzing and employing different dimensions of financial markets. Their collaborative strategies have shaped a withdrawn approach wherein the artists are akin to puppeteers: their production mostly comprises choreographing the labour of others." (João Laia, *Frieze*)

Cecilia Grönberg is an artist, photographer, and the image editor of *OEI* magazine and OEI editör. She is currently working together with Jonas (J) Magnusson on an expanded publishing project centered around two uniquely stratified Swedish plateau mountains, Billingen and Kinnekulle.

Karin Hald is an artist and writer living in Copenhagen, Denmark. In 2016 she established Forlaget Gestus, an exhibition space and publisher for artists who use writing as an essential part of their practice. She holds an MFA from Malmö Art Academy and is currently studying Literary Composition at the University of Gothenburg.

Marcus Harrling is a filmmaker and musician based in Farsta, Sweden. He is currently preparing a live set of audio and video for various UK shows that follow the release of his album *Diagnos*.

Rikard Heberling is a graphic designer living in Stockholm, Sweden. He is currently a researcher in graphic design history at Konstfack University of Arts, Crafts and Design, Stockholm.

Mohomodou Houssouba grew up in Gao, Mali. He studied English at the national teacher's college in Bamako, Mali, and Illinois State University, USA. He writes about history and cultures of northern Mali and coordinates a network that develops modern resources for the Songhay language.

Tim Ingold is Professor of Social Anthropology at the University of Aberdeen and a Fellow of the British Academy and the Royal Society of Edinburgh. His current research explores the interface between anthropology, art, architecture, and design. He is the author of many books, most recently *Anthropology and/as Education* (2018).

Hana Jaber is a historian and researcher living in Paris, France. She is currently a Senior Fellow at the Arab Reform Initiative. Previously she was an Associate Researcher at Chaire d'Histoire du monde arabe contemporain at Collège de France (2010–16). Her ongoing research concerns are population movements and related issues.

Jacob Grønbech Jensen is a graphic designer based in Copenhagen, Denmark.

Sophie Jung is an artist and writer living in London, UK, and Basel, Switzerland. Recent exhibitions include *Lodger* at Blain Southern, London, and *till he looked like a burning bush or a flaming comet* at Sophie Tappeiner, Vienna.

Oscar Lara is an artist based in Stockholm, Sweden, and Lima, Peru. He is currently a PhD candidate at the Royal Institute of Art, Stockholm. His solo show, *Within Heritage Movements*, at the Lima Art Museum (MALI) is among his recent exhibitions.

Lars Bang Larsen is an art historian, writer, and adjunct curator at Moderna Museet in Stockholm, Sweden. He is currently working with Søren Andreasen on a project to follow up on their 2012 picture book *The Critical Mass of Mediation*. He is based in Copenhagen, Denmark.

Doris Lasch is an artist based in Basel, Switzerland.

Leonela Lilja is an artist living in Stockholm, Sweden. She mainly works with found objects, installation, text, and photography. In 2017 she participated in a show at Italienska Palatset, Växjö, Sweden.

Cecilia Luzon lives in Uppsala, Sweden. She is currently a Master's student in Literature and editor-in-chief of the literary magazine *Tydningen*.

Toby Lynas is an artist living in Stockholm, Sweden. He is Head of Operations at the PBSA and has initiated Den Obstinata Enhörningen, a funeral parlor in Stockholm.

Jonas (J) Magnusson is a writer, translator, and the editor-in-chief of *OEI* and of OEI editör. He is currently working together with Cecilia Grönberg on an expanded publishing project centered around two uniquely stratified Swedish plateau mountains, Billingen and Kinnekulle.

Cecilie Hundevad Meng is an artist, writer, and curator based in Copenhagen, Denmark. She runs the exhibition project Forlaget Gestus, an exhibition space and publisher for artists who use writing as an essential part of their practice. In October 2017 she legally changed her name to Kirke Hundevad Meng.

Nanna Nordström is an artist living and working in Stockholm, Sweden. She is currently developing the exhibition *Circular Works* for BS Projects at the HBK Hochschule für Bildende Künste Braunschweig.

Mateusz Nowak is an artist based in Denmark. He holds an MFA from the Royal Danish Academy of Fine Arts. He is currently artist in residence at Wieth-Knudsen Astronomical Observatory in Tisvidleleje.

Kristoffer Ørum is an artist based in Copenhagen, Denmark. His work explores contemporary technological concepts of everyday life, how stories of our lived lives are circulated, and what this circulation means for the ways in which we live our daily lives. He is the initiator of the digital distribution platform Captive Portal and is currently involved in the artistic research project Uncertain Archives at the University of Copenhagen.

Asier Perez is Head of Creativity and Research at Dowayo Service Design. He has recently developed a social behavioral change project in relation to traffic in Manila, the Philippines.

Daniel Pianetti is a designer living in New York City, USA. He is partner at the digital studio No Plans and at the research platform Are.na. With Are.na's team he has been developing a place that helps small communities do research online over time, believing that curiosity is what drives personal knowledge, not algorithms.

Falke Pisano is an artist based in Amsterdam, the Netherlands, and São Paulo, Brazil. In her new series of performances, *VONDERVOTTEIMITTISS*, she takes to questioning ideas that have become powerful because they have been naturalized, and as such (as "nature") have come to be seen as the basis on which humans can establish culture and society.

Lisi Raskin is an Associate Professor and the Department Head of Sculpture at Rhode Island School of Design. She is based in Providence, RI, USA. In the summer of 2018, Raskin will have a two-person exhibition at Fleisher Ollman Gallery in Philadelphia with artist Jesse Harrod. The show will respond to the gallery's inventory of historical work by self-taught artists.

Mikkel Bolt Rasmussen is a cultural critic and author of several books, including *Crisis to Insurrection* (Minor Compositions, 2015) and *Trumps kontrarevolution* (Nemo, 2017). He teaches cultural studies at the University of Copenhagen. He lives and works in Copenhagen, Denmark.

Samuel Richter lives in Uppsala, Sweden, and studies at the Royal Institute of Art, Stockholm.

Hinrich Sachs is a visual artist and writer based in Basel, Switzerland, working in an itinerant fashion. He is currently finalizing *Fog Friend Font*, a multiple author publication project on multilingualism, specifically considering the situation of Inuktitut, the language of the Canadian Inuit.

Gabriel Säll recently graduated from the Royal Institute of Art, Stockholm. He is currently participating in the Berlin Program for Artists in Berlin, Germany.

Eran Schaerf is an artist living and working in Berlin, Germany. His recent installation "Atelier d'assimilation" was exhibited at Zwinger Gallery, Berlin. His recent book, *Frequency-Modulated Scenario* (Archive Books, 2015), focuses on his radio works.

Jacques Henri Sennwald is an artist dividing his time between Amsterdam, the Netherlands, and Lausanne, Switzerland. He is currently working on a series about salt-caked moonlight.

Adam Shiu-Yang Shaw is an artist living and working in Berlin, Germany. Recent exhibitions include *vinegar stone & the language of flowers*, Towards, Toronto, Canada (2017), *Kamias Triennial*, Kamias Special Projects, Quezon City, the Philippines (2017), and *Gabinete de Moda*, Gabinete, Lisbon, Portugal (2017).

Aron Skoog is an artist based in Stockholm, Sweden. He has recently exhibited in Sweden and Denmark, co-edited the journal *Filmögon*, and co-organized a film program with the works of the late artist Richard Vogel.

Simon Starling is an artist living and working in Copenhagen, Denmark. He is currently developing an exhibition for the Musée Régional d'Art Contemporain, Sérignan, France, and a film about Caravaggio in Malta.

Jonathan Terry lives and works in Stockholm, Sweden. He studied fine art in Umeå, Sweden, Oslo, Norway, and at the Royal Institute of Art, Stockholm.

Yusuke Toda is a sculptor, visual artist, and professor at Musashino Art University, Tokyo. He lives in Sayama-shi, Japan. He recently installed a large outdoor sculpture on top of a cliff at the Nagasakibana Resort Camp Site in Mime, Bungotakada, Japan.

Hedda Viå is an artist and physiotherapist living in Stockholm, Sweden. She runs the lecture series *Prothesis, metaphor and the obsolete body*.

Gitte Villesen is an artist living in Berlin, Germany. In 2016 she realized the first part of the photo- and videoinstallation *Deeply immersed in the contents of a learning stone*; the second part, *A stone out of date* (working title), was realized in 2017. A poster-publication, *I stick my hands into the earth, and I think for a while*, was recently published by Archive Books.

Lili von Wallenstein is the pseudonym of a writer, publisher, and criminologist. Her book *Mannen i Damaskus* was published in 2017 under another name. She lives in Stockholm, Sweden.

Apichaya Wanthiang is an artist living in Oslo, Norway. She works with painting, installation, and discursive formats. Her interests lie in the seemingly small and anecdotal as a means to encourage criticality and empathy. She recently exhibited in Kunsthall 3.14 and Hordaland Kunstsenter, Bergen, Norway, and Unge Kunstneres Samfund, Oslo. She is currently working on a dance piece with choreographer Ming-Hwa Yeh, which will be shown in Taipei, Taiwan.

Johan Widén is an artist. Since 2017 he has been living in the small village Väggarp in southern Sweden. During the last couple of years he has, together with writer Ylva Gislén, been developing a large body of works inspired by Selma Lagerlöf's novel *Jerusalem* (1902–03), which will be exhibited at the Palestinian Heritage Museum in Jerusalem in 2018.

Barbara Wien is a gallerist and publisher based in Berlin, Germany. Recent publications of Wiens Verlag include *soon the slugs will meet again* by Tomas Schmit, *50/50* by Vaclav Pozarek, and *An Opaque Wind* by Haegue Yang. An upcoming publication is Dieter Roth's *Collected Interviews*, the first English edition of *Gesammelte Interviews* from 2002.

Filippa Wikner lives and works in Stockholm, Sweden. She is currently studying her final year at the Royal Institute of Art, Stockholm.

Yun Yu is a designer living in Copenhagen, Denmark, and Stockholm, Sweden. She is currently working at e-Types, a Copenhagen-based design consultancy.

Klara Zetterholm is an artist living in Stockholm, Sweden. She recently presented her work in the BA degree show at the Royal Institute of Art, Stockholm.

COLOPHON

NAVIGATION
A PUBLICATION FOR A PLACE
WITHOUT A HISTORICAL CENTER,
CREATED CONTINUOUSLY ANEW
IN MEETINGS AND EVENTS THAT
OCCUR IN EMPOWERED SPACES,
SIMULTANEOUSLY

Onomatopee 162
cabinet project

Editors: Hinrich Sachs, Kirke Hundevad Meng, Samuel Richter, Rikard Heberling
Copy-editing: Laura Schleussner, Sylee Gore, Ruth Buchanan
Translation: Robert McInnes (from French), Jan Salomonsson (from Swedish)
Graphic design: Rikard Heberling
Printed by Printon Trükikoda, Tallinn, 2018

Special thanks to all who contributed with their choice of flotsam and jetsam.
Thanks to Kelechi Azu, Frederic Bruly Bouabré, Robert Filliou, Freek Lomme, Gaia Martino, Judith Rosenthal, Julia Voss, Maja Wismer.
Supported by the Royal Institute of Art as well as by private funders.

This publication acts as the sequel to *3 Days of Navigating*, a program of events and presentations that took place at Index, Moderna Museet, and the Royal Institute of Art in Stockholm, Sweden, between September 21 and 23, 2016. Initiated by Hinrich Sachs, it emerged from the engagement of a group of students from the Royal Institute of Art over the course of a year, together with invited contributors.

ISBN 9789491677915

onomatopee.net